Adam Smith

Selected Philosophical Writings

Edited and Introduced
by James R. Otteson

LIBRARY OF
SCOTTISH
PHILOSOPHY

ia

IMPRINT ACADEMIC

Published in the UK by Imprint Academic
PO Box 200, Exeter EX5 5YX, UK

Published in the USA by Imprint Academic
Philosophy Documentation Center
PO Box 7147, Charlottesville, VA 22906-7147, USA

ISBN 1 84540 001 1

A CIP catalogue record for this book is available from the British Library and US Library of Congress

Contents

3. Languages and Criticism

4: History and Philosophy of Science

5. Correspondence

Series Editor's Note

The principal purpose of volumes in this series is not to provide scholars with accurate editions, but to make the writings of Scottish philosophers accessible to a new generation of modern readers. In accordance with this purpose, certain changes have been made to the original texts:

- Spelling and punctuation have been modernized.
- In some cases, the selected passages have been given new titles.
- Some original footnotes and references have not been included.
- Some extracts have been shortened from their original length.
- Quotations from Greek have been transliterated, and passages in foreign languages translated, or omitted altogether.

Care has been taken to ensure that in no instance do these amendments truncate the argument or alter the meaning intended by the original author. For readers who want to consult the original texts, bibliographical details are provided for each extract.

The Library of Scottish Philosophy was launched at the Third International Reid Symposium on Scottish Philosophy in July 2004 with an initial six volumes. Attractively produced and competitively priced, these appeared just fifteen months after the original suggestion of such a series. This remarkable achievement owes a great deal to the work and commitment of the editors of the individual volumes, but it was only possible because of the energy and enthusiasm of the publisher, Keith Sutherland, and the outstanding work of Jon Cameron, Editorial and Administrative Assistant to the Centre for the Study of Scottish Philosophy.

Acknowledgements

Grateful acknowledgement is made to the Carnegie Trust for the Universities of Scotland for generous financial support for the Library of Scottish Philosophy in general, and to George Stevenson for a subvention for this volume in particular. Acknowledgement is also made to the University of Aberdeen Special Libraries and Collections for the engravings for the cover of this volume of the Edinburgh Faculty of Advocates and of Leith Harbour from *Modern Athens* (1829).

Gordon Graham,
Aberdeen, July 2004

Introduction

Adam Smith was born in 1723 in Kirkcaldy, Scotland, and died in Edinburgh in 1790. Along with figures like his teacher Francis Hutcheson (1694–1746) and his friend David Hume (1711–76), Smith was one of the principals of a period of astonishing learning that has become known as the Scottish Enlightenment. He is the author of two books: the 1759 *Theory of Moral Sentiments* (*TMS*) and the 1776 *Inquiry into the Nature and Causes of the Wealth of Nations* (*WN*). His first book brought him considerable acclaim during his lifetime and was quickly considered one of the great works of moral theory – impressing, for example, such people as Immanuel Kant (1724–1804), who called Smith his '*Liebling*' or 'favourite', and Charles Darwin (1809–82), who in his 1871 *Descent of Man* endorsed and accepted several of Smith's 'striking' conclusions. *TMS* went through fully six revised editions during Smith's lifetime. Since the nineteenth century, however, Smith's fame has largely rested on his second book, which, whether judged by its influence or its greatness, must be considered one of the most important works of the millennium.

Smith matriculated at the University of Glasgow at the age of fourteen in 1737. He considered his instruction at Glasgow, which was heavy in the classics, quite good; the influence of Hutcheson, to whom Smith later referred to as 'the never to be forgotten Dr Hutcheson', was pronounced. After Glasgow, Smith was a Snell exhibitioner at Balliol College, Oxford, with whose level of instruction Smith was, however, not so impressed: 'In the University of Oxford, the greater part of the public professors have, for these many years, given up altogether even the pretence of teaching.' Smith made good use of the libraries at Oxford, however, studying widely in English, French, Greek and Latin literature. He left Oxford and returned to Kirkcaldy in 1746.

In 1748 Smith began giving in Edinburgh 'Lectures on Rhetoric and the *Belles Lettres*', as Kames's biographer Alexander Tytler reports, focusing on literary criticism and the arts of speaking and writing well. It was during this time that Smith met and befriended Hume, who was to become Smith's closest confidant and greatest philosophical influence. Smith left Edinburgh to become Professor of Logic at the University of Glasgow in 1751 and then Professor of Moral Philosophy in 1752. The lectures he gave there eventually crystallized into *The Theory of Moral Sentiments.*

In *TMS,* Smith argues that human beings naturally desire a 'mutual sympathy of sentiments' with their fellows, which means that they long to see their own judgments and sentiments echoed in others. Because we all seek out this 'sympathy' — or 'harmony' or 'concord' of sentiments — much of social life is a give-and-take whereby people alternately try to moderate their own sentiments so that others can 'enter into them' and try to arouse others' sentiments so that they match their own. This market-like negotiation results in the gradual development of shared habits, and then rules, of judgment about moral matters ranging from etiquette to moral duty. This process also gives rise, Smith argues, to an ultimate standard of moral judgment, the 'impartial spectator', whose perspective we routinely seek out in judging both our own and others' conduct. When we use it to judge our own, it is what constitutes our conscience. We consult the impartial spectator simply by asking ourselves what a fully-informed but disinterested person would think about our conduct. If such a person would approve, then we may proceed; if he would disapprove, then we should desist.

Morality on Smith's account is thus an earthly, grounded affair. Although he makes frequent reference to God and the 'Author of Nature', scholars disagree over to what extent such references do any real work in his theory — and thus to what extent Smith's theory of moral sentiments is a relativistic account, eschewing reliance on transcendent, objective rules of morality. One way to understand Smith's account, and to my mind the most promising, is as subscribing to a 'middle-way' objectivity. A community's moral standards are not, so far as we know, eternally commanded by a transcendent being or order, yet neither are they perfectly arbitrary or subject to individual subjective whims. They arise as a consequence of at least two relatively fixed, and certainly objective features of the world: human nature and the physical environment in which human beings find themselves and develop communities. On Smith's account, a community's long-standing moral rules will have stood the test of time only if they turned out in fact to be conducive to the welfare of the members of the community given their actual natures and circumstances. That gives any new member of the community in question considerable reason to follow these rules, even if their origins or their actual connection to welfare remain obscure to him.

Smith's substantive moral picture is heavily influenced by several ancient accounts. There is, for example, a strong strand of Stoicism — as evidenced immediately by the fact that Smith claims that self-command is the virtue that gives all the other virtues 'their principal lustre.' And Smith's conception of the impartial spectator as the ultimate arbiter of propriety and merit bears an intriguing resemblance to Aristotle's *phronemos,* or virtuous man. It may be that for Smith the impartial spectator determines propriety and merit, rather than discovering or reflecting them, just as it may be the actions of the virtuous man that for Aristotle are the true standard of virtue. Whether the impartial spectator creates or merely recognizes moral conduct will in the end depend in large part on where this standard comes from, that is, how it originates. Aristotle does not give a genetic account of his virtuous man, however, which leaves the question open for him; perhaps Smith's historical genealogy of the impartial spectator can be seen as attempting to fill this lacuna in the theory.

A final issue of concern surrounding Smith's moral theory, which I cannot hope to resolve here, is the extent to which Smith is in *TMS* merely *describing* the phenomenon of human morality, as a natural scientist or anthropologist might, or whether he is also making moral *endorsements,* as a person concerned to help people lead good or righteous lives might. Smith is clearly doing at least the former: one of his central goals is to describe the origins, maintenance and development of the human social institution of commonly shared morality. But is he also making or recommending moral judgments? Students of *TMS* disagree about this. My view is that Smith is offering a hypothetical imperative: given your nature and given the nature of human social institutions – which Smith has described in detail in *TMS* – then your best chance of being happy is to follow, at least for the most part, your community's moral traditions. This interpretation would capture what I described above as Smith's 'middle-way' objectivity, and would also reflect his genuine concern for people's welfare. In a key footnote in *TMS,* however, where Smith is discussing the propriety of resentment, he writes,

> Let it be considered too, that the present inquiry is not concerning a matter of right, if I may say so, but concerning a matter of fact. We are not at present examining upon what principles a perfect being would approve of the punishments of bad actions; but upon what principles so weak and imperfect a creature as man actually and in fact approves of it.

In the end it may be that *TMS* contains both descriptive and normative aspects, and that to proclaim it as merely the one or the other is a distortion. But there is no scholarly consensus on the point, so readers will have to assess *TMS* on their own.

In 1763, Smith resigned his post at Glasgow to become the personal tutor of Henry Scott, the Third Duke of Buccleuch, whom Smith accompanied on an eighteen-month tour of France and Switzerland. It was during these travels with the Duke that Smith met François Quesnay (1694–1774), Jacques Turgot (1727–81), and others among the so-called French Physiocrats, who were publicists arguing for a relaxation of trade barriers and *laissez-faire* economic policies. Although Smith had long been developing his own similar ideas, numerous conversations with the Physiocrats no doubt helped him refine and sharpen them. In 1767, Smith returned to Kirkcaldy to continue work on what would become his *Wealth of Nations,* which was published for the first time in 1776.

The reactions to the publication of *WN* were swift, numerous, and, among the principals of the Scottish Enlightenment at least, highly laudatory. Here is Hume's reaction:

> Euge! Belle! Dear Mr. Smith: I am much pleas'd with your Performance, and the Perusal of it has taken me from a State of great Anxiety. It was a Work of so much Expectation, by yourself, by your Friends, and by the Public, that I trembled for its Appearance; but am now much relieved. Not but that the Reading of it necessarily requires so much Attention, and the Public is disposed to give so little, that I shall still doubt for some time of its being very popular: But it has Depth and Solidity and Acuteness, and is so much illustrated by curious Facts, that it must at last take the public Attention.

Here is Hugh Blair, Moderator of the General Assembly of the Church of Scotland and Professor of Rhetoric at the University of Edinburgh: 'You have given me full and Compleat Satisfaction and my Faith is fixed. I do think the Age is highly indebted to you, and I wish they may be duly Sensible of the Obligation.' And William Robertson, historian and Principal of the University of Edinburgh: 'You have formed into a regular and consistent system one of the most intricate and important parts of political science, and . . . I should think your Book will occasion a total change in several important articles in police and finance.' Here is Adam Ferguson, Professor of Moral Philosophy at the University of Edinburgh and author of *Essay on the History of Civil Society:* 'You are surely to reign alone on these subjects, to form the opinions, and I hope to govern at least the coming generations.' And, finally, Thomas Malthus, author of *An Essay on the Principle of Population,* claimed that Smith's *WN* 'has done for political economy, what the *Principia* of Newton did for physics.'

In *WN,* Smith argues against the Mercantilists that real wealth is not mere pieces of metal: it is rather the ability to satisfy one's needs and desires. Since each person wishes to 'better his own condition', the argument of *WN* is that those policies and public institutions should be adopted that best allow each of us to do so. Hence the task of the political economist is to conduct empirical, historical investigations to discover what these policies and institutions are. Upon investigation, Smith argues, it turns out that markets, in which the division of labour is allowed to progress, in which trade is free, and in which taxes and regulations are light, are the most conducive to this end. Smith argues that in market-oriented economies based on private property, each person working to better his own condition will increase the supply, and thus lower the price, of whatever good he is producing; this means that others will in turn be in a better position to afford his goods. Thus each person serving his own ends is led, in Smith's famous phrase, 'by an invisible hand', to simultaneously serve everyone else's ends as well by both providing more plentiful and a greater diversity of goods and by thereby lowering prices. The market, Smith saw, could harness people's industry in the service of their own ends and make it serve everyone else's welfare, even if the welfare of others was not part of the individuals' own motivations.

Smith did not think that everyone is fundamentally selfish in any narrow sense. In opposition to Bernard Mandeville (1670–1733), whose 1714 *Fable of the Bees* he called 'licentious', Smith argued that people's 'self-interest' in fact included the interests of others, in particular their family and friends. Nevertheless Smith did believe that natural benevolence is limited and that whatever other motivations people feel, the desire to better their own conditions is always present. That explains why 'It is not from the benevolence of the butcher, the brewer, or the baker, that we expect our dinner, but from their regard to their own interest.' The genius of the Smithian market mechanism, however, was that it could coordinate the disparate individual efforts of indefinitely many persons and derive an overall benefit for the good of society from them. Much of *WN*'s bulk is concerned with providing historical evidence supporting this theoretical argument.

The conclusions of *WN* are, therefore, largely in favour of limiting political interference in markets. Each individual knows his own situation – including his goals and desires, as well as the opportunities available to him – better than does anyone else, and certainly better than any distant legislator. Hence Smith argues that individuals themselves should be allowed to decide how best to apply and sell their labour or goods, with whom to trade and on what terms, and so on. Smith is withering in his condemnation of meddling legislators who overestimate their ability to direct the lives of others, who legislatively substitute their own distant judgment for that of the individuals with actual local knowledge over whom they rule, and who then use the predictable failures of their decisions as excuses for yet more imprudent intervention.

Yet Smith is equally condemnatory of grasping merchants and businessmen who seek legal protections of their industries or prices. 'People of the same trade seldom meet together', Smith writes, 'even for merriment and diversion, but the conversation ends in a conspiracy against the publick, or in some contrivance to raise prices.' Such merchants proclaim that trade barriers, tariffs and other legal protections are for the good of the country, but Smith exposes these claims as mere special pleading, since they work to increase these particular merchants' profits at the expense not only of other competitors but also of the public at large. Keeping prices up and limiting competition will certainly benefit the privileged businessmen, but such policies just as certainly punish everyone else. Smith argues that the way to deal with such attempts at legalized monopoly is not to regulate them directly, however, but rather to disallow anyone from having any legally enforced privileges in the first place. Markets and open competition are, Smith thinks, better providers of social benefit than short-sighted regulation by politically motivated legislators – who are, after all, often remunerated handsomely by the very merchants and businesses from whom they profess to protect the public.

But Smith is no anarchist, nor even a modern-day libertarian. He argues that the first and central duty of the government is to secure 'justice', which for him means protecting people's lives, property and individual freedom. This will entail a system of police and courts, which Smith argues must be effective and efficient if the market system is going to be able to work. In addition to those basic duties, however, Smith also argues that the government should provide out of general taxation for those goods that would conduce to everyone's benefit but that would not repay any private entrepreneurs to provide. In this category he suggests the building of roads, canals and other public infrastructures. He recommends moreover partially subsidizing primary schooling, in the beliefs that everyone should learn to 'read, write, and account' and that a system of government schooling can ensure this.

But his concerns in this regard go far deeper. As the selections from *WN* contained herein demonstrate, Smith was deeply concerned about the deleterious effects on people's minds that the progressing division of labour would have. 'The man whose whole life is spent in performing a few simple operations', Smith writes, 'of which the effects too are, perhaps, always the same, or very nearly the same, has no occasion to exert his understanding, or to exercise his invention in finding out expedients for removing difficulties which never occur. He naturally loses, therefore, the habit of such exertion, and generally becomes as stupid and ignorant as it is possible for a human creature to become.' So although markets and division of labour provide great material benefits, Smith also believed they can deaden the mind and weaken the character. Nationally subsidized schooling might help in this regard, but it is not clear that Smith thought this would be enough. There has been a trend among some recent commentators to suggest that Smith's undeniable concern for the poor and working portions of society in fact make him rather a precursor to modern progressive liberalism than an icon of classical *laissez-faire* liberalism. Smith's strong general anti-interventionism in economics is problematic for this interpretation, but his concern for the least among us was real and palpable.

By the middle of the nineteenth century, *WN* was regularly cited in British parliament – in its Corn Law debates, for example – and its recommendations of free markets and free trade went on to have great influence in the subsequent political and economic developments not only of the British Isles, but also of most of the Western and even parts of the Eastern world. Smith's influence on the founding of the United States was also great. Among his readers were Benjamin Franklin (1706–90), George Washington (1732–99), Thomas Paine (1737–1809) and Thomas Jefferson (1743–1826). When compiling 'a course of reading' in 1799, Jefferson included *WN* along with John Locke's 1690 *Second Treatise of Government* and Condorcet's 1793 *Esquisse d'un tableau des progrès de l'esprit humain* as the essential books. The English historian Henry Thomas Buckle (1821–62) wrote that *WN* 'is probably the most important book that has ever been written', including the Bible. Today most countries in the world either rely on some version of Smithian market-based economies or are in the process of creating them.

Smith remained in Kirkcaldy until 1778, when he left to become Commissioner of Customs in Edinburgh. During this time he visited regularly with friends, among whom he counted Edmund Burke (1729–97), the chemist Joseph Black (1728–99), the geologist James Hutton (1726–97), Prime Minister Frederick (Lord) North (1732–92) and Prime Minister William Pitt the Younger (1759–1806), and he took active roles in learned organizations like the Oyster Club, the Poker Club, and the Select Society, the last of which including among its members William Robertson, David Hume, Lord Monboddo, Adam Ferguson and Lord Kames. In 1783 Smith was a founding member of the Royal Society of Edinburgh, which exists still today as Scotland's premier national academy of science and letters. Having previously served as the University of Glasgow's Dean of Arts (1760) and Vice-Rector (1761–3), in 1787 he was elected Lord Rector of the university, a post he held until 1789.

During his years in Edinburgh Smith extensively revised both *TMS* and *WN* for new editions. He also reported to Le Duc de La Rochefoucauld in 1785 that during this time 'I [Smith] have likewise two other great works upon the anvil; the one is a sort of Philosophical History of all the different branches of Literature, of Philosophy, Poetry and Eloquence; the other is a sort of theory and History of Law and Government.' Neither of these projects was ever published, however. One week before he died, Smith summoned Black and Hutton to his quarters and asked that they burn his unpublished manuscripts, a request they had been resisting for months. This time Smith insisted. They reluctantly complied, destroying sixteen volumes of manuscripts. It is probable that Smith's philosophical history of literature, philosophy, poetry and eloquence and his theory and history of law and government were among the works that perished in that tragic loss.

Adam Smith died in Edinburgh on 17 July 1790 and is buried in the Canongate kirkyard cemetery off High Street in Edinburgh.

Adam Smith: Selected Philosophical Writings is the first anthology to collect excerpts from a wide range of Smith's extant work. It thus contains selections not only of *TMS* and *WN*, but it also contains, from his lectures on jurisprudence, Smith's discussion of the nature of 'justice'; the origins, development, forms and purpose of government; and the threats to liberty and curbs to tyranny. Also contained herein is Smith's history and philosophy of science in his posthumously published *History of Astronomy*, in which he offers a unique account of the motivations for scientific inquiry and tests his account by looking at the development of astronomy from Pythagoras, Plato and Aristotle through Ptolemy and then to Copernicus, Brahe, Galileo, Kepler, Descartes and Newton.

Strikingly, Smith concludes that their respective philosophical systems are 'mere inventions of the imagination', and not representative of actually existing principles or mechanisms. The collection also includes Smith's philosophy of language as presented in his 'Considerations Concerning the First Formation of Language', which Smith himself thought to be an important original contribution to the anthropological study of human language and which contains an early instance of what Dugald Stewart called Smith's method of 'conjectural history.' Although later editors did not always follow his lead, Smith instructed that this essay be appended to the second and each subsequent edition of *TMS* published during his lifetime. Finally, the collection also contains some of Smith's most important correspondence, including his famous 1756 letter to the *Edinburgh Review* outlining what learned Scots should be reading and studying, his 1776 letter to his publisher William Strahan reporting his first-hand account of the death of his friend Hume, and two of Hume's 1759 letters to Smith, one on the reception in Edinburgh of *TMS* and the other containing Hume's objections to *TMS*.

The goal of this anthology is to provide the reader with some indication of the breadth of Smith's learning and an overview of his thought in a number of areas. The hope is that this will spark the reader's interest in further investigating the work of this seminal figure of the Scottish Enlightenment.

Adam Smith was a true polymath: he was master of several languages and their literatures, a historian of ancient and modern worlds, a philosopher in his own right, and a brilliant observer of human society and behaviour. Although he is principally known today as the father of the discipline now called economics, the scope and reach of his work suggest he is probably better considered the father of empirical sociology. Given, however, the much broader eighteenth-century sense of the term 'moral philosophy', which included all the areas of inquiry related to human nature and action, Smith's own choice might well have been simply 'moral philosopher.'

Bibliography

Primary Sources

The definitive edition of Smith's collected works, which includes student notes on his lectures on jurisprudence, his smaller essays, his letters, and an index to the whole, is the Glasgow edition, published in eight volumes by Oxford University Press in hardcover and by Liberty Fund, Inc. of Indianapolis, Indiana in softcover. There are numerous other editions both of *The Theory of Moral Sentiments* and of *The Wealth of Nations* currently in print.

Secondary Sources

Campbell, R. H. and Skinner, A. S. *Adam Smith.* New York: St. Martin's, 1982.

Campbell, T. D. *Adam Smith's Science of Morals.* London: Allen & Unwin, 1971.

Fleischacker, Samuel. *On Adam Smith's* Wealth of Nations: *A Philosophical Companion.* Princeton, NJ: Princeton University Press, 2004.

Griswold, Charles L., Jr. *Adam Smith and the Virtues of Enlightenment.* Cambridge: Cambridge University Press, 1999.

Haakonssen, Knud. *The Science of a Legislator: The Natural Jurisprudence of David Hume and Adam Smith.* Cambridge: Cambridge University Press, 1981.

Heilbroner, Robert L. *The Worldly Philosophers: The Lives, Times and Ideas of the Great Economic Thinkers.* Sixth edition. New York: Simon and Schuster, 1992. Chapter 3, 'The Wonderful World of Adam Smith.'

Montes, Leonidas. *Adam Smith in Context: A Critical Reassessment of some Central Components of His Thought.* New York: Palgrave Macmillan, 2004.

Muller, Jerry Z. *Adam Smith in His Time and Ours: Designing the Decent Society.* New York: Free Press, 1993.

Otteson, James R. *Adam Smith's Marketplace of Life.* Cambridge: Cambridge University Press, 2002.

Rae, John. *Life of Adam Smith.* London: Macmillan, 1895.

Raphael, D. D. *Adam Smith.* Oxford: Oxford University Press, 1985.

Ross, Ian Simpson. *The Life of Adam Smith.* Oxford: Clarendon, 1995.

Rothschild, Emma. *On Economic Sentiments: Adam Smith, Condorcet, and the Enlightenment.* Cambridge, MA: Harvard University Press, 2001.

Skousen, Mark. *The Making of Modern Economics: The Lives and Ideas of the Great Thinkers.* London: M.E. Sharpe, 2001.

Vivenza, Gloria. *Adam Smith and the Classics.* New York: Oxford University Press, 2001.

Weinstein, Jack Russell. *On Adam Smith.* Belmont, CA: Wadsworth, 2000.

Acknowledgements

This volume would not have been possible without the support of the Centre for the Study of Scottish Philosophy at the University of Aberdeen, and without the learned guidance of the Centre's director, Gordon Graham. The able copy-editing skills of Jon Cameron were also indispensable. The time I spent at the Centre occurred while on sabbatical leave from the University of Alabama and was partially funded by a generous grant from the Earhart Foundation of Ann Arbor, Michigan. I gratefully acknowledge all of their support and help.

Editor's Note

In keeping with the general editorial policy of the Library of Scottish Philosophy series, I have silently modernized the spelling and capitalization of the texts. I note that all italics are in the originals. I have also occasionally, and silently, revised part or section titles where otherwise confusion or repetition would ensue. In a few places I have inserted material into the text or added footnotes; all and only my material appears in square brackets: [ ]. Wherever I have omitted material from the original, I have marked this with an ellipsis. I have largely refrained from adding explanatory footnotes because Smith's texts usually speak for themselves. I have supplied footnotes identifying many of the people Smith names, but I typically provide only their full names and dates — the basic information required to enable readers to investigate them further if they so choose.

One

Moral Theory

PART ONE
Of the Propriety of Action

I: Of the Sense of Propriety

Of Sympathy

How selfish so ever man may be supposed, there are evidently some principles in his nature, which interest him in the fortune of others, and render their happiness necessary to him, though he derives nothing from it except the pleasure of seeing it. Of this kind is pity or compassion, the emotion which we feel for the misery of others, when we either see it, or are made to conceive it in a very lively manner. That we often derive sorrow from the sorrow of others, is a matter of fact too obvious to require any instances to prove it; for this sentiment, like all the other original passions of human nature, is by no means confined to the virtuous and humane, though they may perhaps feel it with the most exquisite sensibility. The greatest ruffian, the most hardened violator of the laws of society, is not altogether without it.

As we have no immediate experience of what other men feel, we can form no idea of the manner in which they are affected, but by conceiving what we ourselves should feel in the like situation. Though our brother is upon the rack, as long as we ourselves are at our ease, our senses will never inform us of what he suffers. They never did, and never can, carry us beyond our own person, and it is by the imagination only that we can form any conception of what are his sensations. Neither can that faculty help us to this any other way, than by representing to us what would be our own, if we were in his case. It is the impressions of our own senses only, not those of his, which our imaginations copy. By the imagination we place ourselves in his situation, we conceive ourselves enduring all the same torments, we enter as it were into his body, and become in some measure the same person with him, and thence form some idea of his sensations, and even feel something which, though weaker in degree, is not altogether unlike them. His agonies, when they are thus brought

From *The Theory of Moral Sentiments* (London and Edinburgh, 1759).

home to ourselves, when we have thus adopted and made them our own, begin at last to affect us, and we then tremble and shudder at the thought of what he feels. For as to be in pain or distress of any kind excites the most excessive sorrow, so to conceive or to imagine that we are in it, excites some degree of the same emotion, in proportion to the vivacity or dullness of the conception.

That this is the source of our fellow-feeling for the misery of others, that it is by changing places in fancy with the sufferer, that we come either to conceive or to be affected by what he feels, may be demonstrated by many obvious observations, if it should not be thought sufficiently evident of itself. When we see a stroke aimed and just ready to fall upon the leg or arm of another person, we naturally shrink and draw back our own leg or our own arm; and when it does fall, we feel it in some measure, and are hurt by it as well as the sufferer. The mob, when they are gazing at a dancer on the slack rope, naturally writhe and twist and balance their own bodies, as they see him do, and as they feel that they themselves must do if in his situation. Persons of delicate fibres and a weak constitution of body complain, that in looking on the sores and ulcers which are exposed by beggars in the streets, they are apt to feel an itching or uneasy sensation in the correspondent part of their own bodies. The horror which they conceive at the misery of those wretches affects that particular part in themselves more than any other; because that horror arises from conceiving what they themselves would suffer, if they really were the wretches whom they are looking upon, and if that particular part in themselves was actually affected in the same miserable manner. The very force of this conception is sufficient, in their feeble frames, to produce that itching or uneasy sensation complained of. Men of the most robust make, observe that in looking upon sore eyes they often feel a very sensible soreness in their own, which proceeds from the same reason; that organ being in the strongest man more delicate, than any other part of the body is in the weakest.

Neither is it those circumstances only, which create pain or sorrow, that call forth our fellow-feeling. Whatever is the passion which arises from any object in the person principally concerned, an analogous emotion springs up, at the thought of his situation, in the breast of every attentive spectator. Our joy for the deliverance of those heroes of tragedy or romance who interest us, is as sincere as our grief for their distress, and our fellow-feeling with their misery is not more real than that with their happiness. We enter into their gratitude towards those faithful friends who did not desert them in their difficulties, and we heartily go along with their resentment against those perfidious traitors who injured, abandoned, or deceived them. In every passion of which the mind of man is susceptible, the emotions of the bystander always correspond to what, by bringing the case home to himself, he imagines should be the sentiments of the sufferer.

Pity and compassion are words appropriated to signify our fellow-feeling with the sorrow of others. Sympathy, though its meaning was, perhaps, originally the same, may now, however, without much impropriety, be made use of to denote our fellow-feeling with any passion whatever.

Upon some occasions sympathy may seem to arise merely from the view of a certain emotion in another person. The passions, upon some occasions, may seem to be transfused from one man to another, instantaneously, and antecedent to any knowledge of what excited them in the person principally concerned. Grief and joy, for example, strongly expressed in the look and gestures of any one, at once affect the spectator with some degree of a like painful or agreeable emotion. A smiling face is, to everybody that sees it, a cheerful object, as a sorrowful countenance, on the other hand, is a melancholy one.

This, however, does not hold universally, or with regard to every passion. There are some passions of which the expressions excite no sort of sympathy, but before we are acquainted with what gave occasion to them, serve rather to disgust and provoke us against them. The furious behaviour of an angry man is more likely to exasperate us against himself than against his enemies. As we are unacquainted with his provocation, we cannot bring his case home to ourselves, nor conceive anything like the passions which it excites. But we plainly see what is the situation of those with whom he is angry, and to what violence they may be exposed from so enraged an adversary. We readily, therefore, sympathize with their fear or resentment, and are immediately disposed to take part against the man from whom they appear to be in so much danger.

If the very appearances of grief and joy inspire us with some degree of the like emotions, it is because they suggest to us the general idea of some good or bad fortune that has befallen the person in whom we observe them: and in these passions this is sufficient to have some little influence upon us. The effects of grief and joy terminate in the person who feels those emotions, of which the expressions do not, like those of resentment, suggest to us the idea of any other person for whom we are concerned, and whose interests are opposite to his. The general idea of good or bad fortune, therefore, creates some concern for the person who has met with it, but the general idea of provocation excites no sympathy with the anger of the man who has received it. Nature, it seems, teaches us to be more averse to enter into this passion, and, till informed of its cause, to be disposed rather to take part against it.

Even our sympathy with the grief or joy of another, before we are informed of the cause of either, is always extremely imperfect. General lamentations, which express nothing but the anguish of the sufferer, create rather a curiosity to inquire into his situation, along with some disposition to sympathize with him, than any actual sympathy that is very sensible. The first question which we ask is, What has befallen you? Till this be answered, though we are uneasy both from the vague idea of his misfortune, and still more from torturing ourselves with conjectures about what it may be, yet our fellow-feeling is not very considerable.

Sympathy, therefore, does not arise so much from the view of the passion, as from that of the situation which excites it. We sometimes feel for another, a passion of which he himself seems to be altogether incapable; because when we put ourselves in his case, that passion arises in our breast from the imagination, though it does not in his from the reality. We blush for the impudence and rudeness of another, though he himself appears to have no sense of the impropriety of his own behaviour; because we cannot help feeling with what confusion we ourselves should be covered, had we behaved in so absurd a manner.

Of all the calamities to which the condition of mortality exposes mankind, the loss of reason appears, to those who have the least spark of humanity, by far the most dreadful, and they behold that last stage of human wretchedness with deeper commiseration than any other. But the poor wretch, who is in it, laughs and sings perhaps, and is altogether insensible of his own misery. The anguish which humanity feels, therefore, at the sight of such an object, cannot be the reflection of any sentiment of the sufferer. The compassion of the spectator must arise altogether from the consideration of what he himself would feel if he was reduced to the same unhappy situation, and, what perhaps is impossible, was at the same time able to regard it with his present reason and judgment.

What are the pangs of a mother, when she hears the moanings of her infant that during the agony of disease cannot express what it feels? In her idea of what it suffers, she joins, to its real helplessness, her own consciousness of that helplessness, and her own terrors for the unknown consequences of its disorder; and out of all these, forms, for her own sorrow, the most complete image of misery and distress. The infant, however, feels only the uneasiness of the present instant, which can never be great. With regard to the future, it is perfectly secure, and in its thoughtlessness and want of foresight, possesses an antidote against fear and anxiety, the great tormentors of the human breast, from which reason and philosophy will, in vain, attempt to defend it, when it grows up to a man.

We sympathize even with the dead, and overlooking what is of real importance in their situation, that awful futurity which awaits them, we are chiefly affected by those circumstances which strike our senses, but can have no influence upon their happiness. It is miserable, we think, to be deprived of the light of the sun; to be shut out from life and conversation; to be laid in the cold grave, a prey to corruption and the reptiles of the earth; to be no more thought of in this world, but to be obliterated, in a little time, from the affections, and almost from the memory, of their dearest friends and relations. Surely, we imagine, we can never feel too much for those who have suffered so dreadful a calamity. The tribute of our fellow-feeling seems doubly due to them now, when they are in danger of being forgot by everybody, and, by the vain honours which we pay to their memory, we endeavour, for our own misery, artificially to keep alive our melancholy remembrance of their misfortune. That our sympathy can afford them no consolation seems to be an addition to their calamity; and to think that all we can do is unavailing, and that, what alleviates all other distress, the regret, the love, and the lamentations of their friends, can yield no comfort to them, serves only to exasperate our sense of their misery. The happiness of the dead, however, most assuredly, is affected by none of these circumstances; nor is it the thought of these things which can ever disturb the profound security of their repose. The idea of that dreary and endless melancholy, which the fancy naturally ascribes to their condition, arises altogether from our joining to the change which has been produced upon them, our own consciousness of that change, from our putting ourselves in their situation, and from our lodging, if I may be allowed to say so, our own living souls in their inanimated bodies, and thence conceiving what would be our emotions in this case. It is from this very illusion of the imagination, that the foresight of our own dissolution is so terrible to us, and that the idea of those circumstances, which undoubtedly can give us no pain when we are dead, makes us miserable while we are alive. And from thence arises one of the most important principles in human nature, the dread of death, the great poison to the happiness, but the great restraint upon the injustice of mankind, which, while it afflicts and mortifies the individual, guards and protects the society.

Of the Pleasure of Mutual Sympathy

But whatever may be the cause of sympathy, or however it may be excited, nothing pleases us more than to observe in other men a fellow feeling with all the emotions of our own breast; nor are we ever so much shocked as by the appearance of the contrary. Those who are fond of deducing all our sentiments from certain refinements of self-love, think themselves at no loss to account, according to their own principles, both for this pleasure and this pain. Man, say they, conscious of his own weakness, and of the need which he has for the assistance of others, rejoices whenever he observes that they adopt his own passions, because he is then assured of that assistance; and grieves whenever he observes the contrary, because he is then assured of their opposition. But both the pleasure and the pain are always felt so instantaneously, and often upon such frivolous occasions, that it seems evident that neither of them can be derived from any such self-interested consideration. A man is mortified when, after having endeavoured to divert the company, he looks round and sees that nobody laughs at his jests but himself. On the contrary, the mirth of the company is highly agreeable to him, and he regards this correspondence of their sentiments with his own as the greatest applause.

Neither does his pleasure seem to arise altogether from the additional vivacity which his mirth may receive from sympathy with theirs, nor his pain from the disappointment he meets with when he misses this pleasure; though both the one and the other, no doubt, do in some measure. When we have read a book or poem so often that we can no longer find any amusement in reading it by ourselves, we can still take pleasure in reading it to a companion. To him it has all the graces of novelty; we enter into the surprise and admiration which it naturally excites in him, but which it is no longer capable of exciting in us; we consider all the ideas which it presents rather in the light in which they appear to him, than in that in which they appear to ourselves, and we are amused by sympathy with his amusement which thus enlivens our own. On the contrary, we should be vexed if he did not seem to be entertained with it, and we could no longer take any pleasure in reading it to him. It is the same case here. The mirth of the company, no doubt, enlivens our own mirth, and their silence, no doubt, disappoints us. But though this may contribute both to the pleasure which we derive from the one, and to the pain which we feel from the other, it is by no means the sole cause of either; and this correspondence of the sentiments of others with our own appears to be a cause of pleasure, and the want of it a cause of pain, which cannot be accounted for in this manner. The sympathy, which my friends express with my joy, might, indeed, give me pleasure by enlivening that joy: but that which they express with my grief could give me none, if it served only to enliven that grief. Sympathy, however, enlivens joy and alleviates grief. It enlivens joy by presenting another source of satisfaction; and it alleviates grief by insinuating into the heart almost the only agreeable sensation which it is at that time capable of receiving.

It is to be observed accordingly, that we are still more anxious to communicate to our friends our disagreeable than our agreeable passions, that we derive still more satisfaction from their sympathy with the former than from that with the latter, and that we are still more shocked by the want of it.

How are the unfortunate relieved when they have found out a person to whom they can communicate the cause of their sorrow? Upon his sympathy they seem to disburthen themselves of a part of their distress: he is not improperly said to share it with them. He not only feels a sorrow of the same kind with that which they feel, but as if he had derived a part of it to himself, what he feels seems to alleviate the weight of what they feel. Yet by relating their misfortunes they in some measure renew their grief. They awaken in their memory the remembrance of those circumstances which occasioned their affliction. Their tears accordingly flow faster than before, and they are apt to abandon themselves to all the weakness of sorrow. They take pleasure, however, in all this, and, it is evident, are sensibly relieved by it; because the sweetness of his sympathy more than compensates the bitterness of that sorrow which, in order to excite this sympathy, they had thus enlivened and renewed. The cruellest insult, on the contrary, which can be offered to the unfortunate, is to appear to make light of their calamities. To seem not to be affected with the joy of our companions is but want of politeness; but not to wear a serious countenance when they tell us their afflictions, is real and gross inhumanity.

Love is an agreeable; resentment, a disagreeable passion; and accordingly we are not half so anxious that our friends should adopt our friendships, as that they should enter into our resentments. We can forgive them though they seem to be little affected with the favours which we may have received, but lose all patience if they seem indifferent about the injuries which may have been done to us: nor are we half so angry with them for not entering into our gratitude, as for not sympathizing with our resentment. They can easily avoid being friends to our friends, but can hardly avoid being enemies to those with whom we are at variance. We seldom resent their being at enmity with the first, though upon that account we may sometimes affect to make an awkward quarrel with them; but we quarrel with them in good earnest if they live in friendship with the last. The agreeable passions of love and joy can satisfy and support the heart without any auxiliary pleasure. The bitter and painful emotions of grief and resentment more strongly require the healing consolation of sympathy.

As the person who is principally interested in any event is pleased with our sympathy, and hurt by the want of it, so we, too, seem to be pleased when we are able to sympathize with him, and to be hurt when we are unable to do so. We run not only to congratulate the successful, but to condole with the afflicted; and the pleasure which we find in the conversation of one whom in all the passions of his heart we can entirely sympathize with, seems to do more than compensate the painfulness of that sorrow with which the view of his situation affects us. On the contrary, it is always disagreeable to feel that we cannot sympathize with him, and instead of being pleased with this exemption from sympathetic pain, it hurts us to find that we cannot share his uneasiness. If we hear a person loudly lamenting his misfortunes, which however, upon bringing the case home to ourselves, we feel, can produce no such violent effect upon us, we are shocked at his grief; and, because we cannot enter into it, call it pusillanimity and weakness. It gives us the spleen, on the other hand, to see another too happy or too much elevated, as we call it, with any little piece of good fortune. We are disobliged even with his joy; and, because we cannot go along with it, call it levity and folly. We are even put out of humour if our companion laughs louder or longer at a joke than we think it deserves; that is, than we feel that we ourselves could laugh at it.

Of the Manner in which We Judge of the Propriety or Impropriety of the Affections of Other Men, by Their Concord or Dissonance with Our Own

When the original passions of the person principally concerned are in perfect concord with the sympathetic emotions of the spectator, they necessarily appear to this last just and proper, and suitable to their objects; and, on the contrary, when, upon bringing the case home to himself, he finds that they do not coincide with what he feels, they necessarily appear to him unjust and improper, and unsuitable to the causes which excite them. To approve of the passions of another, therefore, as suitable to their objects, is the same thing as to observe that we entirely sympathize with them; and not to approve of them as such, is the same thing as to observe that we do not entirely sympathize with them. The man who resents the injuries that have been done to me, and observes that I resent them precisely as he does, necessarily approves of my resentment. The man whose sympathy keeps time to my grief, cannot but admit the reasonableness of my sorrow. He who admires the same poem, or the same picture, and admires them exactly as I do, must surely allow the justness of my admiration. He who laughs at the same joke, and laughs along with me, cannot well deny the propriety of my laughter. On the contrary, the person who, upon these different occasions, either feels no such emotion as that which I feel, or feels none that bears any proportion to mine, cannot avoid disapproving my sentiments on account of their dissonance with his own. If my animosity goes beyond what the indignation of my friend can correspond to; if my grief exceeds what his most tender compassion can go along with; if my admiration is either too high or too low to tally with his own; if I laugh loud and heartily when he only smiles, or, on the contrary, only smile when he laughs loud and heartily; in all these cases, as soon as he comes from considering the object, to observe how I am affected by it, according as there is more or less disproportion between his sentiments and mine, I must incur a greater or less degree of his disapprobation: and upon all occasions his own sentiments are the standards and measures by which he judges of mine. . . .

There are, indeed, some cases in which we seem to approve without any sympathy or correspondence of sentiments, and in which, consequently, the sentiment of approbation would seem to be different from the perception of this coincidence. A little attention, however, will convince us that even in these cases our approbation is ultimately founded upon a sympathy or correspondence of this kind. I shall give an instance in things of a very frivolous nature, because in them the judgments of mankind are less apt to be perverted by wrong systems. We may often approve of a jest, and think the laughter of the company quite just and proper, though we ourselves do not laugh, because, perhaps, we are in a grave humour, or happen to have our attention engaged with other objects. We have learned, however, from experience, what sort of pleasantry is upon most occasions capable of making us laugh, and we observe that this is one of that kind. We approve, therefore, of the laughter of the company, and feel that it is natural and suitable to its object; because, though in our present mood we cannot easily enter into it, we are sensible that upon most occasions we should very heartily join in it.

The same thing often happens with regard to all the other passions. A stranger passes by us in the street with all the marks of the deepest affliction; and we are immediately told that he has just received the news of the death of his father. It is impossible that, in this case, we should not approve of his grief. Yet it may often happen, without any defect of humanity on our part, that, so far from entering into the violence of his sorrow, we should scarce conceive the first movements of concern upon his account. Both he and his father, perhaps, are entirely unknown to us, or we happen to be employed about other things, and do not take time to picture out in our imagination the different circumstances of distress which must occur to him. We have learned, however, from experience, that such a misfortune naturally excites such a degree of sorrow, and we know that if we took time to consider his situation, fully and in all its parts, we should, without doubt, most sincerely sympathize with him. It is upon the consciousness of this conditional sympathy, that our approbation of his sorrow is founded, even in those cases in which that sympathy does not actually take place; and the general rules derived from our preceding experience of what our sentiments would commonly correspond with, correct upon this, as upon many other occasions, the impropriety of our present emotions.

The sentiment or affection of the heart from which any action proceeds, and upon which its whole virtue or vice must ultimately depend, may be considered under two different aspects, or in two different relations; first, in relation to the cause which excites it, or the motive which gives occasion to it; and secondly, in relation to the end which it proposes, or the effect which it tends to produce.

In the suitableness or unsuitableness, in the proportion or disproportion which the affection seems to bear to the cause or object which excites it, consists the propriety or impropriety, the decency or ungracefulness of the consequent action.

In the beneficial or hurtful nature of the effects which the affection aims at, or tends to produce, consists the merit or demerit of the action, the qualities by which it is entitled to reward, or is deserving of punishment . . . .

When we judge in this manner of any affection, as proportioned or disproportioned to the cause which excites it, it is scarce possible that we should make use of any other rule or canon but the correspondent affection in ourselves. If, upon bringing the case home to our own breast, we find that the sentiments which it gives occasion to, coincide and tally with our own, we necessarily approve of them as proportioned and suitable to their objects; if otherwise, we necessarily disapprove of them, as extravagant and out of proportion . . . .

With regard to those objects which are considered without any peculiar relation either to ourselves or to the person whose sentiments we judge of; wherever his sentiments entirely correspond with our own, we ascribe to him the qualities of taste and good judgment. The beauty of a plain, the greatness of a mountain, the ornaments of a building, the expression of a picture, the composition of a discourse, the conduct of a third person, the proportions of different quantities and numbers, the various appearances which the great machine of the universe is perpetually exhibiting, with the secret wheels and springs which produce them; all the general subjects of science and taste, are what we and our companion regard as having no peculiar relation to either of us. We both look at them from the same point of view, and we have no occasion for sympathy, or for that imaginary change of situations from which it arises, in order to produce, with regard to these, the most perfect harmony of sentiments and affections. If, notwithstanding, we are often differently affected, it arises either from the different degrees of attention, which our different habits of life allow us to give easily to the several parts of those complex objects, or from the different degrees of natural acuteness in the faculty of the mind to which they are addressed.

When the sentiments of our companion coincide with our own in things of this kind, which are obvious and easy, and in which, perhaps, we never found a single person who differed from us, though we, no doubt, must approve of them, yet he seems to deserve no praise or admiration on account of them. But when they not only coincide with our own, but lead and direct our own; when in forming them he appears to have attended to many things which we had overlooked, and to have adjusted them to all the various circumstances of their objects; we not only approve of them, but wonder and are surprised at their uncommon and unexpected acuteness and comprehensiveness, and he appears to deserve a very high degree of admiration and applause. For approbation heightened by wonder and surprise, constitutes the sentiment which is properly called admiration, and of which applause is the natural expression. The decision of the man who judges that exquisite beauty is preferable to the grossest deformity, or that twice two are equal to four, must certainly be approved of by all the world, but will not, surely, be much admired. It is the acute and delicate discernment of the man of taste, who distinguishes the minute, and scarce perceptible differences of beauty and deformity; it is the comprehensive accuracy of the experienced mathematician, who unravels, with ease, the most intricate and perplexed proportions; it is the great leader in science and taste, the man who directs and conducts our own sentiments, the extent and superior justness of whose talents astonish us with wonder and surprise, who excites our admiration, and seems to deserve our applause: and upon this foundation is grounded the greater part of the praise which is bestowed upon what are called the intellectual virtues.

The utility of those qualities, it may be thought, is what first recommends them to us; and, no doubt, the consideration of this, when we come to attend to it, gives them a new value. Originally, however, we approve of another man's judgment, not as something useful, but as right, as accurate, as agreeable to truth and reality: and it is evident we attribute those qualities to it for no other reason but because we find that it agrees with our own. Taste, in the same manner, is originally approved of, not as useful, but as just, as delicate, and as precisely suited to its object. The idea of the utility of all qualities of this kind, is plainly an after-thought, and not what first recommends them to our approbation.

With regard to those objects, which affect in a particular manner either ourselves or the person whose sentiments we judge of, it is at once more difficult to preserve this harmony and correspondence, and at the same time, vastly more important. My companion does not naturally look upon the misfortune that has befallen me, or the injury that has been done me, from the same point of view in which I consider them. They affect me much more nearly. We do not view them from the same station, as we do a picture, or a poem, or a system of philosophy, and are, therefore, apt to be very differently affected by them. But I can much more easily overlook the want of this correspondence of sentiments with regard to such indifferent objects as concern neither me nor my companion, than with regard to what interests me so much as the misfortune that has befallen me, or the injury that has been done me. Though you despise that picture, or that poem, or even that system of philosophy, which I admire, there is little danger of our quarrelling upon that account. Neither of us can reasonably be much interested about them. They ought all of them to be matters of great indifference to us both; so that, though our opinions may be opposite, our affections may still be very nearly the same. But it is quite otherwise with regard to those objects by which either you or I are particularly affected. Though your judgments in matters of speculation, though your sentiments in matters of taste, are quite opposite to mine, I can easily overlook this opposition; and if I have any degree of temper, I may still find some entertainment in your conversation, even upon those very subjects. But if you have either no fellow-feeling for the misfortunes I have met with, or none that bears any proportion to the grief which distracts me; or if you have either no indignation at the injuries I have suffered, or none that bears any proportion to the resentment which transports me, we can no longer converse upon these subjects. We become intolerable to one another. I can neither support your company, nor you mine. You are confounded at my violence and passion, and I am enraged at your cold insensibility and want of feeling.

In all such cases, that there may be some correspondence of sentiments between the spectator and the person principally concerned, the spectator must, first of all, endeavour, as much as he can, to put himself in the situation of the other, and to bring home to himself every little circumstance of distress which can possibly occur to the sufferer. He must adopt the whole case of his companion with all its minutest incidents; and strive to render as perfect as possible, that imaginary change of situation upon which his sympathy is founded.

After all this, however, the emotions of the spectator will still be very apt to fall short of the violence of what is felt by the sufferer. Mankind, though naturally sympathetic, never conceive, for what has befallen another, that degree of passion which naturally animates the person principally concerned. That imaginary change of situation, upon which their sympathy is founded, is but momentary. The thought of their own safety, the thought that they themselves are not really the sufferers, continually intrudes itself upon them; and though it does not hinder them from conceiving a passion somewhat analogous to what is felt by the sufferer, hinders them from conceiving any thing that approaches to the same degree of violence. The person principally concerned is sensible of this, and at the same time passionately desires a more complete sympathy. He longs for that relief which nothing can afford him but the entire concord of the affections of the spectators with his own. To see the emotions of their hearts, in every respect, beat time to his own, in the violent and disagreeable passions, constitutes his sole consolation. But he can only hope to obtain this by lowering his passion to that pitch, in which the spectators are capable of going along with him. He must flatten, if I may be allowed to say so, the sharpness of its natural tone, in order to reduce it to harmony and concord with the emotions of those who are about him. What they feel, will, indeed, always be, in some respects, different from what he feels, and compassion can never be exactly the same with original sorrow; because the secret consciousness that the change of situations, from which the sympathetic sentiment arises, is but imaginary, not only lowers it in degree, but, in some measure, varies it in kind, and gives it a quite different modification. These two sentiments, however, may, it is evident, have such a correspondence with one another, as is sufficient for the harmony of society. Though they will never be unisons, they may be concords, and this is all that is wanted or required.

In order to produce this concord, as nature teaches the spectators to assume the circumstances of the person principally concerned, so she teaches this last in some measure to assume those of the spectators. As they are continually placing themselves in his situation, and thence conceiving emotions similar to what he feels; so he is as constantly placing himself in theirs, and thence conceiving some degree of that coolness about his own fortune, with which he is sensible that they will view it. As they are constantly considering what they themselves would feel, if they actually were the sufferers, so he is as constantly led to imagine in what manner he would be affected if he was only one of the spectators of his own situation. As their sympathy makes them look at it, in some measure, with his eyes, so his sympathy makes him look at it, in some measure, with theirs, especially when in their presence and acting under their observation: and as the reflected passion, which he thus conceives, is much weaker than the original one, it necessarily abates the violence of what he felt before he came into their presence, before he began to recollect in what manner they would be affected by it, and to view his situation in this candid and impartial light . . . .

II: Of the Degrees of the Different Passions which are Consistent with Propriety

The propriety of every passion excited by objects peculiarly related to ourselves, the pitch which the spectator can go along with, must lie, it is evident, in a certain mediocrity. If the passion is too high, or if it is too low, he cannot enter into it. Grief and resentment for private misfortunes and injuries may easily, for example, be too high, and in the greater part of mankind they are so. They may likewise, though this more rarely happens, be too low. We denominate the excess, weakness and fury: and we call the defect stupidity, insensibility, and want of spirit. We can enter into neither of them, but are astonished and confounded to see them.

This mediocrity, however, in which the point of propriety consists, is different in different passions. It is high in some, and low in others. There are some passions which it is indecent to express very strongly, even upon those occasions, in which it is acknowledged that we cannot avoid feeling them in the highest degree. And there are others of which the strongest expressions are upon many occasions extremely graceful, even though the passions themselves do not, perhaps, arise so necessarily. The first are those passions with which, for certain reasons, there is little or no sympathy: the second are those with which, for other reasons, there is the greatest. And if we consider all the different passions of human nature, we shall find that they are regarded as decent, or indecent, just in proportion as mankind are more or less disposed to sympathize with them.

Of the Passions which Take Their Origin from the Body

It is indecent to express any strong degree of those passions which arise from a certain situation or disposition of the body; because the company, not being in the same disposition, cannot be expected to sympathize with them. Violent hunger, for example, though upon many occasions not only natural, but unavoidable, is always indecent, and to eat voraciously is universally regarded as a piece of ill manners. There is, however, some degree of sympathy, even with hunger. It is agreeable to see our companions eat with a good appetite, and all expressions of loathing are offensive. The disposition of body which is habitual to a man in health, makes his stomach easily keep time, if I may be allowed so coarse an expression, with the one, and not with the other. We can sympathize with the distress which excessive hunger occasions when we read the description of it in the journal of a siege, or of a sea voyage. We imagine ourselves in the situation of the sufferers, and thence readily conceive the grief, the fear and consternation, which must necessarily distract them. We feel, ourselves, some degree of those passions, and therefore sympathize with them: but as we do not grow hungry by reading the description, we cannot properly, even in this case, be said to sympathize with their hunger.

It is the same case with the passion by which Nature unites the two sexes. Though naturally the most furious of all the passions, all strong expressions of it are upon every occasion indecent, even between persons in whom its most complete indulgence is acknowledged by all laws, both human and divine, to be perfectly innocent. There seems, however, to be some degree of sympathy even with this passion. To talk to a woman as we would to a man is improper: it is expected that their company should inspire us with more gaiety, more pleasantry, and more attention; and an entire insensibility to the fair sex, renders a man contemptible in some measure even to the men . . . .

Of Those Passions which Take Their Origin from a Particular Turn or Habit of the Imagination

Even of the passions derived from the imagination, those which take their origin from a peculiar turn or habit it has acquired, though they may be acknowledged to be perfectly natural, are, however, but little sympathized with. The imaginations of mankind, not having acquired that particular turn, cannot enter into them; and such passions, though they may be allowed to be almost unavoidable in some part of life, are always, in some measure, ridiculous. This is the case with that strong attachment which naturally grows up between two persons of different sexes, who have long fixed their thoughts upon one another. Our imagination not having run in the same channel with that of the lover, we cannot enter into the eagerness of his emotions. If our friend has been injured, we readily sympathize with his resentment, and grow angry with the very person with whom he is angry. If he has received a benefit, we readily enter into his gratitude, and have a very high sense of the merit of his benefactor. But if he is in love, though we may think his passion just as reasonable as any of the kind, yet we never think ourselves bound to conceive a passion of the same kind, and for the same person for whom he has conceived it. The passion appears to everybody, but the man who feels it, entirely disproportioned to the value of the object; and love, though it is pardoned in a certain age because we know it is natural, is always laughed at, because we cannot enter into it. All serious and strong expressions of it appear ridiculous to a third person; and though a lover may be good company to his mistress, he is so to nobody else. He himself is sensible of this; and as long as he continues in his sober senses, endeavours to treat his own passion with raillery and ridicule. It is the only style in which we care to hear of it; because it is the only style in which we ourselves are disposed to talk of it. We grow weary of the grave, pedantic, and long-sentenced love of Cowley and Petrarca,[2] who never have done with exaggerating the violence of their attachments; but the gaiety of Ovid, and the gallantry of Horace, are always agreeable . . . .

Of all the passions, however, which are so extravagantly disproportioned to the value of their objects, love is the only one that appears, even to the weakest minds, to have anything in it that is either graceful or agreeable. In itself, first of all, though it may be ridiculous, it is not naturally odious; and though its consequences are often fatal and dreadful, its intentions are seldom mischievous. And then, though there is little propriety in the passion itself, there is a good deal in some of those which always accompany it. There is in love a strong mixture of humanity, generosity, kindness, friendship, esteem; passions with which, of all others, for reasons which shall be explained immediately, we have the greatest propensity to sympathize, even notwithstanding we are sensible that they are, in some measure, excessive. The sympathy which we feel with them, renders the passion which they accompany less disagreeable, and supports it in our imagination, notwithstanding all the vices which commonly go along with it; though in the one sex it necessarily leads to the last ruin and infamy; and though in the other, where it is apprehended to be least fatal, it is almost always attended with an incapacity for labour, a neglect of duty, a contempt of fame, and even of common reputation. Notwithstanding all this, the degree of sensibility and generosity with which it is supposed to be accompanied, renders it to many the object of vanity; and they are fond of appearing capable of feeling what would do them no honour if they had really felt it.

It is for a reason of the same kind, that a certain reserve is necessary when we talk of our own friends, our own studies, our own professions. All these are objects which we cannot expect should interest our companions in the same degree in which they interest us. And it is for want of this reserve, that the one half of mankind make bad company to the other. A philosopher is company to a philosopher only; the member of a club, to his own little knot of companions.

Of the Unsocial Passions

There is another set of passions, which, though derived from the imagination, yet before we can enter into them, or regard them as graceful or becoming, must always be brought down to a pitch much lower than that to which undisciplined nature would raise them. These are, hatred and resentment, with all their different modifications. With regard to all such passions, our sympathy is divided between the person who feels

---

[2] [Abraham Cowley (1618–67) and Petrarch (Francesco Petrarca, 1304–74)].

them, and the person who is the object of them. The interests of these two are directly opposite. What our sympathy with the person who feels them would prompt us to wish for, our fellow-feeling with the other would lead us to fear. As they are both men, we are concerned for both, and our fear for what the one may suffer, damps our resentment for what the other has suffered. Our sympathy, therefore, with the man who has received the provocation, necessarily falls short of the passion which naturally animates him, not only upon account of those general causes which render all sympathetic passions inferior to the original ones, but upon account of that particular cause which is peculiar to itself, our opposite sympathy with another person. Before resentment, therefore, can become graceful and agreeable, it must be more humbled and brought down below that pitch to which it would naturally rise, than almost any other passion . . . .

Those passions, however, are regarded as necessary parts of the character of human nature. A person becomes contemptible who tamely sits still, and submits to insults, without attempting either to repel or to revenge them. We cannot enter into his indifference and insensibility: we call his behaviour mean-spiritedness, and are as really provoked by it as by the insolence of his adversary. Even the mob are enraged to see any man submit patiently to affronts and ill usage. They desire to see this insolence resented, and resented by the person who suffers from it. They cry to him with fury, to defend, or to revenge himself. If his indignation rouses at last, they heartily applaud, and sympathize with it. It enlivens their own indignation against his enemy, whom they rejoice to see him attack in turn, and are as really gratified by his revenge, provided it is not immoderate, as if the injury had been done to themselves . . . .

It is the same case with those passions we have been just now considering. Their immediate effects are so disagreeable, that even when they are most justly provoked, there is still something about them which disgusts us. These, therefore, are the only passions of which the expressions, as I formerly observed, do not dispose and prepare us to sympathize with them, before we are informed of the cause which excites them . . . . It was, it seems, the intention of Nature, that those rougher and more unamiable emotions, which drive men from one another, should be less easily and more rarely communicated . . . .

If those passions are disagreeable to the spectator, they are not less so to the person who feels them. Hatred and anger are the greatest poison to the happiness of a good mind. There is, in the very feeling of those passions, something harsh, jarring, and convulsive, something that tears and distracts the breast, and is altogether destructive of that composure and tranquillity of mind which is so necessary to happiness, and which is best promoted by the contrary passions of gratitude and love. It is not the value of what they lose by the perfidy and ingratitude of those they live with, which the generous and humane are most apt to regret. Whatever they may have lost, they can generally be very happy without it.

What most disturbs them is the idea of perfidy and ingratitude exercised towards themselves; and the discordant and disagreeable passions which this excites, constitute, in their own opinion, the chief part of the injury which they suffer. . . .

Of the Social Passions

As it is a divided sympathy which renders the whole set of passions just now mentioned, upon most occasions, so ungraceful and disagreeable; so there is another set opposite to these, which a redoubled sympathy renders almost always peculiarly agreeable and becoming. Generosity, humanity, kindness, compassion, mutual friendship and esteem, all the social and benevolent affections, when expressed in the countenance or behaviour, even towards those who are not peculiarly connected with ourselves, please the indifferent spectator upon almost every occasion. His sympathy with the person who feels those passions, exactly coincides with his concern for the person who is the object of them. The interest, which, as a man, he is obliged to take in the happiness of this last, enlivens his fellow-feeling with the sentiments of the other, whose emotions are employed about the same object. We have always, therefore, the strongest disposition to sympathize with the benevolent affections. They appear in every respect agreeable to us. We enter into the satisfaction both of the person who feels them, and of the person who is the object of them. For as to be the object of hatred and indignation gives more pain than all the evil which a brave man can fear from his enemies; so there is a satisfaction in the consciousness of being beloved, which, to a person of delicacy and sensibility, is of more importance to happiness, than all the advantage which he can expect to derive from it. What character is so detestable as that of one who takes pleasure to sow dissension among friends, and to turn their most tender love into mortal hatred? Yet wherein does the atrocity of this so much abhorred injury consist? Is it in depriving them of the frivolous good offices, which, had their friendship continued, they might have expected from one another? It is in depriving them of that friendship itself, in robbing them of each other's affections, from which both derived so much satisfaction; it is in disturbing the harmony of their hearts, and putting an end to that happy commerce which had before subsisted between them. These affections, that harmony, this commerce, are felt, not only by the tender and the delicate, but by the rudest vulgar of mankind, to be of more importance to happiness than all the little services which could be expected to flow from them.

The sentiment of love is, in itself, agreeable to the person who feels it. It sooths and composes the breast, seems to favour the vital motions, and to promote the healthful state of the human constitution; and it is rendered still more delightful by the consciousness of the gratitude and satisfaction which it must excite in him who is the object of it. Their mutual regard renders them happy in one another, and sympathy, with this mutual regard, makes them agreeable to every other person. With what pleasure do we look upon a family, through the whole of which reign mutual love and esteem, where the parents and children are companions for one another, without any other difference than what is made by respectful affection on the one side, and kind indulgence on the other; where freedom and fondness, mutual raillery and mutual kindness, show that no opposition of interest divides the brothers, nor any rivalship of favour sets the sisters at variance, and where every thing presents us with the idea of peace, cheerfulness, harmony, and contentment? On the contrary, how uneasy are we made when we go into a house in which jarring contention sets one half of those who dwell in it against the other; where amidst affected smoothness and complaisance, suspicious looks and sudden starts of passion betray the mutual jealousies which burn within them, and which are every moment ready to burst out through all the restraints which the presence of the company imposes?

Those amiable passions, even when they are acknowledged to be excessive, are never regarded with aversion. There is something agreeable even in the weakness of friendship and humanity. The too tender mother, the too indulgent father, the too generous and affectionate friend, may sometimes, perhaps, on account of the softness of their natures, be looked upon with a species of pity, in which, however, there is a mixture of love, but can never be regarded with hatred and aversion, nor even with contempt, unless by the most brutal and worthless of mankind. It is always with concern, with sympathy and kindness, that we blame them for the extravagance of their attachment. There is a helplessness in the character of extreme humanity which more than anything interests our pity. There is nothing in itself which renders it either ungraceful or disagreeable. We only regret that it is unfit for the world, because the world is unworthy of it, and because it must expose the person who is endowed with it as a prey to the perfidy and ingratitude of insinuating falsehood, and to a thousand pains and uneasinesses, which, of all men, he the least deserves to feel, and which generally too he is, of all men, the least capable of supporting. It is quite otherwise with hatred and resentment. Too violent a propensity to those detestable passions, renders a person the object of universal dread and abhorrence, who, like a wild beast, ought, we think, to be hunted out of all civil society.

Of the Selfish Passions

Besides those two opposite sets of passions, the social and unsocial, there is another which holds a sort of middle place between them; is never either so graceful as is sometimes the one set, nor is ever so odious as is sometimes the other. Grief and joy, when conceived upon account of our own private good or bad fortune, constitute this third set of passions. Even when excessive, they are never so disagreeable as excessive resentment, because no opposite sympathy can ever interest us against them: and when most suitable to their objects, they are never so agreeable as impartial humanity and just benevolence; because no double sympathy can ever interest us for them. There is, however, this difference between grief and joy, that we are generally most disposed to sympathize with small joys and great sorrows. The man who, by some sudden revolution of fortune, is lifted up all at once into a condition of life, greatly above what he had formerly lived in, may be assured that the congratulations of his best friends are not all of them perfectly sincere. An upstart, though of the greatest merit, is generally disagreeable, and a sentiment of envy commonly prevents us from heartily sympathizing with his joy. . . . If the chief part of human happiness arises from the consciousness of being beloved, as I believe it does, those sudden changes of fortune seldom contribute much to happiness. He is happiest who advances more gradually to greatness, whom the public destines to every step of his preferment long before he arrives at it, in whom, upon that account, when it comes, it can excite no extravagant joy, and with regard to whom it cannot reasonably create either any jealousy in those he overtakes, or any envy in those he leaves behind.

Mankind, however, more readily sympathize with those smaller joys which flow from less important causes. It is decent to be humble amidst great prosperity; but we can scarce express too much satisfaction in all the little occurrences of common life, in the company with which we spent the evening last night, in the entertainment that was set before us, in what was said and what was done, in all the little incidents of the present conversation, and in all those frivolous nothings which fill up the void of human life. Nothing is more graceful than habitual cheerfulness, which is always founded upon a peculiar relish for all the little pleasures which common occurrences afford. We readily sympathize with it: it inspires us with the same joy, and makes every trifle turn up to us in the same agreeable aspect in which it presents itself to the person endowed with this happy disposition. Hence it is that youth, the season of gaiety, so easily engages our affections. That propensity to joy which seems even to animate the bloom, and to sparkle from the eyes of youth and beauty, though in a person of the same sex, exalts, even the aged, to a more joyous mood than ordinary. They forget, for a time, their infirmities, and abandon themselves to those agreeable ideas and emotions to which they have long been strangers, but which, when the presence of so much happiness recalls them to their breast, take their place there, like old acquaintance, from whom they are sorry to have ever been parted, and whom they embrace more heartily upon account of this long separation.

It is quite otherwise with grief. Small vexations excite no sympathy, but deep affliction calls forth the greatest. . . . Joy is a pleasant emotion, and we gladly abandon ourselves to it upon the slightest occasion. We readily, therefore, sympathize with it in others, whenever we are not prejudiced by envy. But grief is painful, and the mind, even when it is our own misfortune, naturally resists and recoils from it. We would endeavour either not to conceive it at all, or to shake it off as soon as we have conceived it. Our aversion to grief will not, indeed, always hinder us from conceiving it in our own case upon very trifling occasions, but it constantly prevents us from sympathizing with it in others when excited by the like frivolous causes: for our sympathetic passions are always less irresistible than our original ones . . . .

Our sympathy, on the contrary, with deep distress, is very strong and very sincere. It is unnecessary to give an instance. We weep even at the feigned representation of a tragedy. If you labour, therefore, under any signal calamity, if by some extraordinary misfortune you are fallen into poverty, into diseases, into disgrace and disappointment; even though your own fault may have been, in part, the occasion, yet you may generally depend upon the sincerest sympathy of all your friends, and, as far as interest and honour will permit, upon their kindest assistance too. But if your misfortune is not of this dreadful kind, if you have only been a little baulked in your ambition, if you have only been jilted by your mistress, or are only hen-pecked by your wife, lay your account with the raillery of all your acquaintance.

III: Of the Effects of Prosperity and Adversity Upon the Judgment of Mankind with Regard to the Propriety of Action; and Why it is More Easy to Obtain Their Approbation in the One State Than in the Other

That Though Our Sympathy with Sorrow is Generally a More Lively Sensation than Our Sympathy with Joy, it Commonly Falls Much More Short of the Violence of What is Naturally Felt by the Person Principally Concerned

Our sympathy with sorrow, though not more real, has been more taken notice of than our sympathy with joy. The word sympathy, in its most proper and primitive signification, denotes our fellow-feeling with the sufferings, not that with the enjoyments, of others. A late ingenious and subtle philosopher[3] thought it necessary to prove, by arguments, that we had a real sympathy with joy, and that congratulation was a principle of human nature. Nobody, I believe, ever thought it necessary to prove that compassion was such . . . .

Over and above all this, we often struggle to keep down our sympathy with the sorrow of others. Whenever we are not under the observation of the sufferer, we endeavour, for our own sake, to suppress it as much as

---

[3] [Joseph Butler (1692–1752).]

we can, and we are not always successful. The opposition which we make to it, and the reluctance with which we yield to it, necessarily oblige us to take more particular notice of it. But we never have occasion to make this opposition to our sympathy with joy. If there is any envy in the case, we never feel the least propensity towards it; and if there is none, we give way to it without any reluctance. On the contrary, as we are always ashamed of our own envy, we often pretend, and sometimes really wish to sympathize with the joy of others, when by that disagreeable sentiment we are disqualified from doing so. We are glad, we say, on account of our neighbour's good fortune, when in our hearts, perhaps, we are really sorry. We often feel a sympathy with sorrow when we would wish to be rid of it; and we often miss that with joy when we would be glad to have it. The obvious observation, therefore, which it naturally falls in our way to make, is, that our propensity to sympathize with sorrow must be very strong, and our inclination to sympathize with joy very weak.

Notwithstanding this prejudice, however, I will venture to affirm, that, when there is no envy in the case, our propensity to sympathize with joy is much stronger than our propensity to sympathize with sorrow; and that our fellow-feeling for the agreeable emotion approaches much more nearly to the vivacity of what is naturally felt by the persons principally concerned, than that which we conceive for the painful one...

What can be added to the happiness of the man who is in health, who is out of debt, and has a clear conscience? To one in this situation, all accessions of fortune may properly be said to be superfluous; and if he is much elevated upon account of them, it must be the effect of the most frivolous levity. This situation, however, may very well be called the natural and ordinary state of mankind. Notwithstanding the present misery and depravity of the world, so justly lamented, this really is the state of the greater part of men. The greater part of men, therefore, cannot find any great difficulty in elevating themselves to all the joy which any accession to this situation can well excite in their companion.

But though little can be added to this state, much may be taken from it. Though between this condition and the highest pitch of human prosperity, the interval is but a trifle; between it and the lowest depth of misery the distance is immense and prodigious. Adversity, on this account, necessarily depresses the mind of the sufferer much more below its natural state, than prosperity can elevate him above it. The spectator, therefore, must find it much more difficult to sympathize entirely, and keep perfect time, with his sorrow, than thoroughly to enter into his joy, and must depart much further from his own natural and ordinary temper of mind in the one case than in the other. It is on this account, that though our sympathy with sorrow is often a more pungent sensation than our sympathy with joy, it always falls much more short of the violence of what is naturally felt by the person principally concerned....

Of the Origin of Ambition, and of the Distinction of Ranks

It is because mankind are disposed to sympathize more entirely with our joy than with our sorrow, that we make parade of our riches, and conceal our poverty. Nothing is so mortifying as to be obliged to expose our distress to the view of the public, and to feel, that though our situation is open to the eyes of all mankind, no mortal conceives for us the half of what we suffer. Nay, it is chiefly from this regard to the sentiments of mankind, that we pursue riches and avoid poverty. For to what purpose is all the toil and bustle of this world? What is the end of avarice and ambition, of the pursuit of wealth, of power, and preeminence? Is it to supply the necessities of nature? The wages of the meanest labourer can supply them. We see that they afford him food and clothing, the comfort of a house, and of a family. If we examined his economy with rigour, we should find that he spends a great part of them upon conveniencies, which may be regarded as superfluities, and that, upon extraordinary occasions, he can give something even to vanity and distinction. What then is the cause of our aversion to his situation, and why should those who have been educated in the higher ranks of life, regard it as worse than death, to be reduced to live, even without labour, upon the same simple fare with him, to dwell under the same lowly roof, and to be clothed in the same humble attire? Do they imagine that their stomach is better, or their sleep sounder in a palace than in a cottage? The contrary has been so often observed, and, indeed, is so very obvious, though it had never been observed, that there is nobody ignorant of it. From whence, then, arises that emulation which runs through all the different ranks of men, and what are the advantages which we propose by that great purpose of human life which we call bettering our condition? To be observed, to be attended to, to be taken notice of with sympathy, complacency, and approbation, are all the advantages which we can propose to derive from it. It is the vanity, not the ease, or the pleasure, which interests us. But vanity is always founded upon the belief of our being the object of attention and approbation. The rich man glories in his riches, because he feels that they naturally draw upon him the attention of the world, and that mankind are disposed to go along with him in all those agreeable emotions with which the advantages of his situation so readily inspire him. At the thought of this, his heart seems to swell and dilate itself within him, and he is fonder of his wealth, upon this account, than for all the other advantages it procures him. The poor man, on the contrary, is ashamed of his poverty. He feels that it either places him out of the sight of mankind, or, that if they take any notice of him, they have, however, scarce any fellow-feeling with the misery and distress which he suffers. He is mortified upon both accounts; for though to be overlooked, and to be disapproved of, are things entirely different, yet as obscurity covers us from the daylight of honour and approbation, to feel that we are taken no notice of, necessarily damps the most agreeable hope, and disappoints the most ardent desire, of human nature. The poor man goes out and comes in unheeded, and when in the midst of a crowd is in the same obscurity as if shut up in his own hovel. Those humble cares and painful attentions which occupy those in his situation, afford no amusement to the dissipated and the gay. They turn away their eyes from him, or if the extremity of his distress forces them to look at him, it is only to spurn so disagreeable an object from among them. The fortunate and the proud wonder at the insolence of human wretchedness, that it should dare to present itself before them, and with the loathsome aspect of its misery presume to disturb the serenity of their happiness. The man of rank and distinction, on the contrary, is observed by all the world. Everybody is eager to look at him, and to conceive, at least by sympathy, that joy and exultation with which his circumstances naturally inspire him. His actions are the objects of the public care. Scarce a word, scarce a gesture, can fall from him that is altogether neglected. In a great assembly he is the person upon whom all direct their eyes; it is upon him that their passions seem all to wait with expectation, in order to receive that movement and direction which he shall impress upon them; and if his behaviour is not altogether absurd, he has, every moment, an opportunity of interesting mankind, and of rendering himself the object of the observation and fellow-feeling of everybody about him. It is this, which, notwithstanding the restraint it imposes, notwithstanding the loss of liberty with which it is attended, renders greatness the object of envy, and compensates, in the opinion of mankind, all that toil, all that anxiety, all those mortifications which must be undergone in the pursuit of it; and what is of yet more consequence, all that leisure, all that ease, all that careless security, which are forfeited forever by the acquisition.

When we consider the condition of the great, in those delusive colours in which the imagination is apt to paint it, it seems to be almost the abstract idea of a perfect and happy state. It is the very state which, in all our waking dreams and idle reveries, we had sketched out to ourselves as the final object of all our desires. We feel, therefore, a peculiar sympathy with the satisfaction of those who are in it. We favour all their inclinations, and forward all their wishes. What pity, we think, that anything should spoil and corrupt so agreeable a situation! We could even wish them immortal; and it seems hard to us, that death should at last put an end to such perfect enjoyment. It is cruel, we think, in Nature to compel them from their exalted stations to that humble, but hospitable home, which she has provided for all her children. Great King, live forever! is the compliment, which, after the manner of eastern adulation, we should readily make them, if experience did not teach us its absurdity. Every calamity that befalls them, every injury that is done them, excites in the breast of the spectator ten times more compassion and resentment than he would have felt, had the same things happened to other men. It is the misfortunes of Kings only which afford the proper subjects for tragedy. They resemble, in this respect, the misfortunes of lovers. Those two situations are the chief which interest us upon the theatre; because, in spite of all that reason and experience can tell us to the contrary, the prejudices of the imagination attach to these two states a happiness superior to any other. To disturb, or to put an end to such perfect enjoyment, seems to be the most atrocious of all injuries. The traitor who conspires against the life of his monarch, is thought a greater monster than any other murderer. All the innocent blood that was shed in the civil wars, provoked less indignation than the death of Charles I. A stranger to human nature, who saw the indifference of men about the misery of their inferiors, and the regret and indignation which they feel for the misfortunes and sufferings of those above them, would be apt to imagine, that pain must be more agonizing, and the convulsions of death more terrible to persons of higher rank, than to those of meaner stations.

Upon this disposition of mankind, to go along with all the passions of the rich and the powerful, is founded the distinction of ranks, and the order of society. Our obsequiousness to our superiors more frequently arises from our admiration for the advantages of their situation, than from any private expectations of benefit from their good-will. Their benefits can extend but to a few; but their fortunes interest almost everybody. We are eager to assist them in completing a system of happiness that approaches so near to perfection; and we desire to serve them for their own sake, without any other recompense but the vanity or the honour of obliging them. Neither is our deference to their inclinations founded chiefly, or altogether, upon a regard to the utility of such submission, and to the order of society, which is best supported by it. Even when the order of society seems to require that we should oppose them, we can hardly bring ourselves to do it. That kings are the servants of the people, to be obeyed, resisted, deposed, or punished, as the public conveniency may require, is the doctrine of reason and philosophy; but it is not the doctrine of Nature. Nature would teach us to submit to them for their own sake, to tremble and bow down before their exalted station, to regard their smile as a reward sufficient to compensate any services, and to dread their displeasure, though no other evil were to follow from it, as the severest of all mortifications . . . .

'Love', says my Lord Rochfaucault,[4] 'is commonly succeeded by ambition; but ambition is hardly ever succeeded by love'. That passion, when once it has got entire possession of the breast, will admit neither a rival nor a successor. To those who have been accustomed to the possession, or even to the hope of public admiration, all other pleasures sicken and decay. Of all the discarded statesmen who for their own ease have studied to get the better of ambition, and to despise those honours which they could no longer arrive at, how few have been able to succeed? The greater part have spent their time in the most listless and insipid indo-

---

[4] [François de La Rochefoucauld (1613–80).]

lence, chagrined at the thoughts of their own insignificancy, incapable of being interested in the occupations of private life, without enjoyment, except when they talked of their former greatness, and without satisfaction, except when they were employed in some vain project to recover it. Are you in earnest resolved never to barter your liberty for the lordly servitude of a court, but to live free, fearless, and independent? There seems to be one way to continue in that virtuous resolution; and perhaps but one. Never enter the place from whence so few have been able to return; never come within the circle of ambition; nor ever bring yourself into comparison with those masters of the earth who have already engrossed the attention of half mankind before you.

Of such mighty importance does it appear to be, in the imaginations of men, to stand in that situation which sets them most in the view of general sympathy and attention. And thus, place, that great object which divides the wives of aldermen, is the end of half the labours of human life; and is the cause of all the tumult and bustle, all the rapine and injustice, which avarice and ambition have introduced into this world. People of sense, it is said, indeed despise place; that is, they despise sitting at the head of the table, and are indifferent who it is that is pointed out to the company by that frivolous circumstance, which the smallest advantage is capable of overbalancing. But rank, distinction pre-eminence, no man despises, unless he is either raised very much above, or sunk very much below, the ordinary standard of human nature; unless he is either so confirmed in wisdom and real philosophy, as to be satisfied that, while the propriety of his conduct renders him the just object of approbation, it is of little consequence though he be neither attended to, nor approved of; or so habituated to the idea of his own meanness, so sunk in slothful and sottish indifference, as entirely to have forgot the desire, and almost the very wish, for superiority . . . .

Of the Corruption of Our Moral Sentiments, which is Occasioned by this Disposition to Admire the Rich and the Great, and to Despise or Neglect Persons of Poor and Mean Condition

This disposition to admire, and almost to worship, the rich and the powerful, and to despise, or, at least, to neglect persons of poor and mean condition, though necessary both to establish and to maintain the distinction of ranks and the order of society, is, at the same time, the great and most universal cause of the corruption of our moral sentiments. That wealth and greatness are often regarded with the respect and admiration which are due only to wisdom and virtue; and that the contempt, of which vice and folly are the only proper objects, is often most unjustly bestowed upon poverty and weakness, has been the complaint of moralists in all ages.

We desire both to be respectable and to be respected. We dread both to be contemptible and to be contemned. But, upon coming into the world, we soon find that wisdom and virtue are by no means the sole objects of respect; nor vice and folly, of contempt. We frequently see the respectful attentions of the world more strongly directed towards the rich and the great, than towards the wise and the virtuous. We see frequently the vices and follies of the powerful much less despised than the poverty and weakness of the innocent. To deserve, to acquire, and to enjoy the respect and admiration of mankind, are the great objects of ambition and emulation. Two different roads are presented to us, equally leading to the attainment of this so much desired object; the one, by the study of wisdom and the practice of virtue; the other, by the acquisition of wealth and greatness. Two different characters are presented to our emulation; the one, of proud ambition and ostentatious avidity; the other, of humble modesty and equitable justice. Two different models, two different pictures, are held out to us, according to which we may fashion our own character and behaviour; the one more gaudy and glittering in its colouring; the other more correct and more exquisitely beautiful in its outline: the one forcing itself upon the notice of every wandering eye; the other, attracting the attention of scarce anybody but the most studious and careful observer. They are the wise and the virtuous chiefly, a select, though, I am afraid, but a small party, who are the real and steady admirers of wisdom and virtue. The great mob of mankind are the admirers and worshippers, and, what may seem more extraordinary, most frequently the disinterested admirers and worshippers, of wealth and greatness . . . .

In the middling and inferior stations of life, the road to virtue and that to fortune, to such fortune, at least, as men in such stations can reasonably expect to acquire, are, happily in most cases, very nearly the same. In all the middling and inferior professions, real and solid professional abilities, joined to prudent, just, firm, and temperate conduct, can very seldom fail of success . . . .

In the superior stations of life the case is unhappily not always the same. In the courts of princes, in the drawing-rooms of the great, where success and preferment depend, not upon the esteem of intelligent and well-informed equals, but upon the fanciful and foolish favour of ignorant, presumptuous, and proud superiors; flattery and falsehood too often prevail over merit and abilities. In such societies the abilities to please, are more regarded than the abilities to serve. In quiet and peaceable times, when the storm is at a distance, the prince, or great man, wishes only to be amused, and is even apt to fancy that he has scarce any occasion for the service of anybody, or that those who amuse him are sufficiently able to serve him. The external graces, the frivolous accomplishments of that impertinent and foolish thing called a man of fashion, are commonly more admired than the solid and masculine virtues of a warrior, a statesman, a philosopher, or a legislator. All the great and awful virtues, all the virtues which can fit, either for the council, the senate, or the field, are, by the insolent and insignificant flatterers, who commonly figure the most in such corrupted societies, held in the utmost contempt and derision . . . .

It is from our disposition to admire, and consequently to imitate, the rich and the great, that they are enabled to set, or to lead what is called the fashion. Their dress is the fashionable dress; the language of their conversation, the fashionable style; their air and deportment, the fashionable behaviour. Even their vices and follies are fashionable; and the greater part of men are proud to imitate and resemble them in the very qualities which dishonour and degrade them. Vain men often give themselves airs of a fashionable profligacy, which, in their hearts, they do not approve of, and of which, perhaps, they are really not guilty. They desire to be praised for what they themselves do not think praise-worthy, and are ashamed of unfashionable virtues which they sometimes practice in secret, and for which they have secretly some degree of real veneration. There are hypocrites of wealth and greatness, as well as of religion and virtue; and a vain man is as apt to pretend to be what he is not, in the one way, as a cunning man is in the other. He assumes the equipage and splendid way of living of his superiors, without considering that whatever may be praise-worthy in any of these, derives its whole merit and propriety from its suitableness to that situation and fortune which both require and can easily support the expense. Many a poor man places his glory in being thought rich, without considering that the duties (if one may call such follies by so very venerable a name) which that reputation imposes upon him, must soon reduce him to beggary, and render his situation still more unlike that of those whom he admires and imitates, than it had been originally.

To attain to this envied situation, the candidates for fortune too frequently abandon the paths of virtue; for unhappily, the road which leads to the one, and that which leads to the other, lie sometimes in very opposite directions. But the ambitious man flatters himself that, in the splendid situation to which he advances, he will have so many means of commanding the respect and admiration of mankind, and will be enabled to act with such superior propriety and grace, that the lustre of his future conduct will entirely cover, or efface, the foulness of the steps by which he arrived at that elevation. . . . It is not ease or pleasure, but always honour, of one kind or another, though frequently an honour very ill understood, that the ambitious man really pursues. But the honour of his exalted station appears, both in his own eyes and in those of other people, polluted and defiled by the baseness of the means through which he rose to it. Though by the profusion of every liberal expense; though by excessive indulgence in every profligate pleasure, the wretched, but usual, resource of ruined characters; though by the hurry of public business, or by the prouder and more dazzling tumult of war, he may endeavour to efface, both from his own memory and from that of other people, the remembrance of what he has done; that remembrance never fails to pursue him. He invokes in vain the dark and dismal powers of forgetfulness and oblivion. He remembers himself what he has done, and that remembrance tells him that other people must likewise remember it. Amidst all the gaudy pomp of the most ostentatious greatness; amidst the venal and vile adulation of the great and of the learned; amidst the more innocent, though more foolish, acclamations of the common people; amidst all the pride of conquest and the triumph of successful war, he is still secretly pursued by the avenging furies of shame and remorse; and, while glory seems to surround him on all sides, he himself, in his own imagination, sees black and foul infamy fast pursuing him, and every moment ready to overtake him from behind . . . .

PART TWO

Of Merit and Demerit; Or, of the Objects of Reward and Punishment

I: Of the Sense of Merit and Demerit

There is another set of qualities ascribed to the actions and conduct of mankind, distinct from their propriety or impropriety, their decency or ungracefulness, and which are the objects of a distinct species of approbation and disapprobation. These are Merit and Demerit, the qualities of deserving reward, and of deserving punishment.

It has already been observed, that the sentiment or affection of the heart, from which any action proceeds, and upon which its whole virtue or vice depends, may be considered under two different aspects, or in two different relations: first, in relation to the cause or object which excites it; and, secondly, in relation to the end which it proposes, or to the effect which it tends to produce: that upon the suitableness or unsuitableness, upon the proportion or disproportion, which the affection seems to bear to the cause or object which excites it, depends the propriety or impropriety, the decency or ungracefulness of the consequent action; and that upon the beneficial or hurtful effects which the affection proposes or tends to produce, depends the merit or demerit, the good or ill desert of the action to which it gives occasion. Wherein consists our sense of the propriety or impropriety of actions, has been explained in the former part of this discourse. We come now to consider, wherein consists that of their good or ill desert.

That Whatever Appears to be the Proper Object of Gratitude, Appears to Deserve Reward; and That, in the Same Manner, Whatever Appears to be the Proper Object of Resentment, Appears to Deserve Punishment

To us, therefore, that action must appear to deserve reward, which appears to be the proper and approved object of that sentiment, which most immediately and directly prompts us to reward, or to do good to another. And in the same manner, that action must appear to deserve punishment, which appears to be the proper and approved object of that sentiment which most immediately and directly prompts us to punish, or to inflict evil upon another.

The sentiment which most immediately and directly prompts us to reward, is gratitude; that which most immediately and directly prompts us to punish, is resentment.

To us, therefore, that action must appear to deserve reward, which appears to be the proper and approved object of gratitude; as, on the other hand, that action must appear to deserve punishment, which appears to be the proper and approved object of resentment . . . .

Of the Proper Objects of Gratitude and Resentment

To be the proper and approved object either of gratitude or resentment, can mean nothing but to be the object of that gratitude, and of that resentment, which naturally seems proper, and is approved of.

But these, as well as all the other passions of human nature, seem proper and are approved of, when the heart of every impartial spectator entirely sympathizes with them, when every indifferent bystander entirely enters into, and goes along with them.

He, therefore, appears to deserve reward, who, to some person or persons, is the natural object of a gratitude which every human heart is disposed to beat time to, and thereby applaud: and he, on the other hand, appears to deserve punishment, who in the same manner is to some person or persons the natural object of a resentment which the breast of every reasonable man is ready to adopt and sympathize with. To us, surely, that action must appear to deserve reward, which everybody who knows of it would wish to reward, and therefore delights to see rewarded: and that action must as surely appear to deserve punishment, which everybody who hears of it is angry with, and upon that account rejoices to see punished . . . .

That Where There is No Approbation of the Conduct of the Person Who Confers the Benefit, There is Little Sympathy With the Gratitude of Him Who Receives It: and That, on the Contrary, Where There is No Disapprobation of the Motives of the Person Who Does the Mischief, There is no Sort of Sympathy With the Resentment of Him Who Suffers It

It is to be observed, however, that, how beneficial soever on the one hand, or how hurtful soever on the other, the actions or intentions of the person who acts may have been to the person who is, if I may say so, acted upon, yet if in the one case there appears to have been no propriety in the motives of the agent, if we cannot enter into the affections which influenced his conduct, we have little sympathy with the gratitude of the person who receives the benefit: or if, in the other case, there appears to have been no impropriety in the motives of the agent, if, on the contrary, the affections which influenced his conduct are such as we must necessarily enter into, we can have no sort of sympathy with the resentment of the person who suffers. Little gratitude seems due in the one case and all sort of resentment seems unjust in the other. The one action seems to merit little reward, the other to deserve no punishment . . . .

The Analysis of the Sense of Merit and Demerit

As our sense, therefore, of the propriety of conduct arises from what I shall call a direct sympathy with the affections and motives of the person who acts, so our sense of its merit arises from what I shall call an indirect sympathy with the gratitude of the person who is, if I may say so, acted upon.

As we cannot indeed enter thoroughly into the gratitude of the person who receives the benefit, unless we beforehand approve of the motives of the benefactor, so, upon this account, the sense of merit seems to be a compounded sentiment, and to be made up of two distinct emotions; a direct sympathy with the sentiments of the agent, and an indirect sympathy with the gratitude of those who receive the benefit of his actions . . . .

In the same manner as our sense of the impropriety of conduct arises from a want of sympathy, or from a direct antipathy to the affections and motives of the agent, so our sense of its demerit arises from what I shall here too call an indirect sympathy with the resentment of the sufferer.

As we cannot indeed enter into the resentment of the sufferer, unless our heart beforehand disapproves the motives of the agent, and renounces all fellow-feeling with them; so upon this account the sense of demerit, as well as that of merit, seems to be a compounded sentiment, and to be made up of two distinct emotions; a direct antipathy to the sentiments of the agent, and an indirect sympathy with the resentment of the sufferer.

We may here too, upon many different occasions, plainly distinguish those two different emotions combining and uniting together in our sense of the ill desert of a particular character or action. When we read in history concerning the perfidy and cruelty of a Borgia or a Nero,[5] our heart rises up against the detestable sentiments which influenced their conduct, and renounces with horror and abomination all fellow-feeling with such execrable motives. So far our sentiments are founded upon the direct antipathy to the affections of the agent: and the indirect sympathy with the resentment of the sufferers is still more sensibly felt. When we bring home to ourselves the situation of the persons whom those scourges of mankind insulted, murdered, or betrayed, what indignation do we not feel against such insolent and inhuman oppressors of the earth? Our sympathy with the unavoidable distress of the innocent suf-

---

[5] [Cesare Borgia (1467–1507) and Nero (AD37–68), Roman emperor 55–68.]

ferers is not more real nor more lively, than our fellow-feeling with their just and natural resentment. The former sentiment only heightens the latter, and the idea of their distress serves only to inflame and blow up our animosity against those who occasioned it. When we think of the anguish of the sufferers, we take part with them more earnestly against their oppressors; we enter with more eagerness into all their schemes of vengeance, and feel ourselves every moment wreaking, in imagination, upon such violators of the laws of society, that punishment which our sympathetic indignation tells us is due to their crimes. Our sense of the horror and dreadful atrocity of such conduct, the delight which we take in hearing that it was properly punished, the indignation which we feel when it escapes this due retaliation, our whole sense and feeling, in short, of its ill desert, of the propriety and fitness of inflicting evil upon the person who is guilty of it, and of making him grieve in his turn, arises from the sympathetic indignation which naturally boils up in the breast of the spectator, whenever he thoroughly brings home to himself the case of the sufferer.[6]

---

[6] To ascribe in this manner our natural sense of the ill desert of human actions to a sympathy with the resentment of the sufferer, may seem, to the greater part of people, to be a degradation of that sentiment. Resentment is commonly regarded as so odious a passion, that they will be apt to think it impossible that so laudable a principle, as the sense of the ill desert of vice, should in any respect be founded upon it. They will be more willing, perhaps, to admit that our sense of the merit of good actions is founded upon a sympathy with the gratitude of the persons who receive the benefit of them; because gratitude, as well as all the other benevolent passions, is regarded as an amiable principle, which can take nothing from the worth of whatever is founded upon it. Gratitude and resentment, however, are in every respect, it is evident, counterparts to one another; and if our sense of merit arises from a sympathy with the one, our sense of demerit can scarce miss to proceed from a fellow-feeling with the other.

Let it be considered too that resentment, though, in the degrees in which we too often see it, the most odious, perhaps, of all the passions, is not disapproved of when properly humbled and entirely brought down to the level of the sympathetic indignation of the spectator. When we, who are the bystanders, feel that our own animosity entirely corresponds with that of the sufferer, when the resentment of this last does not in any respect go beyond our own, when no word, no gesture, escapes him that denotes an emotion more violent than what we can keep time to, and when he never aims at inflicting any punishment beyond what we should rejoice to see inflicted, or what we ourselves would upon this account even desire to be the instruments of inflicting, it is impossible that we should not entirely approve of his sentiments. Our own emotion in this case must, in our eyes, undoubtedly justify his. And as experience teaches us how much the greater part of mankind are incapable of this moderation, and how great an effort must be made in order to bring down the rude and undisciplined impulse of resentment to this suitable temper, we cannot avoid conceiving a considerable degree of esteem and admiration for one who appears capable of exerting so much self-command over one of the most ungovernable passions of his nature. When indeed the animosity of the sufferer exceeds, as it almost always does, what we can go along with, as we cannot enter into it, we necessarily disapprove of it. We even

II: Of Justice and Beneficence

Comparison of Those Two Virtues

Actions of a beneficent tendency, which proceed from proper motives, seem alone to require reward; because such alone are the approved objects of gratitude, or excite the sympathetic gratitude of the spectator.

Actions of a hurtful tendency, which proceed from improper motives, seem alone to deserve punishment; because such alone are the approved objects of resentment, or excite the sympathetic resentment of the spectator.

Beneficence is always free, it cannot be extorted by force, the mere want of it exposes to no punishment; because the mere want of beneficence tends to do no real positive evil. It may disappoint of the good which might reasonably have been expected, and upon that account it may justly excite dislike and disapprobation: it cannot, however, provoke any resentment which mankind will go along with. The man who does not recompense his benefactor, when he has it in his power, and when his benefactor needs his assistance, is, no doubt, guilty of the

---

disapprove of it more than we should of an equal excess of almost any other passion derived from the imagination. And this too violent resentment, instead of carrying us along with it, becomes itself the object of our resentment and indignation. We enter into the opposite resentment of the person who is the object of this unjust emotion, and who is in danger of suffering from it. Revenge, therefore, the excess of resentment, appears to be the most detestable of all the passions, and is the object of the horror and indignation of every body. And as in the way in which this passion commonly discovers itself among mankind, it is excessive a hundred times for once that it is moderate, we are very apt to consider it as altogether odious and detestable, because in its most ordinary appearances it is so. Nature, however, even in the present depraved state of mankind, does not seem to have dealt so unkindly with us, as to have endowed us with any principle which is wholly and in every respect evil, or which, in no degree and in no direction, can be the proper object of praise and approbation. Upon some occasions we are sensible that this passion, which is generally too strong, may likewise be too weak. We sometimes complain that a particular person shows too little spirit, and has too little sense of the injuries that have been done to him; and we are as ready to despise him for the defect, as to hate him for the excess of this passion.

Let it be considered too, that the present inquiry is not concerning a matter of right, if I may say so, but concerning a matter of fact. We are not at present examining upon what principles a perfect being would approve of the punishment of bad actions; but upon what principles so weak and imperfect a creature as man actually and in fact approves of it. The principles which I have just now mentioned, it is evident, have a very great effect upon his sentiments; and it seems wisely ordered that it should be so. The very existence of society requires that unmerited and unprovoked malice should be restrained by proper punishments; and consequently, that to inflict those punishments should be regarded as a proper and laudable action. Though man, therefore, be naturally endowed with a desire of the welfare and preservation of society, yet the Author of nature has not entrusted it to his reason to find out that a certain application of

blackest ingratitude. The heart of every impartial spectator rejects all fellow-feeling with the selfishness of his motives, and he is the proper object of the highest disapprobation. But still he does no positive hurt to anybody. He only does not do that good which in propriety he ought to have done. He is the object of hatred, a passion which is naturally excited by impropriety of sentiment and behaviour; not of resentment, a passion which is never properly called forth but by actions which tend to do real and positive hurt to some particular persons. His want of gratitude, therefore, cannot be punished. To oblige him by force to perform what in gratitude he ought to perform, and what every impartial spectator would approve of him for performing, would, if possible, be still more improper than his neglecting to perform it. His benefactor would dishonour himself if he attempted by violence to constrain him to gratitude, and it would be impertinent for any third person, who was not the superior of either, to intermeddle. But of all the duties of beneficence, those which gratitude recommends to us approach nearest to what is called a perfect and complete obligation. What friendship, what generosity, what charity, would prompt us to do with universal approbation, is still more free, and can still less be extorted by force than the duties of gratitude. We talk of the debt of gratitude, not of charity, or generosity, nor even of friendship, when friendship is mere esteem, and has not been enhanced and complicated with gratitude for good offices.

Resentment seems to have been given us by nature for defence, and for defence only. It is the safeguard of justice and the security of innocence. It prompts us to beat off the mischief which is attempted to be done to us, and to retaliate that which is already done; that the offender

---

punishments is the proper means of attaining this end; but has endowed him with an immediate and instinctive approbation of that very application which is most proper to attain it. The economy of nature is in this respect exactly of a piece with what it is upon many other occasions. With regard to all those ends which, upon account of their peculiar importance, may be regarded, if such an expression is allowable, as the favourite ends of nature, she has constantly in this manner not only endowed mankind with an appetite for the end which she proposes, but likewise with an appetite for the means by which alone this end can be brought about, for their own sakes, and independent of their tendency to produce it. Thus self-preservation, and the propagation of the species, are the great ends which Nature seems to have proposed in the formation of all animals. Mankind are endowed with a desire of those ends, and an aversion to the contrary; with a love of life, and a dread of dissolution; with a desire of the continuance and perpetuity of the species, and with an aversion to the thoughts of its entire extinction. But though we are in this manner endowed with a very strong desire of those ends, it has not been entrusted to the slow and uncertain determinations of our reason, to find out the proper means of bringing them about. Nature has directed us to the greater part of these by original and immediate instincts. Hunger, thirst, the passion which unites the two sexes, the love of pleasure, and the dread of pain, prompt us to apply those means for their own sakes, and without any consideration of their tendency to those beneficent ends which the great Director of nature intended to produce by them.

may be made to repent of his injustice, and that others, through fear of the like punishment, may be terrified from being guilty of the like offence. It must be reserved therefore for these purposes, nor can the spectator ever go along with it when it is exerted for any other. But the mere want of the beneficent virtues, though it may disappoint us of the good which might reasonably be expected, neither does, nor attempts to do, any mischief from which we can have occasion to defend ourselves.

There is, however, another virtue, of which the observance is not left to the freedom of our own wills, which may be extorted by force, and of which the violation exposes to resentment, and consequently to punishment. This virtue is justice: the violation of justice is injury: it does real and positive hurt to some particular persons, from motives which are naturally disapproved of. It is, therefore, the proper object of resentment, and of punishment, which is the natural consequence of resentment. As mankind go along with, and approve of the violence employed to avenge the hurt which is done by injustice, so they much more go along with, and approve of, that which is employed to prevent and beat off the injury, and to restrain the offender from hurting his neighbours. The person himself who meditates an injustice is sensible of this, and feels that force may, with the utmost propriety, be made use of, both by the person whom he is about to injure, and by others, either to obstruct the execution of his crime, or to punish him when he has executed it. And upon this is founded that remarkable distinction between justice and all the other social virtues, which has of late been particularly insisted upon by an author of very great and original genius,[7] that we feel ourselves to be under a stricter obligation to act according to justice, than agreeably to friendship, charity, or generosity; that the practice of these last mentioned virtues seems to be left in some measure to our own choice, but that, somehow or other, we feel ourselves to be in a peculiar manner tied, bound, and obliged to the observation of justice. We feel, that is to say, that force may, with the utmost propriety, and with the approbation of all mankind, be made use of to constrain us to observe the rules of the one, but not to follow the precepts of the other.

We must always, however, carefully distinguish what is only blameable, or the proper object of disapprobation, from what force may be employed either to punish or to prevent. That seems blameable which falls short of that ordinary degree of proper beneficence which experience teaches us to expect of everybody; and on the contrary, that seems praise-worthy which goes beyond it. The ordinary degree itself seems neither blameable nor praise-worthy. A father, a son, a brother, who behaves to the correspondent relation neither better nor worse than the greater part of men commonly do, seems properly to deserve neither praise nor blame. He who surprises us by extraordinary and unexpected, though still proper and suitable kindness, or on the contrary by

---

[7] [Henry Home, Lord Kames (1696–1782).]

extraordinary and unexpected, as well as unsuitable unkindness, seems praise-worthy in the one case, and blameable in the other.

Even the most ordinary degree of kindness or beneficence, however, cannot, among equals, be extorted by force. Among equals each individual is naturally, and antecedent to the institution of civil government, regarded as having a right both to defend himself from injuries, and to exact a certain degree of punishment for those which have been done to him. Every generous spectator not only approves of his conduct when he does this, but enters so far into his sentiments as often to be willing to assist him. When one man attacks, or robs, or attempts to murder another, all the neighbours take the alarm, and think that they do right when they run, either to revenge the person who has been injured, or to defend him who is in danger of being so. But when a father fails in the ordinary degree of parental affection towards a son; when a son seems to want that filial reverence which might be expected to his father; when brothers are without the usual degree of brotherly affection; when a man shuts his breast against compassion, and refuses to relieve the misery of his fellow-creatures, when he can with the greatest ease; in all these cases, though everybody blames the conduct, nobody imagines that those who might have reason, perhaps, to expect more kindness, have any right to extort it by force. The sufferer can only complain, and the spectator can intermeddle no other way than by advice and persuasion. Upon all such occasions, for equals to use force against one another, would be thought the highest degree of insolence and presumption....

Though the mere want of beneficence seems to merit no punishment from equals, the greater exertions of that virtue appear to deserve the highest reward. By being productive of the greatest good, they are the natural and approved objects of the liveliest gratitude. Though the breach of justice, on the contrary, exposes to punishment, the observance of the rules of that virtue seems scarce to deserve any reward. There is, no doubt, a propriety in the practice of justice, and it merits, upon that account, all the approbation which is due to propriety. But as it does no real positive good, it is entitled to very little gratitude. Mere justice is, upon most occasions, but a negative virtue, and only hinders us from hurting our neighbour. The man who barely abstains from violating either the person, or the estate, or the reputation of his neighbours, has surely very little positive merit. He fulfils, however, all the rules of what is peculiarly called justice, and does everything which his equals can with propriety force him to do, or which they can punish him for not doing. We may often fulfil all the rules of justice by sitting still and doing nothing.

As every man doth, so shall it be done to him, and retaliation seems to be the great law which is dictated to us by Nature. Beneficence and generosity we think due to the generous and beneficent. Those whose hearts never open to the feelings of humanity, should, we think, be shut out, in the same manner, from the affections of all their fellow-creatures, and be allowed to live in the midst of society, as in a great desert where there is nobody to care for them, or to inquire after them. The violator of the laws of justice ought to be made to feel himself that evil which he has done to another; and since no regard to the sufferings of his brethren is capable of restraining him, he ought to be over-awed by the fear of his own. The man who is barely innocent, who only observes the laws of justice with regard to others, and merely abstains from hurting his neighbours, can merit only that his neighbours in their turn should respect his innocence, and that the same laws should be religiously observed with regard to him.

Of the Sense of Justice, of Remorse, and of the Consciousness of Merit

There can be no proper motive for hurting our neighbour, there can be no incitement to do evil to another, which mankind will go along with, except just indignation for evil which that other has done to us. To disturb his happiness merely because it stands in the way of our own, to take from him what is of real use to him merely because it may be of equal or of more use to us, or to indulge, in this manner, at the expense of other people, the natural preference which every man has for his own happiness above that of other people, is what no impartial spectator can go along with. Every man is, no doubt, by nature, first and principally recommended to his own care; and as he is fitter to take care of himself than of any other person, it is fit and right that it should be so. Every man, therefore, is much more deeply interested in whatever immediately concerns himself, than in what concerns any other man: and to hear, perhaps, of the death of another person, with whom we have no particular connexion, will give us less concern, will spoil our stomach, or break our rest much less than a very insignificant disaster which has befallen ourselves. But though the ruin of our neighbour may affect us much less than a very small misfortune of our own, we must not ruin him to prevent that small misfortune, not even to prevent our own ruin. We must, here, as in all other cases, view ourselves not so much according to that light in which we may naturally appear to ourselves, as according to that in which we naturally appear to others. Though every man may, according to the proverb, be the whole world to himself, to the rest of mankind he is a most insignificant part of it. Though his own happiness may be of more importance to him than that of all the world besides, to every other person it is of no more consequence than that of any other man. Though it may be true, therefore, that every individual, in his own breast, naturally prefers himself to all mankind, yet he dares not look mankind in the face, and avow that he acts according to this principle. He feels that in this preference they can never go along with him, and that how natural soever it may be to him, it must always appear excessive and extravagant to them. When he views himself in the light in which he is conscious that others will view him, he sees that to them he is but one of the multitude in no respect better than any other in it. If he would act so as that the impartial spectator may enter into the principles of his conduct, which is what of all things he has the greatest desire to do, he must, upon this, as upon all other occasions, humble the arrogance of his self-love, and bring it down to something which other men can go along with. They will indulge it so far as to allow him to be more anxious about, and to pursue with more earnest assiduity, his own happiness than that of any other person. Thus far, whenever they place themselves in his situation, they will readily go along with him. In the race for wealth, and honours, and preferments, he may run as hard as he can, and strain every nerve and every muscle, in order to outstrip all his competitors. But if he should justle, or throw down any of them, the indulgence of the spectators is entirely at an end. It is a violation of fair play, which they cannot admit of. This man is to them, in every respect, as good as he: they do not enter into that self-love by which he prefers himself so much to this other, and cannot go along with the motive from which he hurt him. They readily, therefore, sympathize with the natural resentment of the injured, and the offender becomes the object of their hatred and indignation. He is sensible that he becomes so, and feels that those sentiments are ready to burst out from all sides against him.

As the greater and more irreparable the evil that is done, the resentment of the sufferer runs naturally the higher; so does likewise the sympathetic indignation of the spectator, as well as the sense of guilt in the agent. Death is the greatest evil which one man can inflict upon another, and excites the highest degree of resentment in those who are immediately connected with the slain. Murder, therefore, is the most atrocious of all crimes which affect individuals only, in the sight both of mankind, and of the person who has committed it. To be deprived of that which we are possessed of, is a greater evil than to be disappointed of what we have only the expectation. Breach of property, therefore, theft and robbery, which take from us what we are possessed of, are greater crimes than breach of contract, which only disappoints us of what we expected. The most sacred laws of justice, therefore, those whose violation seems to call loudest for vengeance and punishment, are the laws which guard the life and person of our neighbour; the next are those which guard his property and possessions; and last of all come those which guard what are called his personal rights, or what is due to him from the promises of others . . . .

Of the Utility of this Constitution of Nature

It is thus that man, who can subsist only in society, was fitted by nature to that situation for which he was made. All the members of human society stand in need of each others assistance, and are likewise exposed to mutual injuries. Where the necessary assistance is reciprocally afforded from love, from gratitude, from friendship, and esteem, the society flourishes and is happy. All the different members of it are bound together by the agreeable bands of love and affection, and are, as it were, drawn to one common centre of mutual good offices.

But though the necessary assistance should not be afforded from such generous and disinterested motives, though among the different members of the society there should be no mutual love and affection, the society, though less happy and agreeable, will not necessarily be dissolved. Society may subsist among different men, as among different merchants, from a sense of its utility, without any mutual love or affection; and though no man in it should owe any obligation, or be bound in gratitude to any other, it may still be upheld by a mercenary exchange of good offices according to an agreed valuation.

Society, however, cannot subsist among those who are at all times ready to hurt and injure one another. The moment that injury begins, the moment that mutual resentment and animosity take place, all the bands of it are broke asunder, and the different members of which it consisted are, as it were, dissipated and scattered abroad by the violence and opposition of their discordant affections. If there is any society among robbers and murderers, they must at least, according to the trite observation, abstain from robbing and murdering one another. Beneficence, therefore, is less essential to the existence of society than justice. Society may subsist, though not in the most comfortable state, without beneficence; but the prevalence of injustice must utterly destroy it.

Though Nature, therefore, exhorts mankind to acts of beneficence, by the pleasing consciousness of deserved reward, she has not thought it necessary to guard and enforce the practice of it by the terrors of merited punishment in case it should be neglected. It is the ornament which embellishes, not the foundation which supports the building, and which it was, therefore, sufficient to recommend, but by no means necessary to impose. Justice, on the contrary, is the main pillar that upholds the whole edifice. If it is removed, the great, the immense fabric of human society, that fabric which to raise and support seems in this world, if I may say so, to have been the peculiar and darling care of Nature, must in a moment crumble into atoms. In order to enforce the observation of justice, therefore, Nature has implanted in the human breast that consciousness of ill-desert, those terrors of merited punishment which attend upon its violation, as the great safeguards of the association of mankind, to protect the weak, to curb the violent, and to chastise the guilty. Men, though naturally sympathetic, feel so little for another, with whom they have no particular connexion, in comparison of what they feel for themselves; the misery of one, who is merely their fellow-creature, is of so little importance to them in comparison even of a small conveniency of their own; they have it so much in their power to hurt him, and may have so many temptations to do so, that if this principle did not stand up within them in his defence, and overawe them into a respect for his innocence, they would, like wild beasts, be at all times ready to fly upon him; and a man would enter an assembly of men as he enters a den of lions.

In every part of the universe we observe means adjusted with the nicest artifice to the ends which they are intended to produce; and in the mechanism of a plant, or animal body, admire how every thing is contrived for advancing the two great purposes of nature, the support of the individual, and the propagation of the species. But in these, and in all such objects, we still distinguish the efficient from the final cause of their several motions and organizations. The digestion of the food, the circulation of the blood, and the secretion of the several juices which are drawn from it, are operations all of them necessary for the great purposes of animal life. Yet we never endeavour to account for them from those purposes as from their efficient causes, nor imagine that the blood circulates, or that the food digests of its own accord, and with a view or intention to the purposes of circulation or digestion. The wheels of the watch are all admirably adjusted to the end for which it was made, the pointing of the hour. All their various motions conspire in the nicest manner to produce this effect. If they were endowed with a desire and intention to produce it, they could not do it better. Yet we never ascribe any such desire or intention to them, but to the watch-maker, and we know that they are put into motion by a spring, which intends the effect it produces as little as they do. But though, in accounting for the operations of bodies, we never fail to distinguish in this manner the efficient from the final cause, in accounting for those of the mind we are very apt to confound these two different things with one another. When by natural principles we are led to advance those ends, which a refined and enlightened reason would recommend to us, we are very apt to impute to that reason, as to their efficient cause, the sentiments and actions by which we advance those ends, and to imagine that to be the wisdom of man, which in reality is the wisdom of God. Upon a superficial view, this cause seems sufficient to produce the effects which are ascribed to it; and the system of human nature seems to be more simple and agreeable when all its different operations are in this manner deduced from a single principle.

As society cannot subsist unless the laws of justice are tolerably observed, as no social intercourse can take place among men who do not generally abstain from injuring one another; the consideration of this necessity, it has been thought, was the ground upon which we approved of the enforcement of the laws of justice by the punishment of those who violated them . . . .

Such is the account commonly given of our approbation of the punishment of injustice. And so far this account is undoubtedly true, that we frequently have occasion to confirm our natural sense of the propriety and fitness of punishment, by reflecting how necessary it is for preserving the order of society. When the guilty is about to suffer that just retaliation, which the natural indignation of mankind tells them is due to his crimes; when the insolence of his injustice is broken and humbled by the terror of his approaching punishment; when he ceases to be an object of fear, with the generous and humane he begins to be an object of pity. The thought of what he is about to suffer extinguishes their resentment for the sufferings of others to which he has given occasion. They are disposed to pardon and forgive him, and to save him from that punishment, which in all their cool hours they had considered as the retribution due to such crimes. Here, therefore, they have occasion to call to their assistance the consideration of the general interest of society. They counterbalance the impulse of this weak and partial humanity by the dictates of a humanity that is more generous and comprehensive. They reflect that mercy to the guilty is cruelty to the innocent, and oppose to the emotions of compassion which they feel for a particular person, a more enlarged compassion which they feel for mankind.

Sometimes too we have occasion to defend the propriety of observing the general rules of justice by the consideration of their necessity to the support of society. We frequently hear the young and the licentious ridiculing the most sacred rules of morality, and professing, sometimes from the corruption, but more frequently from the vanity of their hearts, the most abominable maxims of conduct. Our indignation rouses, and we are eager to refute and expose such detestable principles. But though it is their intrinsic hatefulness and detestableness, which originally inflames us against them, we are unwilling to assign this as the sole reason why we condemn them, or to pretend that it is merely because we ourselves hate and detest them. The reason, we think, would not appear to be conclusive. Yet why should it not; if we hate and detest them because they are the natural and proper objects of hatred and detestation? But when we are asked why we should not act in such or such a manner, the very question seems to suppose that, to those who ask it, this manner of acting does not appear to be for its own sake the natural and proper object of those sentiments. We must show them, therefore, that it ought to be so for the sake of something else. Upon this account we generally cast about for other arguments, and the consideration which first occurs to us, is the disorder and confusion of society which would result from the universal prevalence of such practices. We seldom fail, therefore, to insist upon this topic.

But though it commonly requires no great discernment to see the destructive tendency of all licentious practices to the welfare of society, it is seldom this consideration which first animates us against them. All men, even the most stupid and unthinking, abhor fraud, perfidy, and injustice, and delight to see them punished. But few men have reflected upon the necessity of justice to the existence of society, how obvious soever that necessity may appear to be . . . .

III: Of the Influence of Fortune Upon the Sentiments of Mankind, With Regard to the Merit or Demerit of Actions

Whatever praise or blame can be due to any action, must belong either, first, to the intention or affection of the heart, from which it proceeds; or, secondly, to the external action or movement of the body, which this affection gives occasion to; or, lastly, to the good or bad consequences, which actually, and in fact, proceed from it. These three different things constitute the whole nature and circumstances of the action, and must be the foundation of whatever quality can belong to it.

That the two last of these three circumstances cannot be the foundation of any praise or blame, is abundantly evident; nor has the contrary ever been asserted by anybody. The external action or movement of the body is often the same in the most innocent and in the most blameable actions. He who shoots a bird, and he who shoots a man, both of them perform the same external movement: each of them draws the trigger of a gun. The consequences which actually, and in fact, happen to proceed from any action, are, if possible, still more indifferent either to praise or blame, than even the external movement of the body. As they depend, not upon the agent, but upon fortune, they cannot be the proper foundation for any sentiment, of which his character and conduct are the objects.

The only consequences for which he can be answerable, or by which he can deserve either approbation or disapprobation of any kind, are those which were some way or other intended, or those which, at least, show some agreeable or disagreeable quality in the intention of the heart, from which he acted. To the intention or affection of the heart, therefore, to the propriety or impropriety, to the beneficence or hurtfulness of the design, all praise or blame, all approbation or disapprobation, of any kind, which can justly be bestowed upon any action, must ultimately belong.

When this maxim is thus proposed, in abstract and general terms, there is nobody who does not agree to it. Its self-evident justice is acknowledged by all the world, and there is not a dissenting voice among all mankind. Everybody allows, that how different soever the accidental, the unintended and unforeseen consequences of different actions, yet, if the intentions or affections from which they arose were, on the one hand, equally proper and equally beneficent, or, on the other, equally improper and equally malevolent, the merit or demerit of the actions is still the same, and the agent is equally the suitable object either of gratitude or of resentment.

But how well soever we may seem to be persuaded of the truth of this equitable maxim, when we consider it after this manner, in abstract, yet when we come to particular cases, the actual consequences which happen to proceed from any action, have a very great effect upon our sentiments concerning its merit or demerit, and almost always either enhance or diminish our sense of both. Scarce, in any one instance, perhaps, will our sentiments be found, after examination, to be entirely regulated by this rule, which we all acknowledge ought entirely to regulate them....

Of the Final Cause of This Irregularity of Sentiments

Such is the effect of the good or bad consequences of actions upon the sentiments both of the person who performs them, and of others; and thus, Fortune, which governs the world, has some influence where we should be least willing to allow her any, and directs in some measure the sentiments of mankind, with regard to the character and conduct both of themselves and others. That the world judges by the event, and not by the design, has been in all ages the complaint, and is the great discouragement of virtue. Everybody agrees to the general maxim, that as the event does not depend on the agent, it ought to have no influence upon our sentiments, with regard to the merit or propriety of his conduct. But when we come to particulars, we find that our sentiments are scarce in any one instance exactly conformable to what this equitable maxim would direct. The happy or unprosperous event of any action, is not only apt to give us a good or bad opinion of the prudence with which it was conducted, but almost always too animates our gratitude or resentment, our sense of the merit or demerit of the design.

Nature, however, when she implanted the seeds of this irregularity in the human breast, seems, as upon all other occasions, to have intended the happiness and perfection of the species. If the hurtfulness of the design, if the malevolence of the affection, were alone the causes which excited our resentment, we should feel all the furies of that passion against any person in whose breast we suspected or believed such designs or affections were harboured, though they had never broke out into any action. Sentiments, thoughts, intentions, would become the objects of punishment; and if the indignation of mankind run as high against them as against actions; if the baseness of the thought which had given birth to no action, seemed in the eyes of the world as much to call aloud for vengeance as the baseness of the action, every court of judicature would become a real inquisition. There would be no safety for the most innocent and circumspect conduct. Bad wishes, bad views, bad designs, might still be suspected; and while these excited the same indignation with bad conduct, while bad intentions were as much resented as bad actions, they would equally expose the person to punishment and resentment. Actions, therefore, which either produce actual evil, or attempt to produce it, and thereby put us in the immediate fear of it, are by the Author of nature rendered the only proper and approved objects of human punishment and resentment. Sentiments, designs, affections, though it is from these that according to cool reason human actions derive their whole merit or demerit, are placed by the great Judge of hearts beyond the limits of every human jurisdiction, and are reserved for the cognizance of his own unerring tribunal. That necessary rule of justice, therefore, that men in this life are liable to punishment for their actions only, not for their designs and intentions, is founded upon this salutary and useful irregularity in human sentiments concerning merit or demerit, which at first sight appears so absurd and unaccountable. But every part of nature, when attentively surveyed, equally demonstrates the providential care of its Author, and we may admire the wisdom and goodness of God even in the weakness and folly of man.

Nor is that irregularity of sentiments altogether without its utility, by which the merit of an unsuccessful attempt to serve, and much more that of mere good inclinations and kind wishes, appears to be imperfect. Man was made for action, and to promote by the exertion of his faculties such changes in the external circumstances both of himself and others, as may seem most favourable to the happiness of all. He must not be satisfied with indolent benevolence, nor fancy himself the friend of mankind, because in his heart he wishes well to the prosperity of the world. That he may call forth the whole vigour of his soul, and strain every nerve, in order to produce those ends which it is the purpose of his being to advance, Nature has taught him, that neither himself nor mankind can be fully satisfied with his conduct, nor bestow upon it the full measure of applause, unless he has actually produced them. He is made to know, that the praise of good intentions, without the merit of good offices, will be but of little avail to excite either the loudest acclamations of the world, or even the highest degree of self-applause. The man who has performed no single action of importance, but whose whole conversation and deportment express the justest, the noblest, and most generous sentiments, can be entitled to demand no very high reward, even though his inutility should be owing to nothing but the want of an opportunity to serve. We can still refuse it him without blame. We can still ask him, What have you done? What actual service can you produce, to entitle you to so great a recompense? We esteem you, and love you; but we owe you nothing. To reward indeed that latent virtue which has been useless only for want of an opportunity to serve, to bestow upon it those honours and preferments, which, though in some measure it may be said to deserve them, it could not with propriety have insisted upon, is the effect of the most divine benevolence. To punish, on the contrary, for the affections of the heart only, where no crime has been committed, is the most insolent and barbarous tyranny. The benevolent affections seem to deserve most praise, when they do not wait till it becomes almost a crime for them not to exert themselves. The malevolent, on the contrary, can scarce be too tardy, too slow, or deliberate . . . .

PART THREE

Of the Foundation of Our Judgments Concerning Our Own Sentiments and Conduct, and of the Sense of Duty

Of the Principle of Self-Approbation and of Self-Disapprobation

In the two foregoing parts of this discourse, I have chiefly considered the origin and foundation of our judgments concerning the sentiments and conduct of others. I come now to consider more particularly the origin of those concerning our own.

The principle by which we naturally either approve or disapprove of our own conduct, seems to be altogether the same with that by which we exercise the like judgments concerning the conduct of other people. We either approve or disapprove of the conduct of another man according as we feel that, when we bring his case home to ourselves, we either can or cannot entirely sympathize with the sentiments and motives which directed it. And, in the same manner, we either approve or disapprove of our own conduct, according as we feel that, when we place ourselves in the situation of another man, and view it, as it were, with his eyes and from his station, we either can or cannot entirely enter into and sympathize with the sentiments and motives which influenced it. We can never survey our own sentiments and motives, we can never form any judgment concerning them; unless we remove ourselves, as it were, from our own natural station, and endeavour to view them as at a certain distance from us. But we can do this in no other way than by endeavouring to view them with the eyes of other people, or as other people are likely to view them. Whatever judgment we can form concerning them, accordingly, must always bear some secret reference, either to what are, or to what, upon a certain condition, would be, or to what, we imagine, ought to be the judgment of others. We endeavour to examine our own conduct as we imagine any other fair and impartial spectator would examine it. If, upon placing ourselves in his situation, we thoroughly enter into all the passions and motives which influenced it, we approve of it, by sympathy with the approbation of this supposed equitable judge. If otherwise, we enter into his disapprobation, and condemn it.

Were it possible that a human creature could grow up to manhood in some solitary place, without any communication with his own species, he could no more think of his own character, of the propriety or demerit of his own sentiments and conduct, of the beauty or deformity of his own mind, than of the beauty or deformity of his own face. All these are objects which he cannot easily see, which naturally he does not look at and with regard to which he is provided with no mirror which can present them to his view. Bring him into society, and he is immediately provided with the mirror which he wanted before. It is placed in the countenance and behaviour of those he lives with, which always mark when they enter into, and when they disapprove of his sentiments; and it is here that he first views the propriety and impropriety of his own passions, the beauty and deformity of his own mind. To a man who from his birth was a stranger to society, the objects of his passions, the external bodies which either pleased or hurt him, would occupy his whole attention. The passions themselves, the desires or aversions, the joys or sorrows, which those objects excited, though of all things the most immediately present to him, could scarce ever be the objects of his thoughts. The idea of them could never interest him so much as to call upon his attentive consideration. The consideration of his joy could in him excite no new joy, nor that of his sorrow any new sorrow: though the consideration of the causes of those passions might often excite both. Bring him into society, and all his own passions will immediately become the causes of new passions. He will observe that mankind approve of some of them, and are disgusted by others. He will be elevated in the one case, and cast down in the other; his desires and aversions, his joys and sorrows, will now often become the causes of new desires and new aversions, new joys and new sorrows: they will now, therefore, interest him deeply, and often call upon his most attentive consideration.

Our first ideas of personal beauty and deformity, are drawn from the shape and appearance of others, not from our own. We soon become sensible, however, that others exercise the same criticism upon us. We are pleased when they approve of our figure, and are disobliged when they seem to be disgusted. We become anxious to know how far our appearance deserves either their blame or approbation. We examine our persons limb by limb, and by placing ourselves before a looking-glass, or by some such expedient, endeavour, as much as possible, to view ourselves at the distance and with the eyes of other people. If, after this examination, we are satisfied with our own appearance, we can more easily support the most disadvantageous judgments of others. If, on the contrary, we are sensible that we are the natural objects of distaste, every appearance of their disapprobation mortifies us beyond all measure. A man who is tolerably handsome, will allow you to laugh at any little irregularity in his person; but all such jokes are commonly unsupportable to one who is really deformed. It is evident, however, that we are anxious about our own beauty and deformity, only upon account of its effect upon others. If we had no connexion with society, we should be altogether indifferent about either.

In the same manner our first moral criticisms are exercised upon the characters and conduct of other people; and we are all very forward to observe how each of these affects us. But we soon learn, that other people are equally frank with regard to our own. We become anxious to know how far we deserve their censure or applause, and whether to them we must necessarily appear those agreeable or disagreeable creatures which they represent us. We begin, upon this account, to examine our own passions and conduct, and to consider how these must appear to them, by considering how they would appear to us if in their situation. We suppose ourselves the spectators of our own behaviour, and endeavour to imagine what effect it would, in this light, produce upon us. This is the only looking-glass by which we can, in some measure, with the eyes of other people, scrutinize the propriety of our own conduct. If in this view it pleases us, we are tolerably satisfied. We can be more indifferent about the applause, and, in some measure, despise the censure of the world; secure that, however misunderstood or misrepresented, we are the natural and proper objects of approbation. On the contrary, if we are doubtful about it, we are often, upon that very account, more anxious to gain their approbation, and, provided we have not already, as they say, shaken hands with infamy, we are altogether distracted at the thoughts of their censure, which then strikes us with double severity.

When I endeavour to examine my own conduct, when I endeavour to pass sentence upon it, and either to approve or condemn it, it is evident that, in all such cases, I divide myself, as it were, into two persons; and that I, the examiner and judge, represent a different character from that other I, the person whose conduct is examined into and judged of. The first is the spectator, whose sentiments with regard to my own conduct I endeavour to enter into, by placing myself in his situation, and by considering how it would appear to me, when seen from that particular point of view. The second is the agent, the person whom I properly call myself, and of whose conduct, under the character of a spectator, I was endeavouring to form some opinion. The first is the judge; the second the person judged of. But that the judge should, in every respect, be the same with the person judged of, is as impossible, as that the cause should, in every respect, be the same with the effect . . . .

Of the Love of Praise, and of That of Praise-Worthiness; and of the Dread of Blame, and of That of Blame-Worthiness

Man naturally desires, not only to be loved, but to be lovely; or to be that thing which is the natural and proper object of love. He naturally dreads, not only to be hated, but to be hateful; or to be that thing which is the natural and proper object of hatred. He desires, not only praise, but praise-worthiness; or to be that thing which, though it should be praised by nobody, is, however, the natural and proper object of praise. He dreads, not only blame, but blame-worthiness; or to be that thing which, though it should be blamed by nobody, is, however, the natural and proper object of blame . . . .

The love and admiration which we naturally conceive for those whose character and conduct we approve of, necessarily dispose us to desire to become ourselves the objects of the like agreeable sentiments, and to be as amiable and as admirable as those whom we love and admire the most. Emulation, the anxious desire that we ourselves should excel, is originally founded in our admiration of the excellence of others. Neither can we be satisfied with being merely admired for what other people are admired. We must at least believe ourselves to be admirable for what they are admirable. But, in order to attain this satisfaction, we must become the impartial spectators of our own character and conduct. We must endeavour to view them with the eyes of other people, or as other people are likely to view them. When seen in this light, if they appear to us as we wish, we are happy and contented. But it greatly confirms this happiness and contentment when we find that other people, viewing them with those very eyes with which we, in imagination only, were endeavouring to view them, see them precisely in the same light in which we ourselves had seen them. Their approbation necessarily confirms our own self-approbation. Their praise necessarily strengthens our own sense of our own praise-worthiness. In this case, so far is the love of praise-worthiness from being derived altogether from that of praise; that the love of praise seems, at least in a great measure, to be derived from that of praise-worthiness . . . .

As ignorant and groundless praise can give no solid joy, no satisfaction that will bear any serious examination, so, on the contrary, it often gives real comfort to reflect, that though no praise should actually be bestowed upon us, our conduct, however, has been such as to deserve it, and has been in every respect suitable to those measures and rules by which praise and approbation are naturally and commonly bestowed … . The man who is conscious to himself that he has exactly observed those measures of conduct which experience informs him are generally agreeable, reflects with satisfaction on the propriety of his own behaviour. When he views it in the light in which the impartial spectator would view it, he thoroughly enters into all the motives which influenced it. He looks back upon every part of it with pleasure and approbation, and though mankind should never be acquainted with what he has done, he regards himself, not so much according to the light in which they actually regard him, as according to that in which they would regard him if they were better informed . . . .

Nature, when she formed man for society, endowed him with an original desire to please, and an original aversion to offend his brethren. She taught him to feel pleasure in their favourable, and pain in their unfavourable regard. She rendered their approbation most flattering and most agreeable to him for its own sake; and their disapprobation most mortifying and most offensive.

But this desire of the approbation, and this aversion to the disapprobation of his brethren, would not alone have rendered him fit for that society for which he was made. Nature, accordingly, has endowed him, not only with a desire of being approved of, but with a desire of being what ought to be approved of; or of being what he himself approves of in other men. The first desire could only have made him wish to appear to be fit for society. The second was necessary in order to render him anxious to be really fit. The first could only have prompted him to the affectation of virtue, and to the concealment of vice. The second was necessary in order to inspire him with the real love of virtue, and with the real abhorrence of vice . . . .

The all-wise Author of Nature has, in this manner, taught man to respect the sentiments and judgments of his brethren; to be more or less pleased when they approve of his conduct, and to be more or less hurt when they disapprove of it. He has made man, if I may say so, the immediate judge of mankind; and has, in this respect, as in many others, created him after his own image, and appointed him his vicegerent upon earth, to superintend the behaviour of his brethren. They are taught by nature, to acknowledge that power and jurisdiction which has thus been conferred upon him, to be more or less humbled and mortified when they have incurred his censure, and to be more or less elated when they have obtained his applause.

But though man has, in this manner, been rendered the immediate judge of mankind, he has been rendered so only in the first instance; and an appeal lies from his sentence to a much higher tribunal, to the tribunal of their own consciences, to that of the supposed impartial and well-informed spectator, to that of the man within the breast, the great judge and arbiter of their conduct. The jurisdictions of those two tribunals are founded upon principles which, though in some respects resembling and akin, are, however, in reality different and distinct. The jurisdiction of the man without, is founded altogether in the desire of actual praise, and in the aversion to actual blame. The jurisdiction of the man within, is founded altogether in the desire of praise-worthiness, and in the aversion to blame-worthiness; in the desire of possessing those qualities, and performing those actions, which we love and admire in other people; and in the dread of possessing those qualities, and performing those actions, which we hate and despise in other people. If the man without should applaud us, either for actions which we have not performed, or for motives which had no influence upon us; the man within can immediately humble that pride and elevation of mind which such groundless acclamations might otherwise occasion, by telling us, that as we know that we do not deserve them, we render ourselves despicable by accepting them. If, on the contrary, the man without should reproach us, either for actions which we never performed, or for motives which had no influence upon those which we may have performed; the man within may immediately correct this false judgment, and assure us, that we are by no means the proper objects of that censure which has so unjustly been bestowed upon us . . . .

In such cases, the only effectual consolation of humbled and afflicted man lies in an appeal to a still higher tribunal, to that of the all-seeing Judge of the world, whose eye can never be deceived, and whose judgments can never be perverted. A firm confidence in the unerring rectitude of this great tribunal, before which his innocence is in due time to be declared, and his virtue to be finally rewarded, can alone support him under the weakness and despondency of his own mind, under the perturbation and astonishment of the man within the breast, whom nature has set up as, in this life, the great guardian, not only of his innocence, but of his tranquillity. Our happiness in this life is thus, upon many occasions, dependent upon the humble hope and expectation of a life to come: a hope and expectation deeply rooted in human nature; which can alone support its lofty ideas of its own dignity; can alone illumine the dreary prospect of its continually approaching mortality, and maintain its cheerfulness under all the heaviest calamities to which, from the disorders of this life, it may sometimes be exposed . . . .

Of the Influence and Authority of Conscience

But though the approbation of his own conscience can scarce, upon some extraordinary occasions, content the weakness of man; though the testimony of the supposed impartial spectator, of the great inmate of the breast, cannot always alone support him; yet the influence and authority of this principle is, upon all occasions, very great; and it is only by consulting this judge within, that we can ever see what relates to ourselves in its proper shape and dimensions; or that we can ever make any proper comparison between our own interests and those of other people.

As to the eye of the body, objects appear great or small, not so much according to their real dimensions, as according to the nearness or distance of their situation; so do they likewise to what may be called the natural eye of the mind: and we remedy the defects of both these organs pretty much in the same manner. In my present situation an immense landscape of lawns, and woods, and distant mountains, seems to do no more than cover the little window which I write by, and to be out of all proportion less than the chamber in which I am sitting. I can form a just comparison between those great objects and the little objects around me, in no other way, than by transporting myself, at least in fancy, to a different station, from whence I can survey both at nearly equal distances, and thereby form some judgment of their real proportions. Habit and experience have taught me to do this so easily and so readily, that I am scarce sensible that I do it; and a man must be, in some measure, acquainted with the philosophy of vision, before he can be thoroughly convinced, how little those distant objects would appear to the eye, if the imagination, from a knowledge of their real magnitudes, did not swell and dilate them.

In the same manner, to the selfish and original passions of human nature, the loss or gain of a very small interest of our own, appears to be of vastly more importance, excites a much more passionate joy or sorrow, a much more ardent desire or aversion, than the greatest concern of another with whom we have no particular connexion. His interests, as long as they are surveyed from this station, can never be put into the balance with our own, can never restrain us from doing whatever may tend to promote our own, how ruinous soever to him. Before we can make any proper comparison of those opposite interests, we must change our position. We must view them, neither from our own place nor yet from his, neither with our own eyes nor yet with his, but from the place and with the eyes of a third person, who has no particular connexion with either, and who judges with impartiality between us. Here, too, habit and experience have taught us to do this so easily and so readily, that we are scarce sensible that we do it; and it requires, in this case too, some degree of reflection, and even of philosophy, to convince us, how little interest we should take in the greatest concerns of our neighbour, how little we should be affected by whatever relates to him, if the sense of propriety and justice did not correct the otherwise natural inequality of our sentiments.

Let us suppose that the great empire of China, with all its myriads of inhabitants, was suddenly swallowed up by an earthquake, and let us consider how a man of humanity in Europe, who had no sort of connexion with that part of the world, would be affected upon receiving intelligence of this dreadful calamity. He would, I imagine, first of all, express very strongly his sorrow for the misfortune of that unhappy people, he would make many melancholy reflections upon the precariousness of human life, and the vanity of all the labours of man which could thus be annihilated in a moment. He would too, perhaps, if he was a man of speculation, enter into many reasonings concerning the effects which this disaster might produce upon the commerce of Europe, and the trade and business of the world in general. And when all this fine philosophy was over, when all these humane sentiments had been once fairly expressed, he would pursue his business or his pleasure, take his repose or his diversion, with the same ease and tranquillity, as if no such accident had happened. The most frivolous disaster which could befall himself would occasion a more real disturbance. If he was to lose his little finger tomorrow, he would not sleep tonight; but, provided he never saw them, he will snore with the most profound security over the ruin of a hundred millions of his brethren, and the destruction of that immense multitude seems plainly an object less interesting to him, than this paltry misfortune of his own. To prevent, therefore, this paltry misfortune to himself, would a man of humanity be willing to sacrifice the lives of a hundred millions of his brethren, provided he had never seen them? Human nature startles with horror at the thought, and the world, in its greatest depravity and corruption, never produced such a villain as could be capable of entertaining it. But what makes this difference? When our passive feelings are almost always so sordid and so selfish, how comes it that our active principles should often be so generous and so noble? When we are always so much more deeply affected by whatever concerns ourselves, than by whatever concerns other men; what is it which prompts the generous, upon all occasions, and the mean upon many, to sacrifice their own interests to the greater interests of others? It is not the soft power of humanity, it is not that feeble spark of benevolence which Nature has lighted up in the human heart, that is thus capable of counteracting the strongest impulses of self-love. It is a stronger power, a more forcible motive, which exerts itself upon such occasions. It is reason, principle, conscience, the inhabitant of the breast, the man within, the great judge and arbiter of our conduct. It is he who, whenever we are about to act so as to affect the happiness of others, calls to us, with a voice capable of astonishing the most presumptuous of our passions, that we are but one of the multitude, in no respect better than any other in it; and that when we prefer ourselves so shamefully and so blindly to others, we become the proper objects of resentment, abhorrence, and execration. It is from him only that we learn the real littleness of ourselves, and of whatever relates to ourselves, and the natural misrepresentations of self-love can be corrected only by the eye of this impartial spectator. It is he who shows us the propriety of generosity and the deformity of injustice; the propriety of resigning the greatest interests of our own, for the yet greater interests of others, and the deformity of doing the smallest injury to another, in order to obtain the greatest benefit to ourselves. It is not the love of our neighbour, it is not the love of mankind, which upon many occasions prompts us to the practice of those divine virtues. It is a stronger love, a more powerful affection, which generally takes place upon such occasions; the love of what is honourable and noble, of the grandeur, and dignity, and superiority of our own characters.

When the happiness or misery of others depends in any respect upon our conduct, we dare not, as self-love might suggest to us, prefer the interest of one to that of many. The man within immediately calls to us, that we value ourselves too much and other people too little, and that, by doing so, we render ourselves the proper object of the contempt and indignation of our brethren . . . .

One individual must never prefer himself so much even to any other individual, as to hurt or injure that other, in order to benefit himself, though the benefit to the one should be much greater than the hurt or injury to the other. The poor man must neither defraud nor steal from the rich, though the acquisition might be much more beneficial to the one than the loss could be hurtful to the other. The man within immediately calls to him, in this case too, that he is no better than his neighbour, and that by this unjust preference he renders himself the proper object of the contempt and indignation of mankind; as well as of the punishment which that contempt and indignation must naturally dispose them to inflict, for having thus violated one of those sacred rules, upon the tolerable observation of which depend the whole security and peace of human society . . . .

The man who should feel no more for the death or distress of his own father, or son, than for those of any other man's father or son, would appear neither a good son nor a good father. Such unnatural indifference, far from exciting our applause, would incur our highest disapprobation. Of those domestic affections, however, some are most apt to offend by their excess, and others by their defect. Nature, for the wisest purposes, has rendered, in most men, perhaps in all men, parental tenderness a much stronger affection than filial piety. The continuance and propagation of the species depend altogether upon the former, and not upon the latter. In ordinary cases, the existence and preservation of the child depend altogether upon the care of the parents. Those of the parents seldom depend upon that of the child. Nature, therefore, has rendered the former affection so strong, that it generally requires not to be excited, but to be moderated; and moralists seldom endeavour to teach us how to indulge, but generally how to restrain our fondness, our excessive attachment, the unjust preference which we are disposed to give to our own children above those of other people . . . .

The great source of both the misery and disorders of human life, seems to arise from over-rating the difference between one permanent situation and another. Avarice over-rates the difference between poverty and riches: ambition, that between a private and a public station: vain-glory, that between obscurity and extensive reputation. The person under the influence of any of those extravagant passions, is not only miserable in his actual situation, but is often disposed to disturb the peace of society, in order to arrive at that which he so foolishly admires. The slightest observation, however, might satisfy him, that, in all the ordinary situations of human life, a well-disposed mind may be equally calm, equally cheerful, and equally contented. Some of those situations may, no doubt, deserve to be preferred to others: but none of them can deserve to be pursued with that passionate ardour which drives us to violate the rules either of prudence or of justice; or to corrupt the future tranquillity of our minds, either by shame from the remembrance of our own folly, or by remorse from the horror of our own injustice. Wherever prudence does not direct, wherever justice does not permit, the attempt to change our situation, the man who does attempt it, plays at the most unequal of all games of hazard, and stakes every thing against scarce any thing . . . .

Of the Nature of Self-Deceit, and of the Origin and Use of General Rules

In order to pervert the rectitude of our own judgments concerning the propriety of our own conduct, it is not always necessary that the real and impartial spectator should be at a great distance. When he is at hand, when he is present, the violence and injustice of our own selfish passions are sometimes sufficient to induce the man within the breast to make a report very different from what the real circumstances of the case are capable of authorizing.

There are two different occasions upon which we examine our own conduct, and endeavour to view it in the light in which the impartial spectator would view it: first, when we are about to act; and secondly, after we have acted. Our views are apt to be very partial in both cases; but they are apt to be most partial when it is of most importance that they should be otherwise . . . .

So partial are the views of mankind with regard to the propriety of their own conduct, both at the time of action and after it; and so difficult is it for them to view it in the light in which any indifferent spectator would consider it. But if it was by a peculiar faculty, such as the moral sense is supposed to be, that they judged of their own conduct, if they were endued with a particular power of perception, which distinguished the beauty or deformity of passions and affections; as their own passions would be more immediately exposed to the view of this faculty, it would judge with more accuracy concerning them, than concerning those of other men, of which it had only a more distant prospect.

This self-deceit, this fatal weakness of mankind, is the source of half the disorders of human life. If we saw ourselves in the light in which others see us, or in which they would see us if they knew all, a reformation would generally be unavoidable. We could not otherwise endure the sight.

Nature, however, has not left this weakness; which is of so much importance, altogether without a remedy; nor has she abandoned us entirely to the delusions of self-love. Our continual observations upon the conduct of others, insensibly lead us to form to ourselves certain general rules concerning what is fit and proper either to be done or to be avoided. Some of their actions shock all our natural sentiments. We hear everybody about us express the like detestation against them. This still further confirms, and even exasperates our natural sense of their deformity. It satisfies us that we view them in the proper light, when we see other people view them in the same light. We resolve never to be guilty of the like, nor ever, upon any account, to render ourselves in this manner the objects of universal disapprobation. We thus naturally lay down to ourselves a general rule, that all such actions are to be avoided, as tending to render us odious, contemptible, or punishable, the objects of all those sentiments for which we have the greatest dread and aversion. Other actions, on the contrary, call forth our approbation, and we hear everybody around us express the same favourable opinion concerning them. Everybody is eager to honour and reward them. They excite all those sentiments for which we have by nature the strongest desire; the love, the gratitude, the admiration of mankind. We become ambitious of performing the like; and thus naturally lay down to ourselves a rule of another kind, that every opportunity of acting in this manner is carefully to be sought after.

It is thus that the general rules of morality are formed. They are ultimately founded upon experience of what, in particular instances, our moral faculties, our natural sense of merit and propriety, approve, or disapprove of. We do not originally approve or condemn particular actions; because, upon examination, they appear to be agreeable or inconsistent with a certain general rule. The general rule, on the contrary, is formed, by finding from experience, that all actions of a certain kind, or circumstanced in a certain manner, are approved or disapproved of. To the man who first saw an inhuman murder committed from avarice, envy, or unjust resentment, and upon one too that loved and trusted the murderer, who beheld the last agonies of the dying person, who heard him, with his expiring breath, complain more of the perfidy and ingratitude of his false friend, than of the violence which had been done to him, there could be no occasion, in order to conceive how horrible such an action was, that he should reflect, that one of the most sacred rules of conduct was what prohibited the taking away the life of an innocent person, that this was a plain violation of that rule, and consequently a very blameable action. His detestation of this crime, it is evident, would arise instantaneously and antecedent to his having formed to himself any such general rule. The general rule, on the contrary, which he might afterwards form, would be founded upon the detestation which he felt necessarily arise in his own breast, at the thought of this, and every other particular action of the same kind . . . .

An amiable action, a respectable action, an horrid action, are all of them actions which naturally excite for the person who performs them, the love, the respect, or the horror of the spectator. The general rules which determine what actions are, and what are not, the objects of each of those sentiments, can be formed no other way than by observing what actions actually and in fact excite them.

When these general rules, indeed, have been formed, when they are universally acknowledged and established, by the concurring sentiments of mankind, we frequently appeal to them as to the standards of judgment, in debating concerning the degree of praise or blame that is due to certain actions of a complicated and dubious nature. They are upon these occasions commonly cited as the ultimate foundations of what is just and unjust in human conduct; and this circumstance seems to have misled several very eminent authors, to draw up their systems in such a manner, as if they had supposed that the original judgments of mankind with regard to right and wrong, were formed like the decisions of a court of judicatory, by considering first the general rule, and then, secondly, whether the particular action under consideration fell properly within its comprehension.

Those general rules of conduct, when they have been fixed in our mind by habitual reflection, are of great use in correcting the misrepresentations of self-love concerning what is fit and proper to be done in our particular situation. The man of furious resentment, if he was to listen to the dictates of that passion, would perhaps regard the death of his enemy, as but a small compensation for the wrong, he imagines, he has received; which, however, may be no more than a very slight provocation. But his observations upon the conduct of others, have taught him how horrible all such sanguinary revenges appear. Unless his education has been very singular, he has laid it down to himself as an inviolable rule, to abstain from them upon all occasions . . . .

Of the Influence and Authority of the General Rules of Morality, and that They are Justly Regarded as the Laws of the Deity

The regard to those general rules of conduct, is what is properly called a sense of duty, a principle of the greatest consequence in human life, and the only principle by which the bulk of mankind are capable of directing their actions . . . .

Without this sacred regard to general rules, there is no man whose conduct can be much depended upon. It is this which constitutes the most essential difference between a man of principle and honour and a worthless fellow. The one adheres, on all occasions, steadily and resolutely to his maxims, and preserves through the whole of his life one even tenor of conduct. The other, acts variously and accidentally, as humour, inclination, or interest chance to be uppermost. Nay, such are the inequalities of humour to which all men are subject, that without this principle, the man who, in all his cool hours, had the most delicate sensibility to the propriety of conduct, might often be led to act absurdly upon the most frivolous occasions, and when it was scarce possible to assign any serious motive for his behaving in this manner. Your friend makes you a visit when you happen to be in a humour which makes it disagreeable to receive him: in your present mood his civility is very apt to appear an impertinent intrusion; and if you were to give way to the views of things which at this time occur, though civil in your temper, you would behave to him with coldness and contempt. What renders you incapable of such a rudeness, is nothing but a regard to the general rules of civility and hospitality, which prohibit it. That habitual reverence which your former experience has taught you for these, enables you to act, upon all such occasions, with nearly equal propriety, and hinders those inequalities of temper, to which all men are subject, from influencing your conduct in any very sensible degree. But if without regard to these general rules, even the duties of politeness, which are so easily observed, and which one can scarce have any serious motive to violate, would yet be so frequently violated, what would become of the duties of justice, of truth, of chastity, of fidelity, which it is often so difficult to observe, and which there may be so many strong motives to violate? But upon the tolerable observance of these duties, depends the very existence of human society, which would crumble into nothing if mankind were not generally impressed with a reverence for those important rules of conduct.

This reverence is still further enhanced by an opinion which is first impressed by nature, and afterwards confirmed by reasoning and philosophy, that those important rules of morality are the commands and laws of the Deity, who will finally reward the obedient, and punish the transgressors of their duty.

This opinion or apprehension, I say, seems first to be impressed by nature. Men are naturally led to ascribe to those mysterious beings, whatever they are, which happen, in any country, to be the objects of religious fear, all their own sentiments and passions. They have no other, they can conceive no other to ascribe to them. Those unknown intelligences which they imagine but see not, must necessarily be formed with some sort of resemblance to those intelligences of which they have experience. During the ignorance and darkness of pagan superstition, mankind seem to have formed the ideas of their divinities with so little delicacy, that they ascribed to them, indiscriminately, all the passions of human nature, those not excepted which do the least honour to our species, such as lust, hunger, avarice, envy, revenge. They could not fail, therefore, to ascribe to those beings, for the excellence of whose nature they still conceived the highest admiration, those sentiments and qualities which are the great ornaments of humanity, and which seem to raise it to a resemblance of divine perfection, the love of virtue and beneficence, and the abhorrence of vice and injustice. The man who was injured, called upon Jupiter to be witness of the wrong that was done to him, and could not doubt, but that divine being would behold it with the same indignation which would animate the meanest of mankind, who looked on when injustice was committed. The man who did the injury, felt himself to be the proper object of the detestation and resentment of mankind; and his natural fears led him to impute the same sentiments to those awful beings, whose presence he could not avoid, and whose power he could not resist. These natural hopes and fears, and suspicions, were propagated by sympathy, and confirmed by education; and the gods were universally represented and believed to be the rewarders of humanity and mercy, and the avengers of perfidy and injustice. And thus religion, even in its rudest form, gave a sanction to the rules of morality, long before the age of artificial reasoning and philosophy. That the terrors of religion should thus enforce the natural sense of duty, was of too much importance to the happiness of mankind, for nature to leave it dependent upon the slowness and uncertainty of philosophical researches.

These researches, however, when they came to take place, confirmed those original anticipations of nature. Upon whatever we suppose that our moral faculties are founded, whether upon a certain modification of reason, upon an original instinct, called a moral sense, or upon some other principle of our nature, it cannot be doubted, that they were given us for the direction of our conduct in this life. They carry along with them the most evident badges of this authority, which denote that they were set up within us to be the supreme arbiters of all our actions, to superintend all our senses, passions, and appetites, and to judge how far each of them was either to be indulged or restrained. Our moral faculties are by no means, as some have pretended, upon a level in this respect with the other faculties and appetites of our nature, endowed with no more right to restrain these last, than these last are to restrain them. No other faculty or principle of action judges of any other. Love does not judge of resentment, nor resentment of love. Those two passions may be opposite to one another, but cannot, with any propriety, be said to approve or disapprove of one another. But it is the peculiar office of those faculties now under our consideration to judge, to bestow censure or applause upon all the other principles of our nature. They may be considered as a sort of senses of which those principles are the objects. Every sense is supreme over its own objects. There is no appeal from the eye with regard to the beauty of colours, nor from the ear with regard to the harmony of sounds, nor from the taste with regard to the agreeableness of flavours. Each of those senses judges in the last resort of its own objects. Whatever gratifies the taste is sweet, whatever pleases the eye is beautiful, whatever soothes the ear is harmonious. The very essence of each of those qualities consists in its being fitted to please the sense to which it is addressed. It belongs to our moral faculties, in the same manner to determine when the ear ought to be soothed, when the eye ought to be indulged, when the taste ought to be gratified, when and how far every other principle of our nature ought either to be indulged or restrained. What is agreeable to our moral faculties, is fit, and right, and proper to be done; the contrary wrong, unfit, and improper. The sentiments which they approve of, are graceful and becoming: the contrary, ungraceful and unbecoming. The very words, right, wrong, fit, improper, graceful, unbecoming, mean only what pleases or displeases those faculties.

Since these, therefore, were plainly intended to be the governing principles of human nature, the rules which they prescribe are to be regarded as the commands and laws of the Deity, promulgated by those vicegerents which he has thus set up within us. All general rules are commonly denominated laws: thus the general rules which bodies observe in the communication of motion, are called the laws of motion. But those general rules which our moral faculties observe in approving or condemning whatever sentiment or action is subjected to their examination, may much more justly be denominated such. They have a much greater resemblance to what are properly called laws, those general rules which the sovereign lays down to direct the conduct of his subjects. Like them they are rules to direct the free actions of men: they are prescribed most surely by a lawful superior, and are attended too with the sanction of rewards and punishments. Those vicegerents of God within us, never fail to punish the violation of them, by the torments of inward shame, and self-condemnation; and on the contrary, always reward obedience with tranquillity of mind, with contentment, and self-satisfaction . . . .

In What Cases the Sense of Duty Ought to be the Sole Principle of Our Conduct; and in What Cases it Ought to Concur With Other Motives

Religion affords such strong motives to the practice of virtue, and guards us by such powerful restraints from the temptations of vice, that many have been led to suppose, that religious principles were the sole laudable motives of action. We ought neither, they said, to reward from gratitude, nor punish from resentment; we ought neither to protect the helplessness of our children, nor afford support to the infirmities of our parents, from natural affection. All affections for particular objects, ought to be extinguished in our breast and one great affection take the place of all others, the love of the Deity, the desire of rendering ourselves agreeable to him, and of directing our conduct, in every respect, according to his will. We ought not to be grateful from gratitude, we ought not to be charitable from humanity, we ought not to be public-spirited from the love of our country, nor generous and just from the love of mankind. The sole principle and motive of our conduct in the performance of all those different duties, ought to be a sense that God has commanded us to perform them. I shall not at present take time to examine this opinion particularly; I shall only observe, that we should not have expected to have found it entertained by any sect, who professed themselves of a religion in which, as it is the first precept to love the Lord our God with all our heart, with all our soul, and with all our strength, so it is the second to love our neighbour as we love ourselves; and we love ourselves surely for our own sakes, and not merely because we are commanded to do so. That the sense of duty should be the sole principle of our conduct is nowhere the precept of Christianity; but that it should be the ruling and the governing one, as philosophy, and as, indeed, common sense directs. It may be a question, however, in what cases our actions ought to arise chiefly or entirely from a sense of duty, or from a regard to general rules; and in what cases some other sentiment or affection ought to concur, and have a principal influence . . . .

The rules of justice may be compared to the rules of grammar; the rules of the other virtues, to the rules which critics lay down for the attainment of what is sublime and elegant in composition. The one, are precise, accurate, and indispensable. The other, are loose, vague, and indeterminate, and present us rather with a general idea of the perfection we ought to aim at, than afford us any certain and infallible directions for acquiring it. A man may learn to write grammatically by rule, with the most absolute infallibility; and so, perhaps, he may be taught to act justly. But there are no rules whose observance will infallibly lead us to the attainment of elegance or sublimity in writing; though there are some which may help us, in some measure, to correct and ascertain the vague ideas which we might otherwise have entertained of those perfections. And there are no rules by the knowledge of which we can infallibly be taught to act upon all occasions with prudence, with just magnanimity, or proper beneficence: though there are some which may enable us to correct and ascertain, in several respects, the imperfect ideas which we might otherwise have entertained of those virtues . . . .

PART FOUR

Of the Effect of Utility Upon the Sentiment of Approbation

Of the Beauty which the Appearance of Utility Bestows Upon All the Productions of Art, and of the Extensive Influence of this Species of Beauty

That utility is one of the principal sources of beauty has been observed by every body, who has considered with any attention what constitutes the nature of beauty. The conveniency of a house gives pleasure to the spectator as well as its regularity, and he is as much hurt when he observes the contrary defect, as when he sees the correspondent windows of different forms, or the door not placed exactly in the middle of the building. That the fitness of any system or machine to produce the end for which it was intended, bestows a certain propriety and beauty upon the whole, and renders the very thought and contemplation of it agreeable, is so very obvious that nobody has overlooked it.

The cause too, why utility pleases, has of late been assigned by an ingenious and agreeable philosopher,[8] who joins the greatest depth of thought to the greatest elegance of expression, and possesses the singular and happy talent of treating the abstrusest subjects not only with the most perfect perspicuity, but with the most lively eloquence. The utility of any object, according to him, pleases the master by perpetually suggesting to him the pleasure or conveniency which it is fitted to promote. Every time he looks at it, he is put in mind of this pleasure; and the object in this manner becomes a source of perpetual satisfaction and enjoyment. The spectator enters by sympathy into the sentiments of the master, and necessarily views the object under the same agreeable aspect. When we visit the palaces of the great, we cannot help conceiving the satisfaction we should enjoy if we ourselves were the masters, and were possessed of so much artful and ingeniously contrived accommodation. A similar account is given why the appearance of inconveniency should render any object disagreeable both to the owner and to the spectator.

[8] [David Hume (1711-76).]

But that this fitness, this happy contrivance of any production of art, should often be more valued, than the very end for which it was intended; and that the exact adjustment of the means for attaining any conveniency or pleasure, should frequently be more regarded, than that very conveniency or pleasure, in the attainment of which their whole merit would seem to consist, has not, so far as I know, been yet taken notice of by anybody. That this however is very frequently the case, may be observed in a thousand instances, both in the most frivolous and in the most important concerns of human life.

When a person comes into his chamber, and finds the chairs all standing in the middle of the room, he is angry with his servant, and rather than see them continue in that disorder, perhaps takes the trouble himself to set them all in their places with their backs to the wall. The whole propriety of this new situation arises from its superior conveniency in leaving the floor free and disengaged. To attain this conveniency he voluntarily puts himself to more trouble than all he could have suffered from the want of it; since nothing was more easy, than to have set himself down upon one of them, which is probably what he does when his labour is over. What he wanted therefore, it seems, was not so much this conveniency, as that arrangement of things which promotes it. Yet it is this conveniency which ultimately recommends that arrangement, and bestows upon it the whole of its propriety and beauty.

A watch, in the same manner, that falls behind above two minutes in a day, is despised by one curious in watches. He sells it perhaps for a couple of guineas, and purchases another at fifty, which will not lose above a minute in a fortnight. The sole use of watches however, is to tell us what o'clock it is, and to hinder us from breaking any engagement, or suffering any other inconveniency by our ignorance in that particular point. But the person so nice with regard to this machine, will not always be found either more scrupulously punctual than other men, or more anxiously concerned upon any other account, to know precisely what time of day it is. What interests him is not so much the attainment of this piece of knowledge, as the perfection of the machine which serves to attain it.

How many people ruin themselves by laying out money on trinkets of frivolous utility? What pleases these lovers of toys is not so much the utility, as the aptness of the machines which are fitted to promote it. All their pockets are stuffed with little conveniencies. They contrive new pockets, unknown in the clothes of other people, in order to carry a greater number. They walk about loaded with a multitude of baubles, in weight and sometimes in value not inferior to an ordinary Jew's-box, some of which may sometimes be of some little use, but all of which might at all times be very well spared, and of which the whole utility is certainly not worth the fatigue of bearing the burden.

Nor is it only with regard to such frivolous objects that our conduct is influenced by this principle; it is often the secret motive of the most serious and important pursuits of both private and public life.

The poor man's son, whom heaven in its anger has visited with ambition, when he begins to look around him, admires the condition of the rich. He finds the cottage of his father too small for his accommodation, and fancies he should be lodged more at his ease in a palace. He is displeased with being obliged to walk a-foot, or to endure the fatigue of riding on horseback. He sees his superiors carried about in machines, and imagines that in one of these he could travel with less inconveniency. He feels himself naturally indolent, and willing to serve himself with his own hands as little as possible; and judges, that a numerous retinue of servants would save him from a great deal of trouble. He thinks if he had attained all these, he would sit still contentedly, and be quiet, enjoying himself in the thought of the happiness and tranquillity of his situation. He is enchanted with the distant idea of this felicity. It appears in his fancy like the life of some superior rank of beings, and, in order to arrive at it, he devotes himself forever to the pursuit of wealth and greatness. To obtain the conveniencies which these afford, he submits in the first year, nay in the first month of his application, to more fatigue of body and more uneasiness of mind than he could have suffered through the whole of his life from the want of them. He studies to distinguish himself in some laborious profession. With the most unrelenting industry he labours night and day to acquire talents superior to all his competitors. He endeavours next to bring those talents into public view, and with equal assiduity solicits every opportunity of employment. For this purpose he makes his court to all mankind; he serves those whom he hates, and is obsequious to those whom he despises. Through the whole of his life he pursues the idea of a certain artificial and elegant repose which he may never arrive at, for which he sacrifices a real tranquillity that is at all times in his power, and which, if in the extremity of old age he should at last attain to it, he will find to be in no respect preferable to that humble security and contentment which he had abandoned for it. It is then, in the last dregs of life, his body wasted with toil and diseases, his mind galled and ruffled by the memory of a thousand injuries and disappointments which he imagines he has met with from the injustice of his enemies, or from the perfidy and ingratitude of his friends, that he begins at last to find that wealth and greatness are mere trinkets of frivolous utility, no more adapted for procuring ease of body or tranquillity of mind than the tweezer-cases of the lover of toys; and like them too, more troublesome to the person who carries them about with him than all the advantages they can afford him are commodious. There is no other real difference between them, except that the conveniencies of the one are somewhat more observable than those of the other. The palaces, the gardens, the equipage, the retinue of the great, are objects of which the obvious conveniency strikes everybody. They do not require that their masters should point out to us wherein consists their utility. Of our own accord we readily enter into it, and by sympathy enjoy and thereby applaud the satisfaction which they are fitted to afford him. But the curiosity of a tooth-pick, of an ear-picker, of a machine for cutting the nails, or of any other trinket of the same kind, is not so obvious. Their conveniency may perhaps be equally great, but it is not so striking, and we do not so readily enter into the satisfaction of the man who possesses them. They are therefore less reasonable subjects of vanity than the magnificence of wealth and greatness; and in this consists the sole advantage of these last. They more effectually gratify that love of distinction so natural to man. To one who was to live alone in a desolate island it might be a matter of doubt, perhaps, whether a palace, or a collection of such small conveniencies as are commonly contained in a tweezer-case, would contribute most to his happiness and enjoyment. If he is to live in society, indeed, there can be no comparison, because in this, as in all other cases, we constantly pay more regard to the sentiments of the spectator, than to those of the person principally concerned, and consider rather how his situation will appear to other people, than how it will appear to himself. If we examine, however, why the spectator distinguishes with such admiration the condition of the rich and the great, we shall find that it is not so much upon account of the superior ease or pleasure which they are supposed to enjoy, as of the numberless artificial and elegant contrivances for promoting this ease or pleasure. He does not even imagine that they are really happier than other people: but he imagines that they possess more means of happiness. And it is the ingenious and artful adjustment of those means to the end for which they were intended, that is the principal source of his admiration. But in the languor of disease and the weariness of old age, the pleasures of the vain and empty distinctions of greatness disappear. To one, in this situation, they are no longer capable of recommending those toilsome pursuits in which they had formerly engaged him. In his heart he curses ambition, and vainly regrets the ease and the indolence of youth, pleasures which are fled forever, and which he has foolishly sacrificed for what, when he has got it, can afford him no real satisfaction. In this miserable aspect does greatness appear to every man when reduced either by spleen or disease to observe with attention his own situation, and to consider what it is that is really wanting to his happiness. Power and riches appear then to be, what they are, enormous and operose machines contrived to produce a few trifling conveniencies to the body, consisting of springs the most nice and delicate, which must be kept in order with the most anxious attention, and which in spite of all our care are ready every moment to burst into pieces, and to crush in their ruins their unfortunate possessor. They are immense fabrics, which it requires the labour of a life to raise, which threaten every moment to overwhelm the person that dwells in them, and which while they stand, though they may save him from some smaller inconveniencies, can protect him from none of the severer inclemencies of the season. They keep off the summer shower, not the winter storm, but leave him always as much, and sometimes more exposed than before, to anxiety, to fear, and to sorrow; to diseases, to danger, and to death.

But though this splenetic philosophy, which in time of sickness or low spirits is familiar to every man, thus entirely depreciates those great objects of human desire, when in better health and in better humour, we never fail to regard them under a more agreeable aspect. Our imagination, which in pain and sorrow seems to be confined and cooped up within our own persons, in times of ease and prosperity expands itself to everything around us. We are then charmed with the beauty of that accommodation which reigns in the palaces and economy of the great; and admire how everything is adapted to promote their ease, to prevent their wants, to gratify their wishes, and to amuse and entertain their most frivolous desires. If we consider the real satisfaction which all these things are capable of affording, by itself and separated from the beauty of that arrangement which is fitted to promote it, it will always appear in the highest degree contemptible and trifling. But we rarely view it in this abstract and philosophical light. We naturally confound it in our imagination with the order, the regular and harmonious movement of the system, the machine or economy by means of which it is produced. The pleasures of wealth and greatness, when considered in this complex view, strike the imagination as something grand and beautiful and noble, of which the attainment is well worth all the toil and anxiety which we are so apt to bestow upon it.

And it is well that nature imposes upon us in this manner. It is this deception which rouses and keeps in continual motion the industry of mankind. It is this which first prompted them to cultivate the ground, to build houses, to found cities and commonwealths, and to invent and improve all the sciences and arts, which ennoble and embellish human life; which have entirely changed the whole face of the globe, have turned the rude forests of nature into agreeable and fertile plains, and made the trackless and barren ocean a new fund of subsistence, and the great high road of communication to the different nations of the earth. The earth by these labours of mankind has been obliged to redouble her natural fertility, and to maintain a greater multitude of inhabitants. It is to no purpose, that the proud and unfeeling landlord views his extensive fields, and without a thought for the wants of his brethren, in imagination consumes himself the whole harvest that grows upon them. The homely and vulgar proverb, that the eye is larger than the belly, never was more fully verified than with regard to him. The capacity of his stomach bears no proportion to the immensity of his desires, and will receive no more than that of the meanest peasant. The rest he is obliged to distribute among those, who prepare, in the nicest manner, that little which he himself makes use of, among those who fit up the palace in which this little is to be consumed, among those who provide and keep in order all the different baubles and trinkets, which are employed in the economy of greatness; all of whom thus derive from his luxury and caprice, that share of the necessaries of life, which they would in vain have expected from his humanity or his justice. The produce of the soil maintains at all times nearly that number of inhabitants which it is capable of maintaining. The rich only select from the heap what is most precious and agreeable. They consume little more than the poor, and in spite of their natural selfishness and rapacity, though they mean only their own conveniency, though the sole end which they propose from the labours of all the thousands whom they employ, be the gratification of their own vain and insatiable desires, they divide with the poor the produce of all their improvements. They are led by an invisible hand to make nearly the same distribution of the necessaries of life, which would have been made, had the earth been divided into equal portions among all its inhabitants, and thus without intending it, without knowing it, advance the interest of the society, and afford means to the multiplication of the species. When Providence divided the earth among a few lordly masters, it neither forgot nor abandoned those who seemed to have been left out in the partition. These last too enjoy their share of all that it produces. In what constitutes the real happiness of human life, they are in no respect inferior to those who would seem so much above them. In ease of body and peace of mind, all the different ranks of life are nearly upon a level, and the beggar, who suns himself by the side of the highway, possesses that security which kings are fighting for.

The same principle, the same love of system, the same regard to the beauty of order, of art and contrivance, frequently serves to recommend those institutions which tend to promote the public welfare. When a patriot exerts himself for the improvement of any part of the public police, his conduct does not always arise from pure sympathy with the happiness of those who are to reap the benefit of it. It is not commonly from a fellow-feeling with carriers and waggoners that a public-spirited man encourages the mending of high roads. When the legislature establishes premiums and other encouragements to advance the linen or woollen manufactures, its conduct seldom proceeds from pure sympathy with the wearer of cheap or fine cloth, and much less from that with the manufacturer or merchant. The perfection of police, the extension of trade and manufactures, are noble and magnificent objects. The contemplation of them pleases us, and we are interested in whatever can tend to advance them. They make part of the great system of government, and the wheels of the political machine seem to move with more harmony and ease by means of them. We take pleasure in beholding the perfection of so beautiful and grand a system, and we are uneasy till we remove any obstruction that can in the least disturb or encumber the regularity of its motions. All constitutions of government, however, are valued only in proportion as they tend to promote the happiness of those who live under them. This is their sole use and end. From a certain spirit of system, however, from a certain love of art and contrivance, we sometimes seem to value the means more than the end, and to be eager to promote the happiness of our fellow-creatures, rather from a view to perfect and improve a certain beautiful and orderly system, than from any immediate sense or feeling of what they either suffer or enjoy. There have been men of the greatest public spirit, who have shown themselves in other respects not very sensible to the feelings of humanity. And on the contrary, there have been men of the greatest humanity, who seem to have been entirely devoid of public spirit. Every man may find in the circle of his acquaintance instances both of the one kind and the other. . . . Would you awaken the industry of the man who seems almost dead to ambition, it will often be to no purpose to describe to him the happiness of the rich and the great; to tell him that they are generally sheltered from the sun and the rain, that they are seldom hungry, that they are seldom cold, and that they are rarely exposed to weariness, or to want of any kind. The most eloquent exhortation of this kind will have little effect upon him. If you would hope to succeed, you must describe to him the conveniency and arrangement of the different apartments in their palaces; you must explain to him the propriety of their equipages, and point out to him the number, the order, and the different offices of all their attendants. If anything is capable of making impression upon him, this will. Yet all these things tend only to keep off the sun and the rain, to save them from hunger and cold, from want and weariness. In the same manner, if you would implant public virtue in the breast of him who seems heedless of the interest of his country, it will often be to no purpose to tell him, what superior advantages the subjects of a well-governed state enjoy; that they are better lodged, that they are better clothed, that they are better fed. These considerations will commonly make no great impression. You will be more likely to persuade, if you describe the great system of public police which procures these advantages, if you explain the connexions and dependencies of its several parts, their mutual subordination to one another, and their general subserviency to the happiness of the society; if you show how this system might be introduced into his own country, what it is that hinders it from taking place there at present, how those obstructions might be removed, and all the several wheels of the machine of government be made to move with more harmony and smoothness, without grating upon one another, or mutually retarding one another's motions . . . .

PART FIVE

Of the Influence of Custom and Fashion Upon the Sentiments of Moral Approbation and Disapprobation

Of the Influence of Custom and Fashion Upon Our Notions of Beauty and Deformity

There are other principles besides those already enumerated, which have a considerable influence upon the moral sentiments of mankind, and are the chief causes of the many irregular and discordant opinions which prevail in different ages and nations concerning what is blameable or praise-worthy. These principles are custom and fashion, principles which extend their dominion over our judgments concerning beauty of every kind.

When two objects have frequently been seen together, the imagination acquires a habit of passing easily from the one to the other. If the first appear, we lay our account that the second is to follow. Of their own accord they put us in mind of one another, and the attention glides easily along them. Though, independent of custom, there should be no real beauty in their union, yet when custom has thus connected them together, we feel an impropriety in their separation. The one we think is awkward when it appears without its usual companion. We miss something which we expected to find, and the habitual arrangement of our ideas is disturbed by the disappointment. A suit of clothes, for example, seems to want something if they are without the most insignificant ornament which usually accompanies them, and we find a meanness or awkwardness in the absence even of a haunch button. When there is any natural propriety in the union, custom increases our sense of it, and makes a different arrangement appear still more disagreeable than it would otherwise seem to be. Those who have been accustomed to see things in a good taste, are more disgusted by whatever is clumsy or awkward. Where the conjunction is improper, custom either diminishes, or takes away altogether, our sense of the impropriety. Those who have been accustomed to slovenly disorder lose all sense of neatness or elegance. The modes of furniture or dress which seem ridiculous to strangers, give no offence to the people who are used to them.

Fashion is different from custom, or rather is a particular species of it. That is not the fashion which everybody wears, but which those wear who are of a high rank, or character. The graceful, the easy, and commanding manners of the great, joined to the usual richness and magnificence of their dress, give a grace to the very form which they happen to bestow upon it. As long as they continue to use this form, it is connected in our imaginations with the idea of something that is genteel and magnificent, and though in itself it should be indifferent, it seems, on account of this relation, to have something about it that is genteel and magnificent too. As soon as they drop it, it loses all the grace, which it had appeared to possess before, and being now used only by the inferior ranks of people, seems to have something of their meanness and awkwardness.

Dress and furniture are allowed by all the world to be entirely under the dominion of custom and fashion. The influence of those principles, however, is by no means confined to so narrow a sphere, but extends itself to whatever is in any respect the object of taste, to music, to poetry, to architecture. The modes of dress and furniture are continually changing, and that fashion appearing ridiculous today which was admired five years ago, we are experimentally convinced that it owed its vogue chiefly or entirely to custom and fashion . . . .

Neither is it only over the productions of the arts, that custom and fashion exert their dominion. They influence our judgments, in the same manner, with regard to the beauty of natural objects. What various and opposite forms are deemed beautiful in different species of things? The proportions which are admired in one animal, are altogether different from those which are esteemed in another. Every class of things has its own peculiar conformation, which is approved of, and has a beauty of its own, distinct from that of every other species. It is upon this account that a learned Jesuit, father Buffier,[9] has determined that the beauty of every object consists in that form and colour, which is most usual among things of that particular sort to which it belongs. Thus, in the human form, the beauty of each feature lies in a certain middle, equally removed from a variety of other forms that are ugly. A beautiful nose, for example, is one that is neither very long, nor very short, neither very straight, nor very crooked, but a sort of middle among all these extremes, and less different from anyone of them, than all of them are from one another. It is the form which Nature seems to have aimed at in them all, which, however, she deviates from in a great variety of ways, and very seldom hits exactly; but to which all those deviations still bear a very strong resemblance . . . .

Of the Influence of Custom and Fashion Upon Moral Sentiments

Since our sentiments concerning beauty of every kind, are so much influenced by custom and fashion, it cannot be expected, that those, concerning the beauty of conduct, should be entirely exempted from the dominion of those principles. Their influence here, however, seems to be much less than it is everywhere else. There is, perhaps, no form of external objects, how absurd and fantastical soever, to which custom will not reconcile us, or which fashion will not render even agreeable. But the characters and conduct of a Nero, or a Claudius,[10] are what no custom will ever reconcile us to, what no fashion will ever render agreeable; but

[9] [Claude Buffier (1661–1737).]

[10] [Claudius (10BC–AD54), Roman emperor AD41–54.]

the one will always be the object of dread and hatred; the other of scorn and derision. The principles of the imagination, upon which our sense of beauty depends, are of a very nice and delicate nature, and may easily be altered by habit and education: but the sentiments of moral approbation and disapprobation, are founded on the strongest and most vigorous passions of human nature; and though they may be somewhat warped, cannot be entirely perverted. . . .

The different situations of different ages and countries are apt, in the same manner, to give different characters to the generality of those who live in them, and their sentiments concerning the particular degree of each quality, that is either blameable or praise-worthy, vary, according to that degree which is usual in their own country, and in their own times. That degree of politeness, which would be highly esteemed, perhaps would be thought effeminate adulation, in Russia, would be regarded as rudeness and barbarism at the court of France. That degree of order and frugality, which, in a Polish nobleman, would be considered as excessive parsimony, would be regarded as extravagance in a citizen of Amsterdam. Every age and country look upon that degree of each quality, which is commonly to be met with in those who are esteemed among themselves, as the golden mean of that particular talent or virtue. And as this varies, according as their different circumstances render different qualities more or less habitual to them, their sentiments concerning the exact propriety of character and behaviour vary accordingly.

Among civilized nations, the virtues which are founded upon humanity, are more cultivated than those which are founded upon self-denial and the command of the passions. Among rude and barbarous nations, it is quite otherwise, the virtues of self-denial are more cultivated than those of humanity. The general security and happiness which prevail in ages of civility and politeness, afford little exercise to the contempt of danger, to patience in enduring labour, hunger, and pain. Poverty may easily be avoided, and the contempt of it therefore almost ceases to be a virtue. The abstinence from pleasure becomes less necessary, and the mind is more at liberty to unbend itself, and to indulge its natural inclinations in all those particular respects.

Among savages and barbarians it is quite otherwise. Every savage undergoes a sort of Spartan discipline, and by the necessity of his situation is inured to every sort of hardship. He is in continual danger: he is often exposed to the greatest extremities of hunger, and frequently dies of pure want. His circumstances not only habituate him to every sort of distress, but teach him to give way to none of the passions which that distress is apt to excite. He can expect from his countrymen no sympathy or indulgence for such weakness. Before we can feel much for others, we must in some measure be at ease ourselves. If our own misery pinches us very severely, we have no leisure to attend to that of our neighbour: and all savages are too much occupied with their own wants and necessities, to give much attention to those of another person. A savage, therefore, whatever be the nature of his distress, expects no sympathy from those about him, and disdains, upon that account, to expose himself, by allowing the least weakness to escape him. His passions, how furious and violent soever, are never permitted to disturb the serenity of his countenance or the composure of his conduct and behaviour. The savages in North America, we are told, assume upon all occasions the greatest indifference, and would think themselves degraded if they should ever appear in any respect to be overcome, either by love, or grief, or resentment. Their magnanimity and self-command, in this respect, are almost beyond the conception of Europeans. . . . When a savage is made prisoner of war, and receives, as is usual, the sentence of death from his conquerors, he hears it without expressing any emotion, and afterwards submits to the most dreadful torments, without ever bemoaning himself, or discovering any other passion but contempt of his enemies. While he is hung by the shoulders over a slow fire, he derides his tormentors, and tells them with how much more ingenuity he himself had tormented such of their countrymen as had fallen into his hands. After he has been scorched and burnt, and lacerated in all the most tender and sensible parts of his body for several hours together, he is often allowed, in order to prolong his misery, a short respite, and is taken down from the stake: he employs this interval in talking upon all indifferent subjects, inquires after the news of the country, and seems indifferent about nothing but his own situation. The spectators express the same insensibility; the sight of so horrible an object seems to make no impression upon them; they scarce look at the prisoner, except when they lend a hand to torment him. At other times they smoke tobacco, and amuse themselves with any common object, as if no such matter was going on. Every savage is said to prepare himself from his earliest youth for this dreadful end. He composes, for this purpose, what they call the song of death, a song which he is to sing when he has fallen into the hands of his enemies, and is expiring under the tortures which they inflict upon him. It consists of insults upon his tormentors, and expresses the highest contempt of death and pain. He sings this song upon all extraordinary occasions, when he goes out to war, when he meets his enemies in the field, or whenever he has a mind to show that he has familiarized his imagination to the most dreadful misfortunes, and that no human event can daunt his resolution, or alter his purpose. The same contempt of death and torture prevails among all other savage nations. There is not a negro from the coast of Africa who does not, in this respect, possess a degree of magnanimity which the soul of his sordid master is too often scarce capable of conceiving. Fortune never exerted more cruelly her empire over mankind, than when she subjected those nations of heroes to the refuse of the jails of Europe, to wretches who possess the virtues neither of the countries which they come from, nor of those which they go to, and whose levity, brutality, and baseness, so justly expose them to the contempt of the vanquished . . . .

All these effects of custom and fashion, however, upon the moral sentiments of mankind, are inconsiderable, in comparison of those which they give occasion to in some other cases; and it is not concerning the general style of character and behaviour, that those principles produce the greatest perversion of judgment, but concerning the propriety or impropriety of particular usages.

The different manners which custom teaches us to approve of in the different professions and states of life, do not concern things of the greatest importance. We expect truth and justice from an old man as well as from a young, from a clergyman as well as from an officer; and it is in matters of small moment only that we look for the distinguishing marks of their respective characters. With regard to these too, there is often some unobserved circumstance which, if it was attended to, would show us, that, independent of custom, there was a propriety in the character which custom had taught us to allot to each profession. We cannot complain, therefore, in this case, that the perversion of natural sentiment is very great. Though the manners of different nations require different degrees of the same quality, in the character which they think worthy of esteem, yet the worst that can be said to happen even here, is that the duties of one virtue are sometimes extended so as to encroach a little upon the precincts of some other. The rustic hospitality that is in fashion among the Poles encroaches, perhaps, a little upon economy and good order; and the frugality that is esteemed in Holland, upon generosity and good-fellowship. The hardiness demanded of savages diminishes their humanity; and, perhaps, the delicate sensibility required in civilized nations sometimes destroys the masculine firmness of the character. In general, the style of manners which takes place in any nation, may commonly upon the whole be said to be that which is most suitable to its situation. Hardiness is the character most suitable to the circumstances of a savage; sensibility to those of one who lives in a very civilized society. Even here, therefore, we cannot complain that the moral sentiments of men are very grossly perverted.

It is not therefore in the general style of conduct or behaviour that custom authorizes the widest departure from what is the natural propriety of action. With regard to particular usages, its influence is often much more destructive of good morals, and it is capable of establishing, as lawful and blameless, particular actions, which shock the plainest principles of right and wrong.

Can there be greater barbarity, for example, than to hurt an infant? Its helplessness, its innocence, its amiableness, call forth the compassion, even of an enemy, and not to spare that tender age is regarded as the most furious effort of an enraged and cruel conqueror. What then should we imagine must be the heart of a parent who could injure that weakness which even a furious enemy is afraid to violate? Yet the exposition, that is, the murder of new-born infants, was a practice allowed in almost all the states of Greece, even among the polite and civilized Athenians; and whenever the circumstances of the parent rendered it inconvenient to bring up the child, to abandon it to hunger, or to wild beasts, was regarded without blame or censure. This practice had probably begun in times of the most savage barbarity. The imaginations of men had been first made familiar with it in that earliest period of society, and the uniform continuance of the custom had hindered them afterwards from perceiving its enormity. We find, at this day, that this practice prevails among all savage nations; and in that rudest and lowest state of society it is undoubtedly more pardonable than in any other. The extreme indigence of a savage is often such that he himself is frequently exposed to the greatest extremity of hunger, he often dies of pure want, and it is frequently impossible for him to support both himself and his child. We cannot wonder, therefore, that in this case he should abandon it. One who, in flying from an enemy, whom it was impossible to resist, should throw down his infant, because it retarded his flight, would surely be excusable; since, by attempting to save it, he could only hope for the consolation of dying with it. That in this state of society, therefore, a parent should be allowed to judge whether he can bring up his child, ought not to surprise us so greatly. In the latter ages of Greece, however, the same thing was permitted from views of remote interest or conveniency, which could by no means excuse it. Uninterrupted custom had by this time so thoroughly authorized the practice, that not only the loose maxims of the world tolerated this barbarous prerogative, but even the doctrine of philosophers, which ought to have been more just and accurate, was led away by the established custom, and upon this, as upon many other occasions, instead of censuring, supported the horrible abuse, by far-fetched considerations of public utility. Aristotle talks of it as of what the magistrate ought upon many occasions to encourage. The humane Plato is of the same opinion, and, with all that love of mankind which seems to animate all his writings, nowhere marks this practice with disapprobation. When custom can give sanction to so dreadful a violation of humanity, we may well imagine that there is scarce any particular practice so gross which it cannot authorize. Such a thing, we hear men every day saying, is commonly done, and they seem to think this a sufficient apology for what, in itself, is the most unjust and unreasonable conduct.

There is an obvious reason why custom should never pervert our sentiments with regard to the general style and character of conduct and behaviour, in the same degree as with regard to the propriety or unlawfulness of particular usages. There never can be any such custom. No society could subsist a moment, in which the usual strain of men's conduct and behaviour was of a piece with the horrible practice I have just now mentioned.

PART SIX
Of the Character of Virtue

I: Of the Order in which Individuals are Recommended by Nature to Our Care and Attention

Every man, as the Stoics used to say, is first and principally recommended to his own care; and every man is certainly, in every respect, fitter and abler to take care of himself than of any other person. Every man feels his own pleasures and his own pains more sensibly than those of other people. The former are the original sensations; the latter the reflected or sympathetic images of those sensations. The former may be said to be the substance; the latter the shadow.

After himself, the members of his own family, those who usually live in the same house with him, his parents, his children, his brothers and sisters are naturally the objects of his warmest affections. They are naturally and usually the persons upon whose happiness or misery his conduct must have the greatest influence. He is more habituated to sympathize with them. He knows better how everything is likely to affect them, and his sympathy with them is more precise and determinate, than it can be with the greater part of other people. It approaches nearer, in short, to what he feels for himself . . . .

II: Of the Order in which Societies are by Nature Recommended to Our Beneficence

The same principles that direct the order in which individuals are recommended to our beneficence, direct that likewise in which societies are recommended to it. Those to which it is, or may be of most importance, are first and principally recommended to it.

The state or sovereignty in which we have been born and educated, and under the protection of which we continue to live, is, in ordinary cases, the greatest society upon whose happiness or misery, our good or bad conduct can have much influence. It is accordingly, by nature, most strongly recommended to us. Not only we ourselves, but all the objects of our kindest affections, our children, our parents, our relations, our friends, our benefactors, all those whom we naturally love and revere the most, are commonly comprehended within it; and their prosperity and safety depend in some measure upon its prosperity and safety. It is by nature, therefore, endeared to us, not only by all our selfish, but by all our private benevolent affections. Upon account of our own connexion with it, its prosperity and glory seem to reflect some sort of honour upon ourselves. When we compare it with other societies of the same kind, we are proud of its superiority, and mortified in some degree, if it appears in any respect below them. All the illustrious characters which it has produced in former times (for against those of our own times envy may sometimes prejudice us a little), its warriors, its statesmen, its poets, its philosophers, and men of letters of all kinds; we are disposed to view with the most partial admiration, and to rank them (sometimes most unjustly) above those of all other nations. The patriot who lays down his life for the safety, or even for the vain-glory of this society, appears to act with the most exact propriety. He appears to view himself in the light in which the impartial spectator naturally and necessarily views him, as but one of the multitude, in the eye of that equitable judge, of no more consequence than any other in it, but bound at all times to sacrifice and devote himself to the safety, to the service, and even to the glory of the greater number. But though this sacrifice appears to be perfectly just and proper, we know how difficult it is to make it, and how few people are capable of making it. His conduct, therefore, excites not only our entire approbation, but our highest wonder and admiration, and seems to merit all the applause which can be due to the most heroic virtue. The traitor, on the contrary, who, in some peculiar situation, fancies he can promote his own little interest by betraying to the public enemy that of his native country; who, regardless of the judgment of the man within the breast, prefers himself, in this respect so shamefully and so basely, to all those with whom he has any connexion; appears to be of all villains the most detestable . . . .

Every independent state is divided into many different orders and societies, each of which has its own particular powers, privileges, and immunities. Every individual is naturally more attached to his own particular order or society, than to any other. His own interest, his own vanity, the interest and vanity of many of his friends and companions, are commonly a good deal connected with it. He is ambitious to extend its privileges and immunities. He is zealous to defend them against the encroachments of every other order or society . . . .

All those different orders and societies are dependent upon the state to which they owe their security and protection. That they are all subordinate to that state, and established only in subserviency to its prosperity and preservation, is a truth acknowledged by the most partial member of every one of them. It may often, however, be hard to convince him that the prosperity and preservation of the state require any diminution of the powers, privileges, and immunities of his own particular order or society. This partiality, though it may sometimes be unjust, may not, upon that account, be useless. It checks the spirit of innovation. It tends to preserve whatever is the established balance among the different orders and societies into which the state is divided; and while it sometimes appears to obstruct some alterations of government which may be fashionable and popular at the time, it contributes in reality to the stability and permanency of the whole system.

The love of our country seems, in ordinary cases, to involve in it two different principles; first, a certain respect and reverence for that constitution or form of government which is actually established; and secondly, an earnest desire to render the condition of our fellow-citizens as safe, respectable, and happy as we can. He is not a citizen who is not disposed to respect the laws and to obey the civil magistrate; and he is certainly not a good citizen who does not wish to promote, by every means in his power, the welfare of the whole society of his fellow-citizens.

In peaceable and quiet times, those two principles generally coincide and lead to the same conduct. The support of the established government seems evidently the best expedient for maintaining the safe, respectable, and happy situation of our fellow-citizens; when we see that this government actually maintains them in that situation. But in times of public discontent, faction, and disorder, those two different principles may draw different ways, and even a wise man may be disposed to think some alteration necessary in that constitution or form of government, which, in its actual condition, appears plainly unable to maintain the public tranquillity. In such cases, however, it often requires, perhaps, the highest effort of political wisdom to determine when a real patriot ought to support and endeavour to re-establish the authority of the old system, and when he ought to give way to the more daring, but often dangerous spirit of innovation.

Foreign war and civil faction are the two situations which afford the most splendid opportunities for the display of public spirit. The hero who serves his country successfully in foreign war gratifies the wishes of the whole nation, and is, upon that account, the object of universal gratitude and admiration. In times of civil discord, the leaders of the contending parties, though they may be admired by one half of their fellow-citizens, are commonly execrated by the other. Their characters and the merit of their respective services appear commonly more doubtful. The glory which is acquired by foreign war is, upon this account, almost always more pure and more splendid than that which can be acquired in civil faction.

The leader of the successful party, however, if he has authority enough to prevail upon his own friends to act with proper temper and moderation (which he frequently has not), may sometimes render to his country a service much more essential and important than the greatest victories and the most extensive conquests. He may re-establish and improve the constitution, and from the very doubtful and ambiguous character of the leader of a party, he may assume the greatest and noblest of all characters, that of the reformer and legislator of a great state; and, by the wisdom of his institutions, secure the internal tranquillity and happiness of his fellow-citizens for many succeeding generations.

Amidst the turbulence and disorder of faction, a certain spirit of system is apt to mix itself with that public spirit which is founded upon the love of humanity, upon a real fellow-feeling with the inconveniencies and distresses to which some of our fellow-citizens may be exposed. This spirit of system commonly takes the direction of that more gentle public spirit; always animates it, and often inflames it even to the madness of fanaticism. The leaders of the discontented party seldom fail to hold out some plausible plan of reformation which, they pretend, will not only remove the inconveniencies and relieve the distresses immediately complained of, but will prevent, in all time coming, any return of the like inconveniencies and distresses. They often propose, upon this account, to new-model the constitution, and to alter, in some of its most essential parts, that system of government under which the subjects of a great empire have enjoyed, perhaps, peace, security, and even glory, during the course of several centuries together. The great body of the party are commonly intoxicated with the imaginary beauty of this ideal system, of which they have no experience, but which has been represented to them in all the most dazzling colours in which the eloquence of their leaders could paint it. Those leaders themselves, though they originally may have meant nothing but their own aggrandizement, become many of them in time the dupes of their own sophistry, and are as eager for this great reformation as the weakest and foolishest of their followers. Even though the leaders should have preserved their own heads, as indeed they commonly do, free from this fanaticism, yet they dare not always disappoint the expectation of their followers; but are often obliged, though contrary to their principle and their conscience, to act as if they were under the common delusion. The violence of the party, refusing all palliatives, all temperaments, all reasonable accommodations, by requiring too much frequently obtains nothing; and those inconveniencies and distresses which, with a little moderation, might in a great measure have been removed and relieved, are left altogether without the hope of a remedy.

The man whose public spirit is prompted altogether by humanity and benevolence, will respect the established powers and privileges even of individuals, and still more those of the great orders and societies, into which the state is divided. Though he should consider some of them as in some measure abusive, he will content himself with moderating, what he often cannot annihilate without great violence. When he cannot conquer the rooted prejudices of the people by reason and persuasion, he will not attempt to subdue them by force; but will religiously observe what, by Cicero, is justly called the divine maxim of Plato, never to use violence to his country no more than to his parents. He will accommodate, as well as he can, his public arrangements to the confirmed habits and prejudices of the people; and will remedy as well as he can, the inconveniencies which may flow from the want of those regulations which the people are averse to submit to. When he cannot establish the right, he will not disdain to ameliorate the wrong; but like Solon, when he cannot establish the best system of laws, he will endeavour to establish the best that the people can bear.

The man of system, on the contrary, is apt to be very wise in his own conceit; and is often so enamoured with the supposed beauty of his own ideal plan of government, that he cannot suffer the smallest deviation from any part of it. He goes on to establish it completely and in all its parts, without any regard either to the great interests, or to the strong prejudices which may oppose it. He seems to imagine that he can arrange the different members of a great society with as much ease as the hand arranges the different pieces upon a chess-board. He does not consider that the pieces upon the chess-board have no other principle of motion besides that which the hand impresses upon them; but that, in the great chess-board of human society, every single piece has a principle of motion of its own, altogether different from that which the legislature might choose to impress upon it. If those two principles coincide and act in the same direction, the game of human society will go on easily and harmoniously, and is very likely to be happy and successful. If they are opposite or different, the game will go on miserably, and the society must be at all times in the highest degree of disorder.

Some general, and even systematical, idea of the perfection of policy and law, may no doubt be necessary for directing the views of the statesman. But to insist upon establishing, and upon establishing all at once, and in spite of all opposition, every thing which that idea may seem to require, must often be the highest degree of arrogance. It is to erect his own judgment into the supreme standard of right and wrong. It is to fancy himself the only wise and worthy man in the commonwealth, and that his fellow-citizens should accommodate themselves to him and not he to them. It is upon this account, that of all political speculators, sovereign princes are by far the most dangerous. This arrogance is perfectly familiar to them. They entertain no doubt of the immense superiority of their own judgment. When such imperial and royal reformers, therefore, condescend to contemplate the constitution of the country which is committed to their government, they seldom see any thing so wrong in it as the obstructions which it may sometimes oppose to the execution of their own will. They hold in contempt the divine maxim of Plato, and consider the state as made for themselves, not themselves for the state. The great object of their reformation, therefore, is to remove those obstructions; to reduce the authority of the nobility; to take away the privileges of cities and provinces, and to render both the greatest individuals and the greatest orders of the state, as incapable of opposing their commands, as the weakest and most insignificant.

III: Of Self-Command

The man who acts according to the rules of perfect prudence, of strict justice, and of proper benevolence, may be said to be perfectly virtuous. But the most perfect knowledge of those rules will not alone enable him to act in this manner: his own passions are very apt to mislead him; sometimes to drive him and sometimes to seduce him to violate all the rules which he himself, in all his sober and cool hours, approves of. The most perfect knowledge, if it is not supported by the most perfect self-command, will not always enable him to do his duty . . . .

The command of each of those two sets of passions [i.e., fear and anger], independent of the beauty which it derives from its utility; from its enabling us upon all occasions to act according to the dictates of prudence, of justice, and of proper benevolence; has a beauty of its own, and seems to deserve for its own sake a certain degree of esteem and admiration. In the one case, the strength and greatness of the exertion excites some degree of that esteem and admiration. In the other, the uniformity, the equality and unremitting steadiness of that exertion. . . .

To act according to the dictates of prudence, of justice, and proper beneficence, seems to have no great merit where there is no temptation to do otherwise. But to act with cool deliberation in the midst of the greatest dangers and difficulties; to observe religiously the sacred rules of justice in spite both of the greatest interests which might tempt, and the greatest injuries which might provoke us to violate them; never to suffer the benevolence of our temper to be damped or discouraged by the malignity and ingratitude of the individuals towards whom it may have been exercised; is the character of the most exalted wisdom and virtue. Self-command is not only itself a great virtue, but from it all the other virtues seem to derive their principal lustre.

PART SEVEN

Of Systems of Moral Philosophy

I: Of the Questions which Ought to be Examined in a Theory of Moral Sentiments

If we examine the most celebrated and remarkable of the different theories which have been given concerning the nature and origin of our moral sentiments, we shall find that almost all of them coincide with some part or other of that which I have been endeavouring to give an account of; and that if every thing which has already been said be fully considered, we shall be at no loss to explain what was the view or aspect of nature which led each particular author to form his particular system. From some one or other of those principles which I have been endeavouring to unfold, every system of morality that ever had any reputation in the world has, perhaps, ultimately been derived. As they are all of them, in this respect, founded upon natural principles, they are all of them in some measure in the right. But as many of them are derived from a partial and imperfect view of nature, there are many of them too in some respects in the wrong.

In treating of the principles of morals there are two questions to be considered. First, wherein does virtue consist? Or what is the tone of temper, and tenor of conduct, which constitutes the excellent and praise-worthy character, the character which is the natural object of esteem, honour, and approbation? And, secondly, by what power or faculty in the mind is it, that this character, whatever it be, is recommended to us? Or in other words, how and by what means does it come to pass, that the mind prefers one tenor of conduct to another, denominates the one right and the other wrong; considers the one as the object of approbation, honour, and reward, and the other of blame, censure, and punishment . . . .

II: Chapter 4 – Of Licentious Systems

All those systems, which I have hitherto given an account of, suppose that there is a real and essential distinction between vice and virtue, whatever these qualities may consist in. There is a real and essential difference between the propriety and impropriety of any affection, between benevolence and any other principle of action, between real prudence and short-sighted folly or precipitate rashness. In the main too all of them contribute to encourage the praise-worthy, and to discourage the blameable disposition . . . .

There is, however, another system which seems to take away altogether the distinction between vice and virtue, and of which the tendency is, upon that account, wholly pernicious: I mean the system of Dr Mandeville.[11] Though the notions of this author are in almost every respect erroneous, there are, however, some appearances in human nature, which, when viewed in a certain manner, seem at first sight to favour them. These, described and exaggerated by the lively and humorous, though coarse and rustic eloquence of Dr Mandeville, have thrown upon his doctrines an air of truth and probability which is very apt to impose upon the unskilful.

Dr Mandeville considers whatever is done from a sense of propriety, from a regard to what is commendable and praise-worthy, as being done from a love of praise and commendation, or as he calls it from vanity. Man, he observes, is naturally much more interested in his own happiness than in that of others, and it is impossible that in his heart he can ever really prefer their prosperity to his own. Whenever he appears to do so, we may be assured that he imposes upon us, and that he is then acting from the same selfish motives as at all other times. Among his other selfish passions, vanity is one of the strongest, and he is always easily flattered and greatly delighted with the applauses of those about him. When he appears to sacrifice his own interest to that of his companions, he knows that this conduct will be highly agreeable to their self-love, and that they will not fail to express their satisfaction by bestowing upon him the most extravagant praises. The pleasure which he expects from this, over-balances, in his opinion, the interest which he abandons in

[11] [Bernard Mandeville (1670–1733).]

order to procure it. His conduct, therefore, upon this occasion, is in reality just as selfish, and arises from just as mean a motive as upon any other. He is flattered, however, and he flatters himself, with the belief that it is entirely disinterested; since, unless this was supposed, it would not seem to merit any commendation either in his own eyes or in those of others. All public spirit, therefore, all preference of public to private interest, is, according to him, a mere cheat and imposition upon mankind; and that human virtue which is so much boasted of, and which is the occasion of so much emulation among men, is the mere offspring of flattery begot upon pride.

Whether the most generous and public-spirited actions may not, in some sense, be regarded as proceeding from self-love, I shall not at present examine. The decision of this question is not, I apprehend, of any importance towards establishing the reality of virtue, since self-love may frequently be a virtuous motive of action. I shall only endeavour to show that the desire of doing what is honourable and noble, of rendering ourselves the proper objects of esteem and approbation, cannot with any propriety be called vanity . . . .

But though these three passions, the desire of rendering ourselves the proper objects of honour and esteem; or of becoming what is honourable and estimable; the desire of acquiring honour and esteem by really deserving those sentiments; and the frivolous desire of praise at any rate, are widely different; though the two former are always approved of, while the latter never fails to be despised; there is, however, a certain remote affinity among them, which, exaggerated by the humorous and diverting eloquence of this lively author, has enabled him to impose upon his readers. There is an affinity between vanity and the love of true glory, as both these passions aim at acquiring esteem and approbation. But they are different in this, that the one is a just, reasonable, and equitable passion, while the other is unjust, absurd, and ridiculous. The man who desires esteem for what is really estimable, desires nothing but what he is justly entitled to, and what cannot be refused him without some sort of injury. He, on the contrary, who desires it upon any other terms, demands what he has no just claim to. The first is easily satisfied, is not apt to be jealous or suspicious that we do not esteem him enough, and is seldom solicitous about receiving many external marks of our regard. The other, on the contrary, is never to be satisfied, is full of jealousy and suspicion that we do not esteem him so much as he desires, because he has some secret consciousness that he desires more than he deserves. The least neglect of ceremony, he considers as a mortal affront, and as an expression of the most determined contempt. He is restless and impatient, and perpetually afraid that we have lost all respect for him, and is upon this account always anxious to obtain new expressions of esteem, and cannot be kept in temper but by continual attendance and adulation . . . .

It is the great fallacy of Dr Mandeville's book to represent every passion as wholly vicious, which is so in any degree and in any direction. It is thus that he treats every thing as vanity which has any reference, either to what are, or to what ought to be the sentiments of others: and it is by means of this sophistry, that he establishes his favourite conclusion, that private vices are public benefits. If the love of magnificence, a taste for the elegant arts and improvements of human life, for whatever is agreeable in dress, furniture, or equipage, for architecture, statuary, painting, and music, is to be regarded as luxury, sensuality, and ostentation, even in those whose situation allows, without any inconveniency, the indulgence of those passions, it is certain that luxury, sensuality, and ostentation are public benefits: since without the qualities upon which he thinks proper to bestow such opprobrious names, the arts of refinement could never find encouragement, and must languish for want of employment. Some popular ascetic doctrines which had been current before his time, and which placed virtue in the entire extirpation and annihilation of all our passions, were the real foundation of this licentious system. It was easy for Dr Mandeville to prove, first, that this entire conquest never actually took place among men; and secondly, that, if it was to take place universally, it would be pernicious to society, by putting an end to all industry and commerce, and in a manner to the whole business of human life. By the first of these propositions he seemed to prove that there was no real virtue, and that what pretended to be such, was a mere cheat and imposition upon mankind; and by the second, that private vices were public benefits, since without them no society could prosper or flourish.

Such is the system of Dr Mandeville, which once made so much noise in the world, and which, though, perhaps, it never gave occasion to more vice than what would have been without it, at least taught that vice, which arose from other causes, to appear with more effrontery, and to avow the corruption of its motives with a profligate audaciousness which had never been heard of before.

But how destructive soever this system may appear, it could never have imposed upon so great a number of persons, nor have occasioned so general an alarm among those who are the friends of better principles, had it not in some respects bordered upon the truth. . . . The author who should assign, as the cause of any natural sentiment, some principle which neither had any connexion with it, nor resembled any other principle which had some such connexion, would appear absurd and ridiculous to the most injudicious and unexperienced reader.

Two

Political Economy

An Inquiry into the Nature and Causes of The Wealth of Nations

READING I[1]

Introduction and Plan of the Work

The annual labour of every nation is the fund which originally supplies it with all the necessaries and conveniences of life which it annually consumes, and which consist always, either in the immediate produce of that labour, or in what is purchased with that produce from other nations.

According therefore, as this produce, or what is purchased with it, bears a greater or smaller proportion to the number of those who are to consume it, the nation will be better or worse supplied with all the necessaries and conveniences for which it has occasion.

But this proportion must in every nation be regulated by two different circumstances; first, by the skill, dexterity, and judgment with which its labour is generally applied; and, secondly, by the proportion between the number of those who are employed in useful labour, and that of those who are not so employed. Whatever be the soil, climate, or extent of territory of any particular nation, the abundance or scantiness of its annual supply must, in that particular situation, depend upon those two circumstances.

The abundance or scantiness of this supply too seems to depend more upon the former of those two circumstances than upon the latter. Among the savage nations of hunters and fishers, every individual who is able to work, is more or less employed in useful labour, and endeavours to provide, as well as he can, the necessaries and conveniencies of life, for himself, or such of his family or tribe as are either too old, or too young, or too infirm to go a hunting and fishing. Such nations, however, are so miserably poor, that, from mere want, they are fre-

[1] From *An Inquiry into the Nature and Causes of the Wealth of Nations* (London, 1776).

quently reduced, or, at least, think themselves reduced, to the necessity sometimes of directly destroying, and sometimes of abandoning their infants, their old people, and those afflicted with lingering diseases, to perish with hunger, or to be devoured by wild beasts. Among civilized and thriving nations, on the contrary, though a great number of people do not labour at all, many of whom consume the produce of ten times, frequently of a hundred times more labour than the greater part of those who work; yet the produce of the whole labour of the society is so great, that all are often abundantly supplied, and a workman, even of the lowest and poorest order, if he is frugal and industrious, may enjoy a greater share of the necessaries and conveniences of life than it is possible for any savage to acquire.

The causes of this improvement, in the productive powers of labour, and the order, according to which its produce is naturally distributed among the different ranks and conditions of men in the society, make the subject of the First Book of this Inquiry.

Whatever be the actual state of the skill, dexterity, and judgment with which labour is applied in any nation, the abundance or scantiness of its annual supply must depend, during the continuance of that state, upon the proportion between the number of those who are annually employed in useful labour, and that of those who are not so employed. The number of useful and productive labourers, it will hereafter appear, is everywhere in proportion to the quantity of capital stock which is employed in setting them to work, and to the particular way in which it is so employed, The Second Book, therefore, treats of the nature of capital stock, of the manner in which it is gradually accumulated, and of the different quantities of labour which it puts into motion, according to the different ways in which it is employed.

Nations tolerably well advanced as to skill, dexterity, and judgment, in the application of labour, have followed very different plans in the general conduct or direction of it; and those plans have not all been equally favourable to the greatness of its produce. The policy of some nations has given extraordinary encouragement to the industry of the country; that of others to the industry of towns. Scarce any nation has dealt equally and impartially with every sort of industry. Since the downfall of the Roman empire, the policy of Europe has been more favourable to arts, manufactures, and commerce, the industry of towns; than to agriculture, the industry of the country. The circumstances which seem to have introduced and established this policy are explained in the Third Book.

Though those different plans were, perhaps, first introduced by the private interests and prejudices of particular orders of men, without any regard to, or foresight of, their consequences upon the general welfare of the society; yet they have given occasion to very different theories of political economy; of which some magnify the importance of that industry which is carried on in towns, others of that which is carried on in the country. Those theories have had a considerable influence, not only upon the opinions of men of learning, but upon, the public conduct of princes and sovereign states, I have endeavoured, in the Fourth Book, to explain, as fully and distinctly as I can, those different theories, and the principal effects which they have produced in different ages and nations.

To explain in what has consisted the revenue of the great body of the people, or what has been the nature of those funds which, in different ages and nations, have supplied their annual consumption, is the object of these Four first Books. The Fifth and last Book treats of the revenue of the sovereign, or commonwealth. In this Book I have endeavoured to show; first, what are the necessary expenses of the sovereign, or commonwealth; which of those expenses ought to be defrayed by the general contribution of the whole society; and which of them, by that of some particular part only, or of some particular members of it; secondly, what are the different methods in which the whole society may be made to contribute towards defraying the expenses incumbent on the whole society, and what are the principal advantages and inconveniencies of each of those methods: and, thirdly and lastly, what are the reasons and causes which have induced almost all modern governments to mortgage some part of this revenue, or to contract debts, and what have been the effects of those debts upon the real wealth, the annual produce of the land and labour of the society.

BOOK I

Of the Causes of Improvement in the Productive Powers of Labour, and of the Order According to which its Produce is Naturally Distributed Among the Different Ranks of the People

Of the Division of Labour

The greatest improvement in the productive powers of labour, and the greater part of the skill, dexterity, and judgment with which it is any where directed, or applied, seem to have been the effects of the division of labour.

The effects of the division of labour, in the general business of society, will be more easily understood, by considering in what manner it operates in some particular manufactures. It is commonly supposed to be carried furthest in some very trifling ones; not perhaps that it really is carried further in them than in others of more importance: but in those trifling manufactures which are destined to supply the small wants of but a small number of people, the whole number of workmen must necessarily be small; and those employed in every different branch of the work can often be collected into the same workhouse, and placed at once under the view of the spectator. In those great manufactures, on the contrary, which are destined to supply the great wants of the great body of the people, every different branch of the work employs so great a number of workmen, that it is impossible to collect them all into the same workhouse. We can seldom see more, at one time, than those employed in one single branch. Though in such manufactures, therefore, the work may really be divided into a much greater number of parts, than in those of a more trifling nature, the division is not near so obvious, and has accordingly been much less observed.

To take an example, therefore, from a very trifling manufacture; but one in which the division of labour has been very often taken notice of, the trade of the pin-maker; a workman not educated to this business (which the division of labour has rendered a distinct trade), nor acquainted with the use of the machinery employed in it (to the invention of which the same division of labour has probably given occasion), could scarce, perhaps, with his utmost industry, make one pin in a day, and certainly could not make twenty. But in the way in which this business is now carried on, not only the whole work is a peculiar trade, but it is divided into a number of branches, of which the greater part are likewise peculiar trades. One man draws out the wire, another straights it, a third cuts it, a fourth points it, a fifth grinds it at the top for receiving the head; to make the head requires two or three distinct operations; to put it on, is a peculiar business, to whiten the pins is another; it is even a trade by itself to put them into the paper; and the important business of making a pin is, in this manner, divided into about eighteen distinct operations, which, in some manufactories, are all performed by distinct hands, though in others the same man will sometimes perform two or three of them. I have seen a small manufactory of this kind where ten men only were employed, and where some of them consequently performed two or three distinct operations. But though they were very poor, and therefore but indifferently accommodated with the necessary machinery, they could, when they exerted themselves, make among them about twelve pounds of pins in a day. There are in a pound upwards of four thousand pins of a middling size. Those ten persons, therefore, could make among them upwards of forty-eight thousand pins in a day. Each person, therefore, making a tenth part of forty-eight thousand pins, might be considered as making four thousand eight hundred pins in a day. But if they had all wrought separately and independently, and without any of them having been educated to this peculiar business, they certainly could not each of them have made twenty, perhaps not one pin in a day; that is, certainly, not the two hundred and fortieth, perhaps not the four thousand eight hundredth part of what they are at present capable of performing, in consequence of a proper division and combination of their different operations.

In every other art and manufacture, the effects of the division of labour are similar to what they are in this very trifling one; though, in many of them, the labour can neither be so much subdivided, nor reduced to so great a simplicity of operation. The division of labour, however, so far as it can be introduced, occasions, in every art, a proportionable increase of the productive powers of labour. The separation of different trades and employments from one another, seems to have taken place, in consequence of this advantage. This separation too is generally carried furthest in those countries which enjoy the highest degree of industry and improvement; what is the work of one man, in a rude state of society, being generally that of several in an improved one. In every improved society, the farmer is generally nothing but a farmer; the manufacturer, nothing but a manufacturer. The labour too which is necessary to produce any one complete manufacture, is almost always divided among a great number of hands. How many different trades are employed in each branch of the linen and woollen manufactures, from the growers of the flax and the wool, to the bleachers and smoothers of the linen, or to the dyers and dressers of the cloth! The nature of agriculture, indeed, does not admit of so many subdivisions of labour, nor of so complete a separation of one business from another, as manufactures. It is impossible to separate so entirely, the business of the grazier from that of the corn-farmer, as the trade of the carpenter is commonly separated from that of the smith. The spinner is almost always a distinct person from the weaver; but the ploughman, the harrower, the sower of the seed, and the reaper of the corn, are often the same. The occasions for those different sorts of labour returning with the different seasons of the year, it is impossible that one man should be constantly employed in anyone of them. This impossibility of making so complete and entire a separation of all the different branches of labour employed in agriculture, is perhaps the reason why the improvement of the productive powers of labour in this art, does not always keep pace with their improvement in manufactures. The most opulent nations, indeed, generally excel all their neighbours in agriculture as well as in manufactures; but they are commonly more distinguished by their superiority in the latter than in the former. Their lands are in general better cultivated, and having more labour and expense bestowed upon them, produce more, in proportion to the extent and natural fertility of the ground. But this superiority of produce is seldom much more than in proportion to the superiority of labour and expense. In agriculture, the labour of the rich country is not always much more productive than that of the poor; or, at least, it is never so much more productive, as it commonly is in manufactures. The corn of the rich country, therefore, will not always, in the same degree of goodness, come cheaper to market than that of the poor. The corn of Poland, in the same degree of goodness, is as cheap as that of France, notwithstanding the superior opulence and improvement of the latter country. The corn of France is, in the corn provinces, fully as good, and in most years nearly about the same price with the corn of England, though, in opulence and improvement, France is perhaps inferior to England. The corn-lands of England, however, are better cultivated than those of France, and the corn-lands of France are said to be much better cultivated than those of Poland. But though the poor country, notwithstanding the inferiority of its cultivation, can, in some measure, rival the rich in the cheapness and goodness of its corn, it can pretend to no such competition in its manufactures; at least if those manufactures suit the soil, climate, and situation of the rich country. The silks of France are better and cheaper than those of England, because the silk manufacture, at least under the present high duties upon the importation of raw silk, does not so well suit the climate of England as that of France. But the hardware and the coarse woollens of England are beyond all comparison superior to those of France, and much cheaper too in the same degree of goodness. In Poland there are said to be scarce any manufactures of any kind, a few of those coarser household manufactures excepted, without which no country can well subsist.

This great increase of the quantity of work, which, in consequence of the division of labour, the same number of people are capable of performing, is owing to three different circumstances . . . .

First, the improvement of the dexterity of the workman necessarily increases the quantity of the work he can perform, and the division of labour, by reducing every man's business to some one simple operation, and by making this operation the sole employment of his life, necessarily increases very much the dexterity of the workman. A common smith, who, though accustomed to handle the hammer, has never been used to make nails, if upon some particular occasion he is obliged to attempt it, will scarce, I am assured, be able to make above two or three hundred nails in a day, and those too very bad ones. A smith who has been accustomed to make nails, but whose sole or principal business has not been that of a nailer, can seldom with his utmost diligence make more than eight hundred or a thousand nails in a day. I have seen several boys under twenty years of age who had never exercised any other trade but that of making nails, and who, when they exerted themselves, could make, each of them, upwards of two thousand three hundred nails in a day. The making of a nail, however, is by no means one of the simplest operations. The same person blows the bellows, stirs or mends the fire as there is occasion, heats the iron, and forges every part of the nail: In forging the head too he is obliged to change his tools. The different operations into which the making of a pin, or of a metal button, is subdivided, are all of them much more simple, and the dexterity of the person, of whose life it has been the sole business to perform them, is usually much greater. The rapidity with which some of the operations of those manufactures are performed, exceeds what the human hand could, by those who had never seen them, be supposed capable of acquiring.

Secondly, the advantage which is gained by saving the time commonly lost in passing from one sort of work to another, is much greater than we should at first view be apt to imagine it. It is impossible to pass very quickly from one kind of work to another, that is carried on in a different place, and with quite different tools. A country weaver, who cultivates a small farm, must lose a good deal of time in passing from his loom to the field, and from the field to his loom. When the two trades can be carried on in the same workhouse, the loss of time is no doubt much less. It is even in this case, however, very considerable. A man commonly saunters a little in turning his hand from one sort of employment to another. When he first begins the new work he is seldom very keen and hearty; his mind, as they say, does not go to it, and for some time he rather trifles than applies to good purpose. The habit of sauntering and of indolent careless application, which is naturally, or rather necessarily acquired by every country workman who is obliged to change his work and his tools every half hour, and to apply his hand in twenty different ways almost every day of his life; renders him almost always slothful and lazy, and incapable of any vigorous application even on the most pressing occasions. Independent, therefore, of his deficiency in point of dexterity, this cause alone must always reduce considerably the quantity of work which he is capable of performing.

Thirdly, and lastly, everybody must be sensible how much labour is facilitated and abridged by the application of proper machinery. It is unnecessary to give any example. I shall only observe, therefore, that the invention of all those machines by which labour is so much facilitated and abridged, seems to have been originally owing to the division of labour. Men are much more likely to discover easier and readier methods of attaining any object, when the whole attention of their minds is directed towards that single object, than when it is dissipated among a great variety of things. But in consequence of the division of labour, the whole of every man's attention comes naturally to be directed towards some one very simple object. It is naturally to be expected, therefore, that some one or other of those who are employed in each particular branch of labour should soon find out easier and readier methods of performing their own particular work, wherever the nature of it admits of such improvement. A great part of the machines made use of in those manufactures in which labour is most subdivided, were originally the inventions of common workmen, who, being each of them employed in some very simple operation, naturally turned their thoughts towards finding out easier and readier methods of performing it. Whoever has been much accustomed to visit such manufactures, must frequently have been shown very pretty machines, which were the inventions of such workmen, in order to facilitate and quicken their own particular part of the work. In the first fire-engines, a boy was constantly employed to open and shut alternately the communication between the boiler and the cylinder, according as the piston either ascended or descended. One of those boys, who loved to play with his companions, observed that, by tying a string from the handle of the valve, which opened this communication, to another part of the machine, the valve would open and shut without his assistance, and leave him at liberty to divert himself with his play-fellows. One of the greatest improvements that has been made upon this machine, since it was first invented, was in this manner the discovery of a boy who wanted to save his own labour.

All the improvements in machinery, however, have by no means been the inventions of those who had occasion to use the machines. Many improvements have been made by the ingenuity of the makers of the machines, when to make them became the business of a peculiar trade; and some by that of those who are called philosophers or men of speculation, whose trade it is, not to do anything, but to observe everything; and who, upon that account, are often capable of combining together the powers of the most distant and dissimilar objects. In the progress of society, philosophy or speculation becomes, like every other employment, the principal or sole trade and occupation of a particular class of citizens. Like every other employment too, it is subdivided into a great number of different branches, each of which affords occupation to a peculiar tribe or class of philosophers; and this subdivision of employment in philosophy, as well as in every other business, improves dexterity, and saves time. Each individual becomes more expert in his own peculiar branch, more work is done upon the whole, and the quantity of science is considerably increased by it.

It is the great multiplication of the productions of all the different arts, in consequence of the division of labour, which occasions, in a well-governed society, that universal opulence which extends itself to the lowest ranks of the people. Every workman has a great quantity of his own work to dispose of beyond what he himself has occasion for; and every other workman being exactly in the same situation, he is enabled to exchange a great quantity of his own goods for a great quantity, or, what comes to the same thing, for the price of a great quantity of theirs. He supplies them abundantly with what they have occasion for, and they accommodate him as amply with what he has occasion for, and a general plenty diffuses itself through all the different ranks of the society.

Observe the accommodation of the most common artificer or day-labourer in a civilized and thriving country, and you will perceive that the number of people of whose industry a part, though but a small part, has been employed in procuring him this accommodation, exceeds all computation. The woollen coat, for example, which covers the day-labourer, as coarse and rough as it may appear, is the produce of the joint labour of a great multitude of workmen. The shepherd, the sorter of the wool, the wool-comber or carder, the dyer, the scribbler, the spinner, the weaver, the fuller, the dresser, with many others, must all join their different arts in order to complete even this homely production. How many merchants and carriers, besides, must have been employed in transporting the materials from some of those workmen to others who often live in a very distant part of the country! How much commerce and navigation in particular, how many ship-builders, sailors, sail-makers, rope-makers, must have been employed in order to bring together the different drugs made use of by the dyer, which often come from the remotest corners of the world! What a variety of labour too is necessary in order to produce the tools of the meanest of those workmen! To say nothing of such complicated machines as the ship of the sailor, the mill of the fuller, or even the loom of the weaver, let us consider only what a variety of labour is requisite in order to form that very simple machine, the shears with which the shepherd clips the wool. The miner, the builder of the furnace for smelting the ore, the feller of the timber, the burner of the charcoal to be made use of in the smelting-house, the brick-maker, the brick-layer, the workmen who attend the furnace, the mill-wright, the forger, the smith, must all of them join their different arts in order to produce them. Were we to examine, in the same manner, all the different parts of his dress and household furniture, the coarse linen shirt which he wears next his skin, the shoes which cover his feet, the bed which he lies on, and all the different parts which compose it, the kitchen-grate at which he prepares his victuals, the coals which he makes use of for that purpose, dug from the bowels of the earth, and brought to him perhaps by a long sea and a long land carriage, all the other utensils of his kitchen, all the furniture of his table, the knives and forks, the earthen or pewter plates upon which he serves up and divides his victuals, the different hands employed in preparing his bread and his beer, the glass window which lets in the heat and the light, and keeps out the wind and the rain, with all the knowledge and art requisite for preparing that beautiful and happy invention, without which these northern parts of the world could scarce have afforded a very comfortable habitation, together with the tools of all the different workmen employed in producing those different conveniencies; if we examine, I say, all these things, and consider what a variety of labour is employed about each of them, we shall be sensible that without the assistance and cooperation of many thousands, the very meanest person in a civilized country could not be provided, even according to, what we very falsely imagine, the easy and simple manner in which he is commonly accommodated. Compared, indeed, with the more extravagant luxury of the great, his accommodation must no doubt appear extremely simple and easy; and yet it may be true, perhaps, that the accommodation of an European prince does not always so much exceed that of an industrious and frugal peasant, as the accommodation of the latter exceeds that of many an African king, the absolute master of the lives and liberties of ten thousand naked savages.

Of the Principle which Gives Occasion to the Division of Labour

This division of labour, from which so many advantages are derived, is not originally the effect of any human wisdom, which foresees and intends that general opulence to which it gives occasion. It is the necessary, though very slow and gradual consequence of a certain propensity in human nature which has in view no such extensive utility; the propensity to truck, barter, and exchange one thing for another.

Whether this propensity be one of those original principles in human nature, of which no further account can be given; or whether, as seems more probable, it be the necessary consequence of the faculties of reason and speech, it belongs not to our present subject to enquire. It is common to all men, and to be found in no other race of animals, which seem to know neither this nor any other species of contracts. Two greyhounds, in running down the same hare, have sometimes the appearance of acting in some sort of concert. Each turns her towards his companion, or endeavours to intercept her when his companion turns her towards himself. This, however, is not the effect of any contract, but of the accidental concurrence of their passions in the same object at that particular time. Nobody ever saw a dog make a fair and deliberate exchange of one bone or another with another dog. Nobody ever saw one animal by its gestures and natural cries signify to another, this is mine, that yours; I am willing to give this for that. When an animal wants to obtain something either of a man or of another animal, it has no other means of persuasion but to gain the favour of those whose service it requires. A puppy fawns upon its dam, and a spaniel endeavours by a thousand attractions to engage the attention of its master who is at dinner, when it wants to be fed by him. Man sometimes uses the same arts with his brethren, and when he has no other means of engaging them to act according to his inclinations, endeavours by every servile and fawning attention to obtain their good will. He has not time, however, to do this upon every occasion. In civilized society he stands at all times in need of the cooperation and assistance of great multitudes, while his whole life is scarce sufficient to gain the friendship of a few persons. In almost every other race of animals each individual, when it is grown up to maturity, is entirely independent, and in its natural state has occasion for the assistance of no other living creature. But man has almost constant occasion for the help of his brethren, and it is in vain for him to expect it from their benevolence only. He will be more likely to prevail if he can interest their self-love in his favour, and show them that it is for their own advantage to do for him what he requires of them. Whoever offers to another a bargain of any kind, proposes to do this. Give me that which I want, and you shall have this which you want, is the meaning of every such offer; and it is in this manner that we obtain from one another the far greater part of those good offices which we stand in need of. It is not from the benevolence of the butcher, the brewer, or the baker, that we expect our dinner, but from their regard to their own interest. We address ourselves, not to their humanity but to their self-love, and never talk to them of our own necessities but of their advantages. Nobody but a beggar chooses to depend chiefly upon the benevolence of his fellow-citizens. Even a beggar does not depend upon it entirely. The charity of well-disposed people, indeed, supplies him with the whole fund of his subsistence. But though this principle ultimately provides him with all the necessaries of life which he has occasion for, it neither does nor can provide him with them as he has occasion for them. The greater part of his occasional wants are supplied in the same manner as those of other people, by treaty, by barter, and by purchase. With the money which one man gives him he purchases food. The old clothes which another bestows upon him he exchanges for other old clothes which suit him better, or for lodging, or for food, or for money, with which he can buy either food, clothes, or lodging, as he has occasion.

As it is by treaty, by barter, and by purchase, that we obtain from one another the greater part of those mutual good offices which we stand in need of, so it is this same trucking disposition which originally gives occasion to the division of labour. In a tribe of hunters or shepherds a particular person makes bows and arrows, for example, with more readiness and dexterity than any other. He frequently exchanges them for cattle or for venison with his companions; and he finds at last that he can in this manner get more cattle and venison, than if he himself went to the field to catch them. From a regard to his own interest, therefore, the making of bows and arrows grows to be his chief business, and he becomes a sort of armourer. Another excels in making the frames and covers of their little huts or moveable houses. He is accustomed to be of use in this way to his neighbours, who reward him in the same manner with cattle and with venison, till at last he finds it his interest to dedicate himself entirely to this employment, and to become a sort of house-carpenter. In the same manner a third becomes a smith or a brazier, a fourth a tanner or dresser of hides or skins, the principal part of the clothing of savages. And thus the certainty of being able to exchange all that surplus part of the produce of his own labour, which is over and above his own consumption, for such parts of the produce of other men's labour as he may have occasion for, encourages every man to apply himself to a particular occupation, and to cultivate and bring to perfection whatever talent or genius he may possess for that particular species of business.

The difference of natural talents in different men is, in reality, much less than we are aware of; and the very different genius which appears to distinguish men of different professions, when grown up to maturity, is not upon many occasions so much the cause, as the effect of the division of labour. The difference between the most dissimilar characters, between a philosopher and a common street porter, for example, seems to arise not so much from nature, as from habit, custom, and education. When they came into the world, and for the first six or eight years of their existence, they were, perhaps, very much alike, and neither their parents nor play-fellows could perceive any remarkable difference. About that age, or soon after, they come to be employed in very different occupations. The difference of talents comes then to be taken notice of, and widens by degrees, till at last the vanity of the philosopher is willing to acknowledge scarce any resemblance. But without the disposition to truck, barter, and exchange, every man must have procured to himself every necessary and conveniency of life which he wanted. All must have had the same duties to perform, and the same work to do, and there could have been no such difference of employment as could alone give occasion to any great difference of talents.

As it is this disposition which forms that difference of talents, so remarkable among men of different professions, so it is this same disposition which renders that difference useful. Many tribes of animals acknowledged to be all of the same species, derive from nature a much more remarkable distinction of genius, than what, antecedent to custom and education, appears to take place among men. By nature a philosopher is not in genius and disposition half so different from a street porter, as a mastiff is from a greyhound, or a greyhound from a spaniel, or this last from a shepherd's dog. Those different tribes of animals, however, though all of the same species, are of scarce any use to one another. The strength of the mastiff is not, in the least, supported either by the swiftness of the greyhound, or by the sagacity of the spaniel, or by the docility of the shepherd's dog. The effects of those different geniuses and talents, for want of the power or disposition to barter and exchange, cannot be brought into a common stock, and do not in the least contribute to the better accommodation and conveniency of the species. Each animal is still obliged to support and defend itself, separately and independently, and derives no sort of advantage from that variety of talents with which nature has distinguished its fellows. Among men, on the contrary, the most dissimilar geniuses are of use to one another; the different produces of their respective talents, by the general disposition to truck, barter, and exchange, being brought, as it were, into a common stock, where every man may purchase whatever part of the produce of other men's talents he has occasion for.

That the Division of Labour is Limited by the Extent of the Market

As it is the power of exchanging that gives occasion to the division of labour, so the extent of this division must always be limited by the extent of that power, or, in other words, by the extent of the market. When the market is very small, no person can have any encouragement to dedicate himself entirely to one employment, for want of the power to exchange all that surplus part of the produce of his own labour, which is over and above his own consumption, for such parts of the produce of other men's labour as he has occasion for.

There are some sorts of industry, even of the lowest kind, which can be carried on nowhere but in a great town. A porter, for example, can find employment and subsistence in no other place. A village is by much too narrow a sphere for him; even an ordinary market town is scarce large enough to afford him constant occupation. In the lone houses and very small villages which are scattered about in so desert a country as the Highlands of Scotland, every farmer must be butcher, baker and brewer for his own family. In such situations we can scarce expect to find even a smith, a carpenter, or a mason, within less than twenty miles of another of the same trade. The scattered families that live at eight or ten miles distance from the nearest of them, must learn to perform themselves a great number of little pieces of work, for which, in more populous countries, they would call in the assistance of those workmen. Country workmen are almost everywhere obliged to apply themselves to all the different branches of industry that have so much affinity to one another as to be employed about the same sort of materials. A country carpenter deals in every sort of work that is made of wood: a country smith in every sort of work that is made of iron. The former is not only a carpenter, but a joiner, a cabinet-maker, and even a carver in wood, as well as a wheel-wright, a plough-wright, a cart and wagon maker. The employments of the latter are still more various. It is impossible there should be such a trade as even that of a nailer in the remote and inland parts of the Highlands of Scotland. Such a workman at the rate of a thousand nails a day, and three hundred working days in the year, will make three hundred thousand nails in the year. But in such a situation it would be impossible to dispose of one thousand, that is, of one day's work in the year . . . .

Of the Origin and Use of Money

When the division of labour has been once thoroughly established, it is but a very small part of a man's wants which the produce of his own labour can supply. He supplies the far greater part of them by exchanging that surplus part of the produce of his own labour, which is over and above his own consumption, for such parts of the produce of other men's labour as he has occasion for. Every man thus lives by exchanging, or becomes in some measure a merchant, and the society itself grows to be what is properly a commercial society.

But when the division of labour first began to take place, this power of exchanging must frequently have been very much clogged and embarrassed in its operations. One man, we shall suppose, has more of a certain commodity than he himself has occasion for, while another has less. The former consequently would be glad to dispose of, and the latter to purchase, a part of this superfluity. But if this latter should chance to have nothing that the former stands in need of, no exchange can be made between them. The butcher has more meat in his shop than he himself can consume, and the brewer and the baker would each of them be willing to purchase a part of it. But they have nothing to offer in exchange, except the different productions of their respective trades, and the butcher is already provided with all the bread and beer which he has immediate occasion for. No exchange can, in this case, be made between them. He cannot be their merchant, nor they his customers; and they are all of them thus mutually less serviceable to one another. In order to avoid the inconveniency of such situations, every prudent man in every period of society, after the first establishment of the division of labour, must naturally have endeavoured to manage his affairs in such a manner, as to have at all times by him, besides the peculiar produce of his own industry, a certain quantity of some one commodity or other, such as he imagined few people would be likely to refuse in exchange for the produce of their industry.

Many different commodities, it is probable, were successively both thought of and employed for this purpose. . . .

In all countries, however, men seem at last to have been determined by irresistible reasons to give the preference, for this employment, to metals above every other commodity. Metals can not only be kept with as little loss as any other commodity, scarce anything being less perishable than they are, but they can likewise, without any loss, be divided into any number of parts, as by fusion those parts can easily be reunited again; a quality which no other equally durable commodities possess, and which more than any other quality renders them fit to be the instruments of commerce and circulation. The man who wanted to buy salt, for example, and had nothing but cattle to give in exchange for it, must have been obliged to buy salt to the value of a whole ox, or a whole sheep at a time. He could seldom buy less than this, because what he was to give for it could seldom be divided without loss; and if he had a mind to buy more, he must, for the same reasons, have been obliged to buy double or triple the quantity, the value, to wit, of two or three oxen, or of two or three sheep. If, on the contrary, instead of sheep or oxen, he had metals to give in exchange for it, he could easily proportion the quantity of the metal to the precise quantity of the commodity which he had immediate occasion for.

Different metals have been made use of by different nations for this purpose. Iron was the common instrument of commerce among the ancient Spartans; copper among the ancient Romans; and gold and silver among all rich and commercial nations. . . .

It is in this manner that money has become in all civilized nations the universal instrument of commerce, by the intervention of which goods of all kinds are bought and sold, or exchanged for one another. . . .

The word VALUE, it is to be observed, has two different meanings, and sometimes expresses the utility of some particular object, and sometimes the power of purchasing other goods which the possession of that object conveys. The one may be called 'value in use'; the other, 'value in exchange'. The things which have the greatest value in use have frequently little or no value in exchange; and, on the contrary, those which have the greatest value in exchange have frequently little or no value in use. Nothing is more useful than water: but it will purchase scarce anything; scarce anything can be had in exchange for it. A diamond, on the contrary, has scarce any value in use; but a great quantity of other goods may frequently be had in exchange for it. . . .

Of the Real and Nominal Price of Commodities, or of Their Price in Labour, and Their Price in Money

Every man is rich or poor according to the degree in which he can afford to enjoy the necessaries, conveniencies, and amusements of human life. But after the division of labour has once thoroughly taken place, it is but a very small part of these with which a man's own labour can supply him. The far greater part of them he must derive from the labour of other people, and he must be rich or poor according to the quantity of that labour which he can command, or which he can afford to purchase. The value of any commodity, therefore, to the person who possesses it, and who means not to use or consume it himself, but to exchange it for other commodities, is equal to the quantity of labour which it enables him to purchase or command. Labour, therefore, is the real measure of the exchangeable value of all commodities.

The real price of every thing, what every thing really costs to the man who wants to acquire it, is the toil and trouble of acquiring it. What every thing is really worth to the man who has acquired it, and who wants to dispose of it or exchange it for something else, is the toil and trouble which it can save to himself, and which it can impose upon other people. What is bought with money or with goods is purchased by labour as much as what we acquire by the toil of our own body. That money or those goods indeed save us this toil. They contain the value of a certain quantity of labour which we exchange for what is supposed at the time to contain the value of an equal quantity. Labour was the first price, the original purchase-money that was paid for all things. It was not by gold or by silver, but by labour, that all the wealth of the world was originally purchased; and its value, to those who possess it and who want to exchange it for some new productions, is precisely equal to the quantity of labour which it can enable them to purchase or command . . . .

But though labour be the real measure of the exchangeable value of all commodities, it is not that by which their value is commonly estimated. It is often difficult to ascertain the proportion between two different quantities of labour. The time spent in two different sorts of work will not always alone determine this proportion. The different degrees of hardship endured, and of ingenuity exercised, must likewise be taken into account. There may be more labour in an hour's hard work than in two hours easy business; or in an hour's application to a trade which it cost ten years labour to learn, than in a month's industry at an ordinary and obvious employment. But it is not easy to find any accurate measure either of hardship or ingenuity. In exchanging indeed the different productions of different sorts of labour for one another, some allowance is commonly made for both. It is adjusted, however, not by any accurate measure, but by the higgling and bargaining of the market, according to that sort of rough equality which, though not exact, is sufficient for carrying on the business of common life.

Every commodity besides, is more frequently exchanged for, and thereby compared with, other commodities than with labour. It is more natural, therefore, to estimate its exchangeable value by the quantity of some other commodity than by that of the labour which it can purchase. The greater part of people too understand better what is meant by a quantity of a particular commodity, than by a quantity of labour. The one is a plain palpable object; the other an abstract notion, which, though it can be made sufficiently intelligible, is not altogether so natural and obvious.

But when barter ceases, and money has become the common instrument of commerce, every particular commodity is more frequently exchanged for money than for any other commodity. The butcher seldom carries his beef or his mutton to the baker, or the brewer, in order to exchange them for bread or for beer, but he carries them to the market, where he exchanges them for money, and afterwards exchanges that money for bread and for beer. The quantity of money which he gets for them regulates too the quantity of bread and beer which he can afterwards purchase. It is more natural and obvious to him, therefore, to estimate their value by the quantity of money, the commodity for which he immediately exchanges them, than by that of bread and beer, the commodities for which he can exchange them only by the intervention of another commodity; and rather to say that his butcher's meat is worth threepence or fourpence a pound, than that it is worth three or four pounds of bread, or three or four quarts of small beer. Hence it comes to pass, that the exchangeable value of every commodity is more frequently estimated by the quantity of money, than by the quantity either of labour or of any other commodity which can be had in exchange for it.

Gold and silver, however, like every other commodity, vary in their value, are sometimes cheaper and sometimes dearer, sometimes of easier and sometimes of more difficult purchase. The quantity of labour which any particular quantity of them can purchase or command, or the quantity of other goods which it will exchange for, depends always upon the fertility or barrenness of the mines which happen to be known about the time when such exchanges are made. The discovery of the abundant mines of America reduced, in the sixteenth century, the value of gold and silver in Europe to about a third of what it had been before. As it cost less labour to bring those metals from the mine to the market, so when they were brought thither they could purchase or command less labour; and this revolution in their value, though perhaps the greatest, is by no means the only one of which history gives some account. But as a measure of quantity, such as the natural foot, fathom, or handful, which is continually varying in its own quantity, can never be an accurate measure of the quantity of other things; so a commodity which is itself continually varying in its own value, can never be an accurate measure of the value of other commodities. Equal quantities of labour, at all times and places, may be said to be of equal value to the labourer. In his ordinary state of health, strength and spirits; in the ordinary degree of his skill and dexterity, he must always lay down the same portion of his ease, his liberty, and his happiness. The price which he pays must always be the same, whatever may be the quantity of goods which he receives in return for it. Of these, indeed, it may sometimes purchase a greater and sometimes a smaller quantity; but it is their value which varies, not that of the labour which purchases them. At all times and places that is dear which it is difficult to come at, or which it costs much labour to acquire; and that cheap which is to be had easily, or with very little labour. Labour alone, therefore, never varying in its own value, is alone the ultimate and real standard by which the value of all commodities can at all times and places be estimated and compared. It is their real price; money is their nominal price only.

But though equal quantities of labour are always of equal value to the labourer, yet to the person who employs him they appear sometimes to be of greater and sometimes of smaller value. He purchases them sometimes with a greater and sometimes with a smaller quantity of goods, and to him the price of labour seems to vary like that of all other things. It appears to him dear in the one case, and cheap in the other. In reality, however, it is the goods which are cheap in the one case, and dear in the other.

In this popular sense, therefore, labour, like commodities, may be said to have a real and a nominal price. Its real price may be said to consist in the quantity of the necessaries and conveniencies of life which are given for it; its nominal price, in the quantity of money. The labourer is rich or poor, is well or ill rewarded, in proportion to the real, not to the nominal price of his labour . . . .

Labour, therefore, it appears evidently, is the only universal, as well as the only accurate measure of value, or the only standard by which we can compare the values of different commodities at all times and at all places. We cannot estimate, it is allowed, the real value of different commodities from century to century by the quantities of silver which were given for them. We cannot estimate it from year to year by the quantities of corn. By the quantities of labour we can, with the greatest accuracy, estimate it both from century to century and from year to year. From century to century, corn is a better measure than silver, because, from century to century, equal quantities of corn will command the same quantity of labour more nearly than equal quantities of silver. From year to year, on the contrary, silver is a better measure than corn, because equal quantities of it will more nearly command the same quantity of labour . . . .

Of the Component Parts of the Price of Commodities

In that early and rude state of society which precedes both the accumulation of stock and the appropriation of land, the proportion between the quantities of labour necessary for acquiring different objects seems to be the only circumstance which can afford any rule for exchanging them for one another. If among a nation of hunters, for example, it usually costs twice the labour to kill a beaver which it does to kill a deer, one beaver should naturally exchange for or be worth two deer. It is natural that what is usually the produce of two days or two hours labour, should be worth double of what is usually the produce of one day's or one hour's labour.

If the one species of labour should be more severe than the other, some allowance will naturally be made for this superior hardship; and the produce of one hour's labour in the one way may frequently exchange for that of two hours labour in the other.

Or if the one species of labour requires an uncommon degree of dexterity and ingenuity, the esteem which men have for such talents, will naturally give a value to their produce, superior to what would be due to the time employed about it. Such talents can seldom be acquired but in consequence of long application, and the superior value of their produce may frequently be no more than a reasonable compensation for the time and labour which must be spent in acquiring them. In the advanced state of society, allowances of this kind, for superior hardship and superior skill, are commonly made in the wages of labour; and something of the same kind must probably have taken place in its earliest and rudest period.

In this state of things, the whole produce of labour belongs to the labourer; and the quantity of labour commonly employed in acquiring or producing any commodity, is the only circumstance which can regulate the quantity of labour which it ought commonly to purchase, command, or exchange for.

As soon as stock has accumulated in the hands of particular persons, some of them will naturally employ it in setting to work industrious people, whom they will supply with materials and subsistence, in order to make a profit by the sale of their work, or by what their labour adds to the value of the materials. In exchanging the complete manufacture either for money, for labour, or for other goods, over and above what may be sufficient to pay the price of the materials, and the wages of the workmen, something must be given for the profits of the undertaker of the work who hazards his stock in this adventure. The value which the workmen add to the materials, therefore, resolves itself in this case into two parts, of which the one pays their wages, the other the profits of their employer upon the whole stock of materials and wages which he advanced. He could have no interest to employ them, unless he expected from the sale of their work something more than what was sufficient to replace his stock to him; and he could have no interest to employ a great stock rather than a small one, unless his profits were to bear some proportion to the extent of his stock.

The profits of stock, it may perhaps be thought, are only a different name for the wages of a particular sort of labour, the labour of inspection and direction. They are, however, altogether different, are regulated by quite different principles, and bear no proportion to the quantity, the hardship, or the ingenuity of this supposed labour of inspection and direction. They are regulated altogether by the value of the stock employed, and are greater or smaller in proportion to the extent of this stock. Let us suppose, for example, that in some particular place, where the common annual profits of manufacturing stock are ten percent there are two different manufactures, in each of which twenty workmen are employed at the rate of fifteen pounds a year each, or at the expense of three hundred a year in each manufactory. Let us suppose too, that the coarse materials annually wrought up in the one cost only seven hundred pounds, while the finer materials in the other cost seven thousand. The capital annually employed in the one will in this case amount only to one thousand pounds; whereas that employed in the other will amount to seven thousand three hundred pounds. At the rate of ten percent therefore, the undertaker of the one will expect an yearly profit of about one hundred pounds only; while that of the other will expect about seven hundred and thirty pounds. But though their profits are so very different, their labour of inspection and direction may be either altogether or very nearly the same. In many great works, almost the whole labour of this kind is committed to some principal clerk. His wages properly express the value of this labour of inspection and direction. Though in settling them some regard is had commonly, not only to his labour and skill, but to the trust which is reposed in him, yet they never bear any regular proportion to the capital of which he oversees the management; and the owner of this capital, though he is thus discharged of almost all labour, still expects that his profits should bear a regular proportion to his capital. In the price of commodities, therefore, the profits of stock constitute a component part altogether different from the wages of labour, and regulated by quite different principles . . . .

As soon as the land of any country has all become private property, the landlords, like all other men, love to reap where they never sowed, and demand a rent even for its natural produce. The wood of the forest, the grass of the field, and all the natural fruits of the earth, which, when land was in common, cost the labourer only the trouble of gathering them, come, even to him, to have an additional price fixed upon them. He must then pay for the licence to gather them; and must give up to the landlord a portion of what his labour either collects or produces. This portion, or, what comes to the same thing, the price of this portion, constitutes the rent of land, and in the price of the greater part of commodities makes a third component part.

The real value of all the different component parts of price, it must be observed, is measured by the quantity of labour which they can, each of them, purchase or command. Labour measures the value not only of that part of price which resolves itself into labour, but of that which resolves itself into rent, and of that which resolves itself into profit . . . .

Of the Natural and Market Price of Commodities

There is in every society or neighbourhood an ordinary or average rate both of wages and profit in every different employment of labour and stock. This rate is naturally regulated, as I shall show hereafter, partly by the general circumstances of the society, their riches or poverty, their advancing, stationary, or declining condition; and partly by the particular nature of each employment.

There is likewise in every society or neighbourhood an ordinary or average rate of rent, which is regulated too, as I shall show hereafter, partly by the general circumstances of the society or neighbourhood in which the land is situated, and partly by the natural or improved fertility of the land.

These ordinary or average rates may be called the natural rates of wages, profit, and rent, at the time and place in which they commonly prevail.

When the price of any commodity is neither more nor less than what is; sufficient to pay the rent of the land, the wages of the labour, and the, profits of the stock employed in raising, preparing, and bringing it to market, according to their natural rates, the commodity is then sold for what may be called its natural price.

The commodity is then sold precisely for what it is worth, or for what it really costs the person who brings it to market; for though in common language what is called the prime cost of any commodity does not comprehend the profit of the person who is to sell it again, yet if he sells it at a price which does not allow him the ordinary rate of profit in his neighbourhood, he is evidently a loser by the trade; since by employing his stock in some other way he might have made that profit. His profit, besides, is his revenue, the proper fund of his subsistence. As, while he is preparing and bringing the goods to market, he advances to his workmen their wages, or their subsistence; so he advances to himself, in the same manner, his own subsistence, which is generally suitable to the profit which he may reasonably expect from the sale of his goods. Unless they yield him this profit, therefore, they do not repay him what they may very properly be said to have really cost him.

Though the price, therefore, which leaves him this profit, is not always the lowest at which a dealer may sometimes sell his goods, it is the lowest at which he is likely to sell them for any considerable time; at least where there is perfect liberty, or where he may change his trade as often as he pleases.

The actual price at which any commodity is commonly sold is called its market price. It may either be above, or below, or exactly the same with its natural price.

The market price of every particular commodity is regulated by the proportion between the quantity which is actually brought to market, and the demand of those who are willing to pay the natural price of the commodity, or the whole value of the rent, labour, and profit, which must be paid in order to bring it thither. Such people may be called the effectual demanders, and their demand the effectual demand; since it may be sufficient to effectuate the bringing of the commodity to market. It is different from the absolute demand. A very poor man may be said in some sense to have a demand for a coach and six; he might like to have it; but his demand is not an effectual demand, as the commodity can never be brought to market in order to satisfy it.

When the quantity of any commodity which is brought to market falls short of the effectual demand, all those who are willing to pay the whole value of the rent, wages, and profit, which must be paid in order to bring it thither, cannot be supplied with the quantity which they want. Rather than want it altogether, some of them will be willing to give more. A competition will immediately begin among them, and the market price will rise more or less above the natural price, according as either the greatness of the deficiency, or the wealth and wanton luxury of the competitors, happen to animate more or less the eagerness of the competition. Among competitors of equal wealth and luxury the same deficiency will generally occasion a more or less eager competition, according as the acquisition of the commodity happens to be of more or less importance to them. Hence the exorbitant price of the necessaries of life during the blockade of a town or in a famine.

When the quantity brought to market exceeds the effectual demand, it cannot be all sold to those who are willing to pay the whole value of the rent, wages and profit, which must be paid in order to bring it thither. Some part must be sold to those who are willing to pay less, and the low price which they give for it must reduce the price of the whole. The market price will sink more or less below the natural price, according as the greatness of the excess increases more or less the competition of the sellers, or according as it happens to be more or less important to them to get immediately rid of the commodity. The same excess in the importation of perishable, will occasion a much greater competition than in that of durable commodities; in the importation of oranges, for example, than in that of old iron.

When the quantity brought to market is just sufficient to supply the effectual demand and no more, the market price naturally comes to be either exactly, or as nearly as can be judged of, the same with the natural price. The whole quantity upon hand can be disposed of for this price, and cannot be disposed of for more. The competition of the different dealers obliges them all to accept of this price, but does not oblige them to accept of less.

The quantity of every commodity brought to market naturally suits itself to the effectual demand. It is the interest of all those who employ their land, labour, or stock, in bringing any commodity to market, that the quantity never should exceed the effectual demand; and it is the interest of all other people that it never should fall short of that demand.

If at any time it exceeds the effectual demand, some of the component parts of its price must be paid below their natural rate. If it is rent, the interest of the landlords will immediately prompt them to withdraw a part of their land; and if it is wages or profit, the interest of the labourers in the one case, and of their employers in the other, will prompt them to withdraw a part of their labour or stock from this employment. The quantity brought to market will soon be no more than sufficient to supply the effectual demand. All the different parts of its price will rise to their natural rate, and the whole price to its natural price.

If, on the contrary, the quantity brought to market should at any time fall short of the effectual demand, some of the component parts of its price must rise above their natural rate. If it is rent, the interest of all other landlords will naturally prompt them to prepare more land for the raising of this commodity; if it is wages or profit, the interest of all other labourers and dealers will soon prompt them to employ more labour and stock in preparing and bringing it to market. The quantity brought thither will soon be sufficient to supply the effectual demand. All the different parts of its price will soon sink to their natural rate, and the whole price to its natural price.

The natural price, therefore, is, as it were, the central price, to which the prices of all commodities are continually gravitating. Different accidents may sometimes keep them suspended a good deal above it, and sometimes force them down even somewhat below it. But whatever may be the obstacles which hinder them from settling in this centre of repose and continuance, they are constantly tending towards it.

The whole quantity of industry annually employed in order to bring any commodity to market, naturally suits itself in this manner to the effectual demand. It naturally aims at bringing always that precise quantity thither which may be sufficient to supply, and no more than supply, that demand.

But in some employments the same quantity of industry will in different years produce very different quantities of commodities; while in others it will produce always the same, or very nearly the same. The same number of labourers in husbandry will, in different years, produce very different quantities of corn, wine, oil, hops, etc. But the same number of spinners and weavers will every year produce the same or very nearly the same quantity of linen and woollen cloth. It is only the average produce of the one species of industry which can be suited in any respect to the effectual demand; and as its actual produce is frequently much greater and frequently much less than its average produce, the quantity of the commodities brought to market will sometimes exceed a good deal, and sometimes fall short a good deal of the effectual demand. Even though that demand therefore should continue always the same, their market price will be liable to great fluctuations, will sometimes fall a good deal below, and sometimes rise a good deal above their natural price. In the other species of industry, the produce of equal quantities of labour being always the same or very nearly the same, it can be more exactly suited to the effectual demand. While that demand continues the same, therefore, the market price of the commodities is likely to do so too, and to be either altogether, or as nearly as can be judged of, the same with the natural price. That the price of linen and woollen cloth is liable neither to such frequent nor to such great variations as the price of corn, every man's experience will inform him. The price of the one species of commodities varies only with the variations in the demand: That of the other varies, not only with the variations in the demand, but with the much greater and more frequent variations in the quantity of what is brought to market in order to supply that demand.

The occasional and temporary fluctuations in the market price of any commodity fall chiefly upon those parts of its price which resolve themselves into wages and profit. That part which resolves itself into rent is less affected by them. A rent certain in money is not in the least affected by them either in its rate or in its value. A rent which consists either in a certain proportion or in a certain quantity of the rude produce, is no doubt affected in its yearly value by all the occasional and temporary fluctuations in the market price of that rude produce: but it is seldom affected by them in its yearly rate. In settling the terms of the lease, the landlord and farmer endeavour, according to their best judgment, to adjust that rate, not to the temporary and occasional, but to the average and ordinary price of the produce . . . .

But though the market price of every particular commodity is in this manner continually gravitating, if one may say so, towards the natural price, yet sometimes particular accidents, sometimes natural causes, and sometimes particular regulations of police, may, in many commodities, keep up the market price, for a long time together, a good deal above the natural price.

When by an increase in the effectual demand, the market price of some particular commodity happens to rise a good deal above the natural price, those who employ their stocks in supplying that market are generally careful to conceal this change. If it was commonly known, their great profit would tempt so many new rivals to employ their stocks in the same way, that, the effectual demand being fully supplied, the market price would soon be reduced to the natural price, and perhaps for some time even below it. If the market is at a great distance from the residence of those who supply it, they may sometimes be able to keep the secret for several years together, and may so long enjoy their extraordinary profits without any new rivals. Secrets of this kind, however, it must be acknowledged, can seldom be long kept; and the extraordinary profit can last very little longer than they are kept.

Secrets in manufactures are capable of being longer kept than secrets in trade. A dyer who has found the means of producing a particular colour with materials which cost only half the price of those commonly made use of, may, with good management, enjoy the advantage of his discovery as long as he lives, and even leave it as a legacy to his posterity. His extraordinary gains arise from the high price which is paid for his private labour. They properly consist in the high wages of that labour. But as they are repeated upon every part of his stock, and as their whole amount bears, upon that account, a regular proportion to it, they are commonly considered as extraordinary profits of stock.

Such enhancements of the market price are evidently the effects of particular accidents, of which, however, the operation may sometimes last for many years together . . . .

A monopoly granted either to an individual or to a trading company has the same effect as a secret in trade or manufactures. The monopolists, by keeping the market constantly under-stocked, by never fully supplying the effectual demand, sell their commodities much above the natural price, and raise their emoluments, whether they consist in wages or profit, greatly above their natural rate.

The price of monopoly is upon every occasion the highest which can be got. The natural price, or the price of free competition, on the contrary, is the lowest which can be taken, not upon every occasion, indeed, but for any considerable time together. The one is upon every occasion the highest which can be squeezed out of the buyers, or which, it is supposed, they will consent to give: The other is the lowest which the sellers can commonly afford to take, and at the same time continue their business.

The exclusive privileges of corporations, statutes of apprenticeship, and all those laws which restrain, in particular employments, the competition to a smaller number than might otherwise go into them, have the same tendency, though in a less degree. They are a sort of enlarged monopolies, and may frequently, for ages together and in whole classes of employments, keep up the market price of particular commodities above the natural price, and maintain both the wages of the labour and the profits of the stock employed about them somewhat above their natural rate.

Such enhancements of the market price may last as long as the regulations of police which give occasion to them.

The market price of any particular commodity, though it may continue long above, can seldom continue long below its natural price. Whatever part of it was paid below the natural rate, the persons whose interest it affected would immediately feel the loss, and would immediately withdraw either so much land, or so much labour, or so much stock, from being employed about it, that the quantity brought to market would soon be no more than sufficient to supply the effectual demand. Its market price, therefore, would soon rise to the natural price. This at least would be the case where there was perfect liberty . . . .

Of the Wages of Labour

The produce of labour constitutes the natural recompense or wages of labour.

In that original state of things, which precedes both the appropriation of land and the accumulation of stock, the whole produce of labour belongs to the labourer. He has neither landlord nor master to share with him.

Had this state continued, the wages of labour would have augmented with all those improvements in its productive powers, to which the division of labour gives occasion. All things would gradually have become cheaper. They would have been produced by a smaller quantity of labour; and as the commodities produced by equal quantities of labour would naturally in this state of things be exchanged for one another, they would have been purchased likewise with the produce of a smaller quantity.

But though all things would have become cheaper in reality, in appearance many things might have become dearer than before, or have been exchanged for a greater quantity of other goods. Let us suppose, for example, that in the greater part of employments the productive powers of labour had been improved to tenfold, or that a day's labour could produce ten times the quantity of work which it had done originally; but that in a particular employment they had been improved only to double, or that a day's labour could produce only twice the quantity of work which it had done before. In exchanging the produce of a day's labour in the greater part of employments, for that of a day's labour in this particular one, ten times the original quantity of work in them would purchase only twice the original quantity in it. Any particular quantity in it, therefore, a pound weight, for example, would appear to be five times dearer than before. In reality, however, it would be twice as cheap. Though it required five times the quantity of other goods to purchase it, it would require only half the quantity of labour either to purchase or to produce it. The acquisition, therefore, would be twice as easy as before.

But this original state of things, in which the labourer enjoyed the whole produce of his own labour, could not last beyond the first introduction of the appropriation of land and the accumulation of stock. It was at an end, therefore, long before the most considerable improvements were made in the productive powers of labour, and it would be to no purpose to trace farther what might have been its effects upon the recompense or wages of labour.

As soon as land becomes private property, the landlord demands a share of almost all the produce which the labourer can either raise, or collect from it. His rent makes the first deduction from the produce of the labour which is employed upon land.

It seldom happens that the person who tills the ground has wherewithal to maintain himself till he reaps the harvest. His maintenance is generally advanced to him from the stock of a master, the farmer who employs him, and who would have no interest to employ him, unless he was to share in the produce of his labour, or unless his stock was to be replaced to him with a profit. This profit makes a second deduction from the produce of the labour which is employed upon land.

The produce of almost all other labour is liable to the like deduction of profit. In all arts and manufactures the greater part of the workmen stand in need of a master to advance them the materials of their work, and their wages and maintenance till it be completed. He shares in the produce of their labour, or in the value which it adds to the materials upon which it is bestowed; and in this share consists his profit.

It sometimes happens, indeed, that a single independent workman has stock sufficient both to purchase the materials of his work, and to maintain himself till it be completed. He is both master and workman, and enjoys the whole produce of his own labour, or the whole value which it adds to the materials upon which it is bestowed. It includes what are usually two distinct revenues, belonging to two distinct persons, the profits of stock, and the wages of labour . . . .

What are the common wages of labour depends everywhere upon the contract usually made between those two parties, whose interests are by no means the same. The workmen desire to get as much, the masters to give as little as possible. The former are disposed to combine in order to raise, the latter in order to lower the wages of labour.

It is not, however, difficult to foresee which of the two parties must, upon all ordinary occasions, have the advantage in the dispute, and force the other into a compliance with their terms. The masters, being fewer in number, can combine much more easily; and the law, besides, authorizes, or at least does not prohibit their combinations, while it prohibits those of the workmen. We have no acts of parliament against combining to lower the price of work; but many against combining to raise it. In all such disputes the masters can hold out much longer. A landlord, a farmer, a master manufacturer, or merchant, though they did not employ a single workman, could generally live a year or two upon the stocks which they have already acquired. Many workmen could not subsist a week, few could subsist a month, and scarce any a year without employment. In the long-run the workman may be as necessary to his master as his master is to him; but the necessity is not so immediate.

We rarely hear, it has been said, of the combinations of masters; though frequently of those of workmen. But whoever imagines, upon this account, that masters rarely combine, is as ignorant of the world as of the subject. Masters are always and everywhere in a sort of tacit, but constant and uniform combination, not to raise the wages of labour above their actual rate. To violate this combination is everywhere a most unpopular action, and a sort of reproach to a master among his neighbours and equals. We seldom, indeed, hear of this combination, because it is the usual, and one may say, the natural state of things which nobody ever hears of. Masters too sometimes enter into particular combinations to sink the wages of labour even below this rate. These are always conducted with the utmost silence and secrecy, till the moment of execution, and when the workmen yield, as they sometimes do, without resistance, though severely felt by them, they are never heard of by other people. Such combinations, however, are frequently resisted by a contrary defensive combination of the workmen; who sometimes too, without any provocation of this kind, combine of their own accord to raise the price of their labour. Their usual pretences are, sometimes the high price of provisions; sometimes the great profit which their masters make by their work. But whether their combinations be offensive or defensive, they are always abundantly heard of. In order to bring the point to a speedy decision, they have always recourse to the loudest clamour, and sometimes to the most shocking violence and outrage. They are desperate, and act with the folly and extravagance of desperate men, who must either starve, or frighten their masters into an immediate compliance with their demands. The masters upon these occasions are just as clamorous upon the other side, and never cease to call aloud for the assistance of the civil magistrate, and the rigorous execution of those laws which have been enacted with so much severity against the combinations of servants, labourers, and journeymen. The workmen, accordingly, very seldom derive any advantage from the violence of those tumultuous combinations, which, partly from the interposition of the civil magistrate, partly from the superior steadiness of the masters, partly from the necessity which the greater part of the workmen are under of submitting for the sake of present subsistence, generally end in nothing, but the punishment or ruin of the ringleaders.

But though in disputes with their workmen, masters must generally have the advantage, there is however a certain rate below which it seems impossible to reduce, for any considerable time, the ordinary wages even of the lowest species of labour.

A man must always live by his work, and his wages must at least be sufficient to maintain him. They must even upon most occasions be somewhat more; otherwise it would be impossible for him to bring up a family, and the race of such workmen could not last beyond the first generation . . . .

There are certain circumstances, however, which sometimes give the labourers an advantage, and enable them to raise their wages considerably above this rate; evidently the lowest which is consistent with common humanity.

When in any country the demand for those who live by wages; labourers, journeymen, servants of every kind, is continually increasing; when every year furnishes employment for a greater number than had been employed the year before, the workmen have no occasion to combine in order to raise their wages. The scarcity of hands occasions a competition among masters, who bid against one another, in order to get workmen, and thus voluntarily break through the natural combination of masters not to raise wages.

The demand for those who live by wages, it is evident, cannot increase but in proportion to the increase of the funds which are destined for the payment of wages. These funds are of two kinds; first, the revenue which is over and above what is necessary for the maintenance; and, secondly, the stock which is over and above what is necessary for the employment of their masters.

When the landlord, annuitant, or moneyed man, has a greater revenue than what he judges sufficient to maintain his own family, he employs either the whole or a part of the surplus in maintaining one or more menial servants. Increase this surplus, and he will naturally increase the number of those servants.

When an independent workman, such as a weaver or shoe-maker, has got more stock than what is sufficient to purchase the materials of his own work, and to maintain himself till he can dispose of it, he naturally employs one or more journeymen with the surplus, in order to make a profit by their work. Increase this surplus, and he will naturally increase the number of his journeymen.

The demand for those who live by wages, therefore, necessarily increases with the increase of the revenue and stock of every country, and cannot possibly increase without it. The increase of revenue and stock is the increase of national wealth. The demand for those who live by wages, therefore, naturally increases with the increase of national wealth, and cannot possibly increase without it.

It is not the actual greatness of national wealth, but its continual increase, which occasions a rise in the wages of labour. It is not, accordingly, in the richest countries, but in the most thriving, or in those which are growing rich the fastest, that the wages of labour are highest. England is certainly, in the present times, a much richer country than any part of North America. The wages of labour, however, are much higher in North America than in any part of England. . . . The price of provisions is everywhere in North America much lower than in England. A dearth has never been known there. In the worst seasons, they have always had a sufficiency for themselves, though less for exportation. If the money price of labour, therefore, be higher than it is anywhere in the mother country, its real price, the real command of the necessaries and conveniencies of life which it conveys to the labourer, must be higher in a still greater proportion.

But though North America is not yet so rich as England, it is much more thriving, and advancing with much greater rapidity to the further acquisition of riches. The most decisive mark of the prosperity of any country is the increase of the number of its inhabitants. In Great Britain, and most other European countries, they are not supposed to double in less than five hundred years. In the British colonies in North America, it has been found, that they double in twenty or five-and-twenty years. Nor in the present times is this increase principally owing to the continual importation of new inhabitants, but to the great multiplication of the species. Those who live to old age, it is said, frequently see there from fifty to a hundred, and sometimes many more, descendants from their own body. Labour is there so well rewarded that a numerous family of children, instead of being a burthen is a source of opulence and prosperity to the parents. The labour of each child, before it can leave their house, is computed to be worth a hundred pounds clear gain to them. A young widow with four or five young children, who, among the middling or inferior ranks of people in Europe, would have so little chance for a second husband, is there frequently courted as a sort of fortune. The value of children is the greatest of all encouragements to marriage. We cannot, therefore, wonder that the people in North America should generally marry very young. Notwithstanding the great increase occasioned by such early marriages, there is a continual complaint of the scarcity of hands in North America. The demand for labourers, the funds destined for maintaining them, increase, it seems, still faster than they can find labourers to employ . . . .

Is this improvement in the circumstances of the lower ranks of the people to be regarded as an advantage or as an inconveniency to the society? The answer seems at first sight abundantly plain. Servants, labourers and workmen of different kinds, make up the far greater part of every great political society. But what improves the circumstances of the greater part can never be regarded as an inconveniency to the whole. No society can surely be flourishing and happy, of which the far greater part of the members are poor and miserable. It is but equity, besides, that they who feed, clothe and lodge the whole body of the people, should have such a share of the produce of their own labour as to be themselves tolerably well fed, clothed and lodged.

Poverty, though it no doubt discourages, does not always prevent marriage. It seems even to be favourable to generation. A half-starved Highland woman frequently bears more than twenty children, while a pampered fine lady is often incapable of bearing any, and is generally exhausted by two or three. Barrenness, so frequent among women of fashion, is very rare among those of inferior station. Luxury in the fair sex, while it enflames perhaps the passion for enjoyment, seems always to weaken, and frequently to destroy altogether, the powers of generation.

But poverty, though it does not prevent the generation, is extremely unfavourable to the rearing of children. The tender plant is produced, but in so cold a soil and so severe a climate, soon withers and dies. It is not uncommon, I have been frequently told, in the Highlands of Scotland for a mother who has borne twenty children not to have two alive. Several officers of great experience have assured me, that so far from recruiting their regiment, they have never been able to supply it with drums and fifes from all the soldiers' children that were born in it. A greater number of fine children, however, is seldom seen anywhere than about a barrack of soldiers. Very few of them, it seems, arrive at the age of thirteen or fourteen. In some places one half the children born die before they are four years of age; in many places before they are seven; and in almost all places before they are nine or ten. This great mortality, however, will everywhere be found chiefly among the children of the common people, who cannot afford to tend them with the same care as those of better station. Though their marriages are generally more fruitful than those of people of fashion, a smaller proportion of their children arrive at maturity. In foundling hospitals, and among the children brought up by parish charities, the mortality is still greater than among those of the common people.

Every species of animals naturally multiplies in proportion to the means of their subsistence, and no species can ever multiply beyond it. But in civilized society it is only among the inferior ranks of people that the scantiness of subsistence can set limits to the further multiplication of the human species; and it can do so in no other way than by destroying a great part of the children which their fruitful marriages produce.

The liberal reward of labour, by enabling them to provide better for their children, and consequently to bring up a greater number, naturally tends to widen and extend those limits. It deserves to be remarked too, that it necessarily does this as nearly as possible in the proportion which the demand for labour requires. If this demand is continually increasing, the reward of labour must necessarily encourage in such a manner the marriage and multiplication of labourers, as may enable them to supply that continually increasing demand by a continually increasing population. If the reward should at any time be less than what was requisite for this purpose, the deficiency of hands would soon raise it; and if it should at any time be more, their excessive multiplication would soon lower it to this necessary rate. The market would be so much under-stocked with labour in the one case, and so much over-stocked in the other, as would soon force back its price to that proper rate which the circumstances of the society required. It is in this manner that the demand for men, like that for any other commodity, necessarily regulates the production of men; quickens it when it goes on too slowly, and stops it when it advances too fast. It is this demand which regulates and determines the state of propagation in all the different countries of the world, in North America, in Europe, and in China; which renders it rapidly progressive in the first, slow and gradual in the second, and altogether stationary in the last.

The wear and tear of a slave, it has been said, is at the expense of his master; but that of a free servant is at his own expense. The wear and tear of the latter, however, is, in reality, as much at the expense of his master as that of the former. The wages paid to journeymen and servants of every kind must be such as may enable them, one with another, to continue the race of journeymen and servants, according as the increasing, diminishing, or stationary demand of the society may happen to require. But though the wear and tear of a free servant be equally at the expense of his master, it generally costs him much less than that of a slave. The fund destined for replacing or repairing, if I may say so, the wear and tear of the slave, is commonly managed by a negligent master or careless overseer. That destined for performing the same office with regard to the free man, is managed by the free man himself. The disorders which generally prevail in the economy of the rich, naturally introduce themselves into the management of the former: The strict frugality and parsimonious attention of the poor as naturally establish themselves in that of the latter. Under such different management, the same purpose must require very different degrees of expense to execute it. It appears, accordingly, from the experience of all ages and nations, I believe, that the work done by freemen comes cheaper in the end than that performed by slaves. It is found to do so even at Boston, New York, and Philadelphia, where the wages of common labour are so very high.

The liberal reward of labour, therefore, as it is the effect of increasing wealth, so it is the cause of increasing population. To complain of it is to lament over the necessary effect and cause of the greatest public prosperity.

It deserves to be remarked, perhaps, that it is in the progressive state, while the society is advancing to the further acquisition, rather than when it has acquired its full complement of riches, that the condition of the labouring poor, of the great body of the people, seems to be the happiest and the most comfortable. It is hard in the stationary, and miserable in the declining state. The progressive state is in reality the cheerful and the hearty state to all the different orders of the society. The stationary is dull; the declining, melancholy.

The liberal reward of labour, as it encourages the propagation, so it increases the industry of the common people. The wages of labour are the encouragement of industry, which, like every other human quality, improves in proportion to the encouragement it receives. A plentiful subsistence increases the bodily strength of the labourer, and the comfortable hope of bettering his condition, and of ending his days perhaps in ease and plenty, animates him to exert that strength to the utmost. Where wages are high, accordingly, we shall always find the workmen more active diligent, and expeditious, than where they are low; in England, for example, than in Scotland; in the neighbourhood of great towns, than in remote country places. Some workmen, indeed, when they can earn in four days what will maintain them through the week, will be idle the other three. This, however, is by no means the case with the greater part.

Workmen, on the contrary, when they are liberally paid by the piece, are very apt to over-work themselves, and to ruin their health and constitution in a few years. A carpenter in London, and in some other places, is not supposed to last in his utmost vigour above eight years. Something of the same kind happens in many other trades, in which the workmen are paid by the piece; as they generally are in manufactures, and even in country labour, wherever wages are higher than ordinary. Almost every class of artificers is subject to some peculiar infirmity occasioned by excessive application to their peculiar species of work . . . .

Excessive application during four days of the week, is frequently the real cause of the idleness of the other three, so much and so loudly complained of. Great labour, either of mind or body, continued for several days together, is in most men naturally followed by a great desire of relaxation, which, if not restrained by force or by some strong necessity, is almost irresistible. It is the call of nature, which requires to be relieved by some indulgence, sometimes of ease only, but sometimes too of dissipation and diversion. If it is not complied with, the consequences are often dangerous, and sometimes fatal, and such as almost always, sooner or later, bring on the peculiar infirmity of the trade. If masters would always listen to the dictates of reason and humanity, they have frequently occasion rather to moderate, than to animate the application of many of their workmen. It will be found, I believe, in every sort of trade, that the man who works so moderately, as to be able to work constantly, not only preserves his health the longest, but, in the course of the year, executes the greatest quantity of work . . . .

Inequalities Arising From the Nature of the Employments Themselves

The five following are the principal circumstances which, so far as I have been able to observe, make up for a small pecuniary gain in some employments, and counter-balance a great one in others: first, the agreeableness or disagreeableness of the employments themselves; secondly, the easiness and cheapness, or the difficulty and expense of learning them; thirdly, the constancy or inconstancy of employment in them; fourthly, the small or great trust which must be reposed in those who exercise them; and, fifthly, the probability or improbability of success in them.

First, the wages of labour vary with the ease or hardship, the cleanliness or dirtiness, the honourableness or dishonourableness of the employment. . . . Honour makes a great part of the reward of all honourable professions. In point of pecuniary gain, all things considered, they are generally under-recompensed, as I shall endeavour to show by and by. Disgrace has the contrary effect. The trade of a butcher is a brutal and an odious business; but it is in most places more profitable than the greater part of common trades. The most detestable of all employments, that of public executioner, is in proportion to the quantity of work done, better paid than any common trade whatever.

Hunting and fishing, the most important employments of mankind in the rude state of society, become in its advanced state their most agreeable amusements, and they pursue for pleasure what they once followed from necessity. In the advanced state of society, therefore, they are all very poor people who follow as a trade, what other people pursue as a pastime. Fishermen have been so since the time of Theocritus. A poacher is everywhere a very poor man in Great Britain. In countries where the rigour of the law suffers no poachers, the licensed hunter is not in a much better condition. The natural taste for those employments makes more people follow them than can live comfortably by them, and the produce of their labour, in proportion to its quantity, comes always too cheap to market to afford anything but the most scanty subsistence to the labourers . . . .

Secondly, the wages of labour vary with the easiness and cheapness, or the difficulty and expense of learning the business.

When any expensive machine is erected, the extraordinary work to be performed by it before it is worn out, it must be expected, will replace the capital laid out upon it, with at least the ordinary profits. A man educated at the expense of much labour and time to any of those employments which require extraordinary dexterity and skill, may be compared to one of those expensive machines. The work which he learns to perform, it must be expected, over and above the usual wages of common labour, will replace to him the whole expense of his education, with at least the ordinary profits of an equally valuable capital. It must do this too in a reasonable time, regard being had to the very uncertain duration of human life, in the same manner as to the more certain duration of the machine.

The difference between the wages of skilled labour and those of common labour, is founded upon this principle . . . .

Education in the ingenious arts and in the liberal professions, is still more tedious and expensive. The pecuniary recompense, therefore, of painters and sculptors, of lawyers and physicians, ought to be much more liberal: and it is so accordingly . . . .

Thirdly, The wages of labour in different occupations vary with the constancy or inconstancy of employment.

Employment is much more constant in some trades than in others. In the greater part of manufactures, a journeyman may be pretty sure of employment almost every day in the year that he is able to work. A mason or bricklayer, on the contrary, can work neither in hard frost nor in foul weather, and his employment at all other times depends upon the occasional calls of his customers. He is liable, in consequence, to be frequently without any. What he earns, therefore, while he is employed, must not only maintain him while he is idle, but make him some compensation for those anxious and desponding moments which the thought of so precarious a situation must sometimes occasion . . . .

Fourthly, the wages of labour vary according to the small or great trust which must be reposed in the workmen.

The wages of goldsmiths and jewellers are everywhere superior to those of many other workmen, not only of equal, but of much superior ingenuity; on account of the precious materials with which they are entrusted . . . .

Fifthly, the wages of labour in different employments vary according to the probability or improbability of success in them . . . .

Those professions keep their level, however, with other occupations, and, notwithstanding these discouragements, all the most generous and liberal spirits are eager to crowd into them. Two different causes contribute to recommend them. First, the desire of the reputation which attends upon superior excellence in any of them; and, secondly, the natural confidence which every man has more or less, not only in his own abilities, but in his own good fortune.

To excel in any profession, in which but few arrive at mediocrity, is the most decisive mark of what is called genius or superior talents. The public admiration which attends upon such distinguished abilities, makes always a part of their reward; a greater or smaller in proportion as it is higher or lower in degree. It makes a considerable part of that reward in the profession of physic; a still greater perhaps in that of law; in poetry and philosophy it makes almost the whole . . . .

Inequalities Occasioned by the Policy of Europe

Such are the inequalities in the whole of the advantages and disadvantages of the different employments of labour and stock, which the defect of any of the three requisites above-mentioned must occasion, even where there is the most perfect liberty. But the policy of Europe, by not leaving things at perfect liberty, occasions other inequalities of much greater importance.

It does this chiefly in the three following ways. First, by restraining the competition in some employments to a smaller number than would otherwise be disposed to enter into them; secondly, by increasing it in others beyond what it naturally would be; and, thirdly, by obstructing the free circulation of labour and stock, both from employment to employment and from place to place.

First, the policy of Europe occasions a very important inequality in the whole of the advantages and disadvantages of the different employments of labour and stock, by restraining the competition in some employments to a smaller number than might otherwise be disposed to enter into them.

The exclusive privileges of corporations are the principal means it makes use of for this purpose.

The exclusive privilege of an incorporated trade necessarily restrains the competition, in the town where it is established, to those who are free of the trade. To have served an apprenticeship in the town, under a master properly qualified, is commonly the necessary requisite for obtaining this freedom. The bye-laws of the corporation regulate sometimes the number of apprentices which any master is allowed to have, and almost always the number of years which each apprentice is obliged to serve. The intention of both regulations is to restrain the competition to a much smaller number than might otherwise be disposed to enter into the trade. The limitation of the number of apprentices restrains it directly. A long term of apprenticeship restrains it more indirectly, but as effectually, by increasing the expense of education . . . .

The property which every man has in his own labour, as it is the original foundation of all other property, so it is the most sacred and inviolable. The patrimony of a poor man lies in the strength and dexterity of his hands; and to hinder him from employing this strength and dexterity in what manner he thinks proper without injury to his neighbour, is a plain violation of this most sacred property. It is a manifest encroachment upon the just liberty both of the workman, and of those who might be disposed to employ him. As it hinders the one from working at what he thinks proper, so it hinders the others from employing whom they think proper. To judge whether he is fit to be employed, may surely be trusted to the discretion of the employers whose interest it so much concerns. The affected anxiety of the law-giver lest they should employ an improper person, is evidently as impertinent as it is oppressive.

The institution of long apprenticeships can give no security that insufficient workmanship shall not frequently be exposed to public sale. When this is done it is generally the effect of fraud, and not of inability; and the longest apprenticeship can give no security against fraud. Quite different regulations are necessary to prevent this abuse . . . .

The institution of long apprenticeships has no tendency to form young people to industry. A journeyman who works by the piece is likely to be industrious, because he derives a benefit from every exertion of his industry. An apprentice is likely to be idle, and almost always is so, because he has no immediate interest to be otherwise. In the inferior employments, the sweets of labour consist altogether in the recompense of labour. They who are soonest in a condition to enjoy the sweets of it, are likely soonest to conceive a relish for it, and to acquire the early habit of industry. A young man naturally conceives an aversion to labour, when for a long time he receives no benefit from it. The boys who are put out apprentices from public charities are generally bound for more than the usual number of years, and they generally turn out very idle and worthless . . . .

It is to prevent this reduction of price, and consequently of wages and profit, by restraining that free competition which would most certainly occasion it, that all corporations, and the greater part of corporation laws, have been established. In order to erect a corporation, no other authority in ancient times was requisite in many parts of Europe, but that of the town corporate in which it was established. In England, indeed, a charter from the king was likewise necessary. But this prerogative of the crown seems to have been reserved rather for extorting money from the subject, than for the defence of the common liberty against such oppressive monopolies. Upon paying a fine to the king, the charter seems generally to have been readily granted; and when any particular class of artificers or traders thought proper to act as a corporation without a charter, such adulterine guilds, as they were called, were not always disfranchised upon that account, but obliged to fine annually to the king for permission to exercise their usurped privileges. The immediate inspection of all corporations, and of the bye-laws which they might think proper to enact for their own government, belonged to the town corporate in which they were established; and whatever discipline was exercised over them, proceeded commonly, not from the king, but from that greater incorporation of which the subordinate ones were only parts or members . . . .

People of the same trade seldom meet together, even for merriment and diversion, but the conversation ends in a conspiracy against the public, or in some contrivance to raise prices. It is impossible indeed to prevent such meetings, by any law which either could be executed, or would be consistent with liberty and justice. But though the law cannot hinder people of the same trade from sometimes assembling together, it ought to do nothing to facilitate such assemblies; much less to render them necessary.

A regulation which obliges all those of the same trade in a particular town to enter their names and places of abode in a public register, facilitates such assemblies. It connects individuals who might never otherwise be known to one another, and gives every man of the trade a direction where to find every other man of it.

A regulation which enables those of the same trade to tax themselves in order to provide for their poor, their sick, their widows and orphans, by giving them a common interest to manage, renders such assemblies necessary.

An incorporation not only renders them necessary, but makes the act of the majority binding upon the whole. In a free trade an effectual combination cannot be established but by the unanimous consent of every single trader, and it cannot last longer than every single trader continues of the same mind. The majority of a corporation can enact a byelaw with proper penalties, which will limit the competition more effectually and more durably than any voluntary combination whatever.

The pretence that corporations are necessary for the better government of the trade, is without any foundation. The real and effectual discipline which is exercised over a workman, is not that of his corporation, but that of his customers. It is the fear of losing their employment which restrains his frauds and corrects his negligence. An exclusive corporation necessarily weakens the force of this discipline. A particular set of workmen must then be employed, let them behave well or ill. It is upon this account that in many large incorporated towns no tolerable workmen are to be found, even in some of the most necessary trades. If you would have your work tolerably executed, it must be done in the suburbs, where the workmen having no exclusive privilege, have nothing but their character to depend upon, and you must then smuggle it into the town as well as you can.

It is in this manner that the policy of Europe, by restraining the competition in some employments to a smaller number than would otherwise be disposed to enter into them, occasions a very important inequality in the whole of the advantages and disadvantages of the different employments of labour and stock . . . .

Thirdly, the policy of Europe, by obstructing the free circulation of labour and stock both from employment to employment, and from place to place, occasions in some cases a very inconvenient inequality in the whole of the advantages and disadvantages of their different employments . . . .

BOOK II

Of the Nature, Accumulation, and Employment of Stock

Introduction

In that rude state of society in which there is no division of labour, in which exchanges are seldom made, and in which every man provides every thing for himself, it is not necessary that any stock should be accumulated or stored up beforehand in order to carry on the business of the society. Every man endeavours to supply by his own industry his own occasional wants as they occur. When he is hungry, he goes to the forest to hunt; when his coat is worn out, he clothes himself with the skin of the first large animal he kills: and when his hut begins to go to ruin, he repairs it, as well as he can, with the trees and the turf that are nearest it.

But when the division of labour has once been thoroughly introduced, the produce of a man's own labour can supply but a very small part of his occasional wants. The far greater part of them are supplied by the produce of other men's labour, which he purchases with the produce, or, what is the same thing, with the price of the produce of his own. But this purchase cannot be made till such time as the produce of his own labour has not only been completed, but sold. A stock of goods of different kinds, therefore, must be stored up somewhere sufficient to maintain him, and to supply him with the materials and tools of his work till such time, at least, as both these events can be brought about. A weaver cannot apply himself entirely to his peculiar business, unless there is beforehand stored up somewhere, either in his own possession or in that of some other person, a stock sufficient to maintain him, and to supply him with the materials and tools of his work, till he has not only completed, but sold his web. This accumulation must, evidently, be previous to his applying his industry for so long a time to such a peculiar business.

As the accumulation of stock must, in the nature of things, be previous to the division of labour, so labour can be more and more subdivided in proportion only as stock is previously more and more accumulated. The quantity of materials which the same number of people can work up, increases in a great proportion as labour comes to be more and more subdivided; and as the operations of each workman are gradually reduced to a greater degree of simplicity, a variety of new machines come to be invented for facilitating and abridging those operations. As the division of labour advances, therefore, in order to give constant employment to an equal number of workmen, an equal stock of provisions, and a greater stock of materials and tools than what would have been necessary in a ruder state of things, must be accumulated beforehand. But the number of workmen in every branch of business generally increases with the division of labour in that branch, or rather it is the increase of their number which enables them to class and subdivide themselves in this manner.

As the accumulation of stock is previously necessary for carrying on this great improvement in the productive powers of labour, so that accumulation naturally leads to this improvement. The person who employs his stock in maintaining labour, necessarily wishes to employ it in such a manner as to produce as great a quantity of work as possible. He endeavours, therefore, both to make among his workmen the most proper distribution of employment, and to furnish them with the best machines which he can either invent or afford to purchase. His abilities in both these respects are generally in proportion to the extent of his stock, or to the number of people whom it can employ. The quantity of industry, therefore, not only increases in every country with the increase of the stock which employs it, but, in consequence of that increase, the same quantity of industry produces a much greater quantity of work.

Such are in general the effects of the increase of stock upon industry and its productive powers . . . .

Of the Accumulation of Capital, or of Productive and Unproductive Labour

There is one sort of labour which adds to the value of the subject upon which it is bestowed: There is another which has no such effect. The former, as it produces a value, may be called productive; the latter, unproductive labour. Thus the labour of a manufacturer adds, generally, to the value of the materials which he works upon, that of his own maintenance, and of his master's profit. The labour of a menial servant, on the contrary, adds to the value of nothing. Though the manufacturer has his wages advanced to him by his master, he, in reality, costs him no expense, the value of those wages being generally restored, together with a profit, in the improved value of the subject upon which his labour is bestowed. But the maintenance of a menial servant never is restored. A man grows rich by employing a multitude of manufacturers: He grows poor, by maintaining a multitude of menial servants. The labour of the latter, however, has its value, and deserves its reward as well as that of the former. But the labour of the manufacturer fixes and realizes itself in some particular subject or vendible commodity, which lasts for some time at least after that labour is past. It is, as it were, a certain quantity of labour stocked and stored up to be employed, if necessary, upon some other occasion. That subject, or what is the same thing, the price of that subject, can afterwards, if necessary, put into motion a quantity of labour equal to that which had originally produced it. The labour of the menial servant, on the contrary, does not fix or realize itself in any particular subject or vendible commodity. His services generally perish in the very instant of their performance, and seldom leave any trace or value behind them, for which an equal quantity of service could afterwards be procured.

The labour of some of the most respectable orders in the society is, like that of menial servants, unproductive of any value, and does not fix or realize itself in any permanent subject, or vendible commodity, which endures after that labour is past, and for which an equal quantity of labour could afterwards be procured. The sovereign, for example, with all the officers both of justice and war who serve under him, the whole army and navy, are unproductive labourers. They are the servants of the public, and are maintained by a part of the annual produce of the industry of other people. Their service, how honourable, how useful, or how necessary soever, produces nothing for which an equal quantity of service can afterwards be procured. The protection, security, and defence of the commonwealth, the effect of their labour this year, will not purchase its protection, security, and defence, for the year to come. In the same class must be ranked, some both of the gravest and most important, and some of the most frivolous professions: churchmen, lawyers, physicians, men of letters of all kinds; players, buffoons, musicians, opera-singers, opera-dancers, etc. The labour of the meanest of these has a certain value, regulated by the very same principles which regulate that of every other sort of labour; and that of the noblest and most useful, produces nothing which could afterwards purchase or procure an equal quantity of labour. Like the declamation of the actor, the harangue of the orator, or the tune of the musician, the work of all of them perishes in the very instant of its production.

Both productive and unproductive labourers, and those who do not labour at all, are all equally maintained by the annual produce of the land and labour of the country. This produce, how great soever, can never be infinite, but must have certain limits. According, therefore, as a smaller or greater proportion of it is in any one year employed in maintaining unproductive hands, the more in the one case and the less in the other will remain for the productive, and the next year's produce will be greater or smaller accordingly; the whole annual produce, if we except the spontaneous productions of the earth, being the effect of productive labour . . . .

Whatever part of his stock a man employs as a capital, he always expects it to be replaced to him with a profit. He employs it, therefore, in maintaining productive hands only; and after having served in the function of a capital to him, it constitutes a revenue to them. Whenever he employs any part of it in maintaining unproductive hands of any kind, that part is, from that moment, withdrawn from his capital, and placed in his stock reserved for immediate consumption.

Unproductive labourers, and those who do not labour at all, are all maintained by revenue; either, first, by that part of the annual produce which is originally destined for constituting a revenue to some particular persons, either as the rent of land or as the profits of stock; or, secondly, by that part which, though originally destined for replacing a capital and for maintaining productive labourers only, yet when it comes into their hands, whatever part of it is over and above their necessary subsistence, may be employed in maintaining indifferently either productive or unproductive hands. Thus, not only the great landlord or the rich merchant, but even the common workman, if his wages are considerable, may maintain a menial servant; or he may sometimes go to a play or a puppet-show, and contribute his share towards maintaining one set of unproductive labourers; or he may pay some taxes, and thus help to maintain another set, more honourable and useful, indeed, but equally unproductive. No part of the annual produce, however, which had been originally destined to replace a capital, is ever directed towards maintaining unproductive hands, till after it has put into motion its full complement of productive labour, or all that it could put into motion in the way in which it was employed. The workman must have earned his wages by work done, before he can employ any part of them in this manner. That part too is generally but a small one. It is his spare revenue only, of which productive labourers have seldom a great deal. They generally have some, however; and in the payment of taxes the greatness of their number may compensate, in some measure, the smallness of their contribution. The rent of land and the profits of stock are everywhere, therefore, the principal sources from which unproductive hands derive their subsistence. These are the two sorts of revenue of which the owners have generally most to spare. They might both maintain indifferently either productive or unproductive hands. They seem, however, to have some predilection for the latter. The expense of a great lord feeds generally more idle than industrious people. The rich merchant, though with his capital he maintains industrious people only, yet by his expense, that is, by the employment of his revenue, he feeds commonly the very same sort as the great lord.

The proportion, therefore, between the productive and unproductive hands, depends very much in every country upon the proportion between that part of the annual produce, which, as soon as it comes either from the ground or from the hands of the productive labourers, is destined for replacing a capital, and that which is destined for constituting a revenue, either as rent, or as profit. This proportion is very different in rich from what it is in poor countries . . . .

The proportion between capital and revenue, therefore, seems everywhere to regulate the proportion between industry and idleness. Wherever capital predominates, industry prevails: wherever revenue, idleness. Every increase or diminution of capital, therefore, naturally tends to increase or diminish the real quantity of industry, the number of productive hands, and consequently the exchangeable value of the annual produce of the land and labour of the country, the real wealth and revenue of all its inhabitants.

Capitals are increased by parsimony, and diminished by prodigality and misconduct.

Whatever a person saves from his revenue he adds to his capital, and either employs it himself in maintaining an additional number of productive hands, or enables some other person to do so, by lending it to him for an interest, that is, for a share of the profits. As the capital of an individual can be increased only by what he saves from his annual revenue or his annual gains, so the capital of a society, which is the same with that of all the individuals who compose it, can be increased only in the same manner.

Parsimony, and not industry, is the immediate cause of the increase of capital. Industry, indeed, provides the subject which parsimony accumulates. But whatever industry might acquire, if parsimony did not save and store up, the capital would never be the greater.

Parsimony, by increasing the fund which is destined for the maintenance of productive hands, tends to increase the number of those hands whose labour adds to the value of the subject upon which it is bestowed. It tends therefore to increase the exchangeable value of the annual produce of the land and labour of the country. It puts into motion an additional quantity of industry, which gives an additional value to the annual produce.

What is annually saved is as regularly consumed as what is annually spent, and nearly in the same time too; but it is consumed by a different set of people. That portion of his revenue which a rich man annually spends, is in most cases consumed by idle guests, and menial servants, who leave nothing behind them in return for their consumption. That portion which he annually saves, as for the sake of the profit it is immediately employed as a capital, is consumed in the same manner, and nearly in the same time too, but by a different set of people, by labourers, manufacturers, and artificers, who reproduce with a profit the value of their annual consumption. His revenue, we shall suppose, is paid him in money. Had he spent the whole, the food, clothing, and lodging which the whole could have purchased, would have been distributed among the former set of people. By saving a part of it, as that part is for the sake of the profit immediately employed as a capital either by himself or by some other person, the food, clothing, and lodging, which may be purchased with it, are necessarily reserved for the latter. The consumption is the same, but the consumers are different.

By what a frugal man annually saves, he not only affords maintenance to an additional number of productive hands, for that or the ensuing year, but, like the founder of a public workhouse, he establishes as it were a perpetual fund for the maintenance of an equal number in all times to come. The perpetual allotment and destination of this fund, indeed, is not always guarded by any positive law, by any trust-right or deed of mort-main. It is always guarded, however, by a very powerful principle, the plain and evident interest of every individual to whom any share of it shall ever belong. No part of it can ever afterwards be employed to maintain any but productive hands, without an evident loss to the person who thus perverts it from its proper destination.

The prodigal perverts it in this manner. By not confining his expense within his income, he encroaches upon his capital. Like him who perverts the revenues of some pious foundation to profane purposes, he pays the wages of idleness with those funds which the frugality of his forefathers had, as it were, consecrated to the maintenance of industry. By diminishing the funds destined for the employment of productive labour, he necessarily diminishes, so far as it depends upon him, the quantity of that labour which adds a value to the subject upon which it is bestowed, and, consequently, the value of the annual produce of the land and labour of the whole country, the real wealth and revenue of its inhabitants. If the prodigality of some was not compensated by the frugality of others, the conduct of every prodigal, by feeding the idle with the bread of the industrious, tends not only to beggar himself, but to impoverish his country . . . .

Whatever, therefore, we may imagine the real wealth and revenue of a country to consist in, whether in the value of the annual produce of its land and labour, as plain reason seems to dictate; or in the quantity of the precious metals which circulate within it, as vulgar prejudices suppose; in either view of the matter, every prodigal appears to be a public enemy, and every frugal man a public benefactor.

The effects of misconduct are often the same as those of prodigality. Every injudicious and unsuccessful project in agriculture, mines, fisheries, trade, or manufactures, tends in the same manner to diminish the funds destined for the maintenance of productive labour. In every such project, though the capital is consumed by productive hands only, yet, as by the injudicious manner in which they are employed, they do not reproduce the full value of their consumption, there must always be some diminution in what would otherwise have been the productive funds of the society.

It can seldom happen, indeed, that the circumstances of a great nation can be much affected either by the prodigality or misconduct of individuals; the profusion or imprudence of some being always more than compensated by the frugality and good conduct of others.

With regard to profusion, the principle, which prompts to expense, is the passion for present enjoyment; which, though sometimes violent and very difficult to be restrained, is in general only momentary and occasional. But the principle which prompts to save, is the desire of bettering our condition, a desire which, though generally calm and dispassionate, comes with us from the womb, and never leaves us till we go into the grave. In the whole interval which separates those two moments, there is scarce perhaps a single instant in which any man is so perfectly and completely satisfied with his situation, as to be without any wish of alteration or improvement, of any kind. An augmentation of fortune is the means by which the greater part of men propose and wish to better their condition. It is the means the most vulgar and the most obvious; and the most likely way of augmenting their fortune, is to save and accumulate some part of what they acquire, either regularly and annually, or upon some extraordinary occasions. Though the principle of expense, therefore, prevails in almost all men upon some occasions, and in some men upon almost all occasions, yet in the greater part of men, taking the whole course of their life at an average, the principle of frugality seems not only to predominate, but to predominate very greatly . . . .

Great nations are never impoverished by private, though they sometimes are by public prodigality and misconduct. The whole, or almost the whole public revenue, is in most countries employed in maintaining unproductive hands. Such are the people who compose a numerous and splendid court, a great ecclesiastical establishment, great fleets and armies, who in time of peace produce nothing, and in time of war acquire nothing which can compensate the expense of maintaining them, even while the war lasts. Such people, as they themselves produce nothing, are all maintained by the produce of other men's labour. When multiplied, therefore, to an unnecessary number, they may in a particular year consume so great a share of this produce, as not to leave a sufficiency for maintaining the productive labourers, who should reproduce it next year. The next year's produce, therefore, will be less than that of the foregoing, and if the same disorder should continue, that of the third year will be still less than that of the second. Those unproductive hands, who should be maintained by a part only of the spare revenue of the people, may consume so great a share of their whole revenue, and thereby oblige so great a number to encroach upon their capitals, upon the funds destined for the maintenance of productive labour, that all the frugality and good conduct of individuals may not be able to compensate the waste and degradation of produce occasioned by this violent and forced encroachment.

This frugality and good conduct, however, is upon most occasions; it appears from experience, sufficient to compensate, not only the private prodigality and misconduct of individuals, but the public extravagance of government. The uniform, constant, and uninterrupted effort of every man to better his condition, the principle from which public and national, as well as private opulence is originally derived, is frequently powerful enough to maintain the natural progress of things toward improvement, in spite both of the extravagance of government, and of the greatest errors of administration. Like the unknown principle of animal life, it frequently restores health and vigour to the constitution, in spite, not only of the disease, but of the absurd prescriptions of the doctor . . . .

In each of those periods [of England's history], however, there was, not only much private and public profusion, many expensive and unnecessary wars, great perversion of the annual produce from maintaining productive to maintaining unproductive hands; but sometimes, in the confusion of civil discord, such absolute waste and destruction of stock, as might be supposed, not only to retard, as it certainly did, the natural accumulation of riches, but to have left the country, at the end of the period, poorer than at the beginning. Thus, in the happiest and most fortunate period of them all, that which has passed since the restoration, how many disorders and misfortunes have occurred, which, could they have been foreseen, not only the impoverishment, but the total ruin of the country would have been expected from them? . . . In the course of the four French wars, the nation has contracted more than a hundred and forty-five millions of debt, over and above all the other extraordinary annual expense which they occasioned, so that the whole cannot be computed at less than two hundred millions. So great a share of the annual produce of the land and labour of the country, has, since the revolution, been employed upon different occasions, in maintaining an extraordinary number of unproductive hands. But had not those wars given this particular direction to so large a capital, the greater part of it would naturally have been employed in maintaining productive hands, whose labour would have replaced, with a profit, the whole value of their consumption. The value of the annual produce of the land and labour of the country, would have been considerably increased by it every year, and every year's increase would have augmented still more that of the following year. More houses would have been built, more lands would have been improved, and those which had been improved before would have been better cultivated, more manufactures would have been established, and those which had been established before would have been more extended; and to what height the real wealth and revenue of the country might, by this time, have been raised, it is not perhaps very easy even to imagine.

But though the profusion of government must, undoubtedly, have retarded the natural progress of England towards wealth and improvement, it has not been able to stop it. The annual produce of its land and labour is, undoubtedly, much greater at present than it was either at the restoration or at the revolution. The capital, therefore, annually employed in cultivating this land, and in maintaining this labour, must likewise be much greater. In the midst of all the exactions of government, this capital has been silently and gradually accumulated by the private frugality and good conduct of individuals, by their universal, continual, and uninterrupted effort to better their own condition. It is this effort, protected by law and allowed by liberty to exert itself in the manner that is most advantageous, which has maintained the progress of England towards opulence and improvement in almost all former times, and which, it is to be hoped, will do so in all future times. England, however, as it has never been blessed with a very parsimonious government, so parsimony has at no time been the characteristic virtue of its inhabitants. It is the highest impertinence and presumption, therefore, in kings and ministers, to pretend to watch over the economy of private people, and to restrain their expense either by sumptuary laws, or by prohibiting the importation of foreign luxuries. They are themselves always, and without any exception, the greatest spendthrifts in the society. Let them look well after their own expense, and they may safely trust private people with theirs. If their own extravagance does not ruin the state, that of their subjects never will.

As frugality increases, and prodigality diminishes the public capital, so the conduct of those, whose expense just equals their revenue, without either accumulating or encroaching, neither increases nor diminishes it. Some modes of expense, however, seem to contribute more to the growth of public opulence than others.

The revenue of an individual may be spent, either in things which are consumed immediately, and in which one day's expense can neither alleviate nor support that of another; or it may be spent in things more durable, which can therefore be accumulated, and in which every day's expense may, as he chooses, either alleviate or support and heighten the effect of that of the following day. A man of fortune, for example, may either spend his revenue in a profuse and sumptuous table, and in maintaining a great number of menial servants, and a multitude of dogs and horses; or contenting himself with a frugal table and few attendants, he may lay out the greater part of it in adorning his house or his country villa, in useful or ornamental buildings, in useful or ornamental furniture, in collecting books, statues, pictures; or in things more frivolous, jewels, baubles, ingenious trinkets of different kinds; or, what is most trifling of all, in amassing a great wardrobe of fine clothes, like the favourite and minister of a great prince who died a few years ago. Were two men of equal fortune to spend their revenue, the one chiefly in the one way, the other in the other, the magnificence of the person whose expense had been chiefly in durable commodities, would be continually increasing, every day's expense contributing something to support and heighten the effect of that of the following day: that of the other, on the contrary, would be no greater at the end of the period than at the beginning. The former too would, at the end of the period, be the richer man of the two. He would have a stock of goods of some kind or other, which, though it might not be worth all that it cost, would always be worth something. No trace or vestige of the expense of the latter would remain, and the effects of ten or twenty years profusion would be as completely annihilated as if they had never existed . . . .

BOOK III

Of the Different Progress of Opulence in Different Nations

Of the Natural Progress of Opulence

The great commerce of every civilized society, is that carried on between the inhabitants of the town and those of the country. It consists in the exchange of rude for manufactured produce, either immediately, or by the intervention of money, or of some sort of paper which represents money. The country supplies the town with the means of subsistence, and the materials of manufacture. The town repays this supply by sending back a part of the manufactured produce to the inhabitants of the country. The town in which there neither is nor can be any reproduction of substances, may very properly be said to gain its whole wealth and subsistence from the country. We must not, however, upon this account, imagine that the gain of the town is the loss of the country. The gains of both are mutual and reciprocal, and the division of labour is in this, as in all other cases, advantageous to all the different persons employed in the various occupations into which it is subdivided. The inhabitants of the country purchase of the town a greater quantity of manufactured goods, with the produce of a much smaller quantity of their own labour, than they must have employed had they attempted to prepare them themselves. The town affords a market for the surplus produce of the country, or what is over and above the maintenance of the cultivators, and it is there that the inhabitants of the country exchange it for something else which is in demand among them. The greater the number and revenue of the inhabitants of the town, the more extensive is the market which it affords to those of the country; and the more extensive that market, it is always the more advantageous to a great number. The corn which grows within a mile of the town, sells there for the same price with that which comes from twenty miles distance. But the price of the latter must generally, not only pay the expense of raising and bringing it to market, but afford too the ordinary profits of agriculture to the farmer. The proprietors and cultivators of the country, therefore, which lies in the neighbourhood of the town, over and above the ordinary profits of agriculture, gain, in the price of what they sell, the whole value of the carriage of the like produce that is brought from more distant parts, and they save, besides, the whole value of this carriage in the price of what they buy. Compare the cultivation of the lands in the neighbourhood of any considerable town, with that of those which lie at some distance from it, and you will easily satisfy yourself how much the country is benefited by the commerce of the town. Among all the absurd speculations that have been propagated concerning the balance of trade, it has never been pretended that either the country loses by its commerce with the town, or the town by that with the country which maintains it.

As subsistence is, in the nature of things, prior to conveniency and luxury, so the industry which procures the former, must necessarily be prior to that which ministers to the latter. The cultivation and improvement of the country, therefore, which affords subsistence, must, necessarily, be prior to the increase of the town, which furnishes only the means of conveniency and luxury. It is the surplus produce of the country only, or what is over and above the maintenance of the cultivators, that constitutes the subsistence of the town, which can therefore increase only with the increase of this surplus produce. The town, indeed, may not always derive its whole subsistence from the country in its neighbourhood, or even from the territory to which it belongs, but from very distant countries; and this, though it forms no exception from the general rule, has occasioned considerable variations in the progress of opulence in different ages and nations.

That order of things which necessity imposes in general, though not in every particular country, is, in every particular country, promoted by the natural inclinations of man. If human institutions had never thwarted those natural inclinations, the towns could nowhere have increased beyond what the improvement and cultivation of the territory in which they were situated could support; till such time, at least, as the whole of that territory was completely cultivated and improved. Upon equal, or nearly equal profits, most men will choose to employ their capitals rather in the improvement and cultivation of land, than either in manufactures or in foreign trade. The man who employs his capital in land, has it more under his view and command, and his fortune is much less liable to accidents than that of the trader, who is obliged frequently to commit it, not only to the winds and the waves, but to the more uncertain elements of human folly and injustice, by giving great credits in distant countries to men, with whose character and situation he can seldom be thoroughly acquainted. The capital of the landlord, on the contrary, which is fixed in the improvement of his land, seems to be as well secured as the nature of human affairs can admit of. The beauty of the country besides, the pleasures of a country life, the tranquillity of mind which it promises, and wherever the injustice of human laws does not disturb it, the independency which it really affords, have charms that more or less attract everybody; and as to cultivate the ground was the original destination of man, so in every stage of his existence he seems to retain a predilection for this primitive employment.

Without the assistance of some artificers, indeed, the cultivation of land cannot be carried on, but with great inconveniency and continual interruption. Smiths, carpenters, wheel-wrights, and plough-wrights, masons, and bricklayers, tanners, shoemakers, and tailors, are people, whose service the farmer has frequent occasion for. Such artificers too stand, occasionally, in need of the assistance of one another; and as their residence is not, like that of the farmer, necessarily tied down to a precise spot, they naturally settle in the neighbourhood of one another, and thus form a small town or village. The butcher, the brewer, and the baker, soon join them, together with many other artificers and retailers, necessary or useful for supplying their occasional wants, and who contribute still further to augment the town. The inhabitants of the town and those of the country are mutually the servants of one another. The town is a continual fair or market, to which the inhabitants of the country resort, in order to exchange their rude for manufactured produce. It is this commerce which supplies the inhabitants of the town both with the materials of their work, and the means of their subsistence. The quantity of the finished work which they sell to the inhabitants of the country, necessarily regulates the quantity of the materials and provisions which they buy. Neither their employment nor subsistence, therefore, can augment, but in proportion to the augmentation of the demand from the country for finished work; and this demand can augment only in proportion to the extension of improvement and cultivation. Had human institutions, therefore, never disturbed the natural course of things, the progressive wealth and increase of the towns would, in every political society, be consequential, and in proportion to the improvement and cultivation of the territory or country.

In our North American colonies, where uncultivated land is still to be had upon easy terms, no manufactures for distant sale have ever yet been established in any of their towns. When an artificer has acquired a little more stock than is necessary for carrying on his own business in supplying the neighbouring country, he does not, in North America, attempt to establish with it a manufacture for more distant sale, but employs it in the purchase and improvement of uncultivated land. From artificer he becomes planter, and neither the large wages nor the easy subsistence which that country affords to artificers, can bribe him rather to work for other people than for himself. He feels that an artificer is the servant of his customers, from whom he derives his subsistence; but that a planter who cultivates his own land, and derives his necessary subsistence from the labour of his own family, is really a master, and independent of all the world.

In countries, on the contrary, where there is either no uncultivated land, or none that can be had upon easy terms, every artificer who has acquired more stock than he can employ in the occasional jobs of the neighbourhood, endeavours to prepare work for more distant sale. The smith erects some sort of iron, the weaver some sort of linen or woollen manufactory. Those different manufactures come, in process of time, to be gradually subdivided, and thereby improved and refined in a great variety of ways, which may easily be conceived, and which it is therefore unnecessary to explain any further . . . .

According to the natural course of things, therefore, the greater part of the capital of every growing society is, first, directed to agriculture, afterwards to manufactures, and last of all to foreign commerce. This order of things is so very natural, that in every society that had any territory, it has always, I believe, been in some degree observed. Some of their lands must have been cultivated before any considerable towns could be established, and some sort of coarse industry of the manufacturing kind must have been carried on in those towns, before they could well think of employing themselves in foreign commerce.

But though this natural order of things must have taken place in some degree in every such society, it has, in all the modern states of Europe, been, in many respects, entirely inverted. The foreign commerce of some of their cities has introduced all their finer manufactures, or such as were fit for distant sale; and manufactures and foreign commerce together, have given birth to the principal improvements of agriculture. The manners and customs which the nature of their original government introduced, and which remained after that government was greatly altered, necessarily forced them into this unnatural and retrograde order.

How the Commerce of the Towns Contributed to the Improvement of the Country

The increase and riches of commercial and manufacturing towns, contributed to the improvement and cultivation of the countries to which they belonged, in three different ways.

First, by affording a great and ready market for the rude produce of the country, they gave encouragement to its cultivation and further improvement. This benefit was not even confined to the countries in which they were situated, but extended more or less to all those with which they had any dealings. To all of them they afforded a market for some part either of their rude or manufactured produce, and consequently gave some encouragement to the industry and improvement of all. Their own country, however, on account of its neighbourhood, necessarily derived the greatest benefit from this market. Its rude produce being charged with less carriage, the traders could pay the growers a better price for it, and yet afford it as cheap to the consumers as that of more distant countries.

Secondly, the wealth acquired by the inhabitants of cities was frequently employed in purchasing such lands as were to be sold, of which a great part would frequently be uncultivated. Merchants are commonly ambitious of becoming country gentlemen, and when they do, they are generally the best of all improvers. A merchant is accustomed to employ his money chiefly in profitable projects; whereas a mere country gentleman is accustomed to employ it chiefly in expense. The one often sees his money go from him and return to him again with a profit: the other, when once he parts with it, very seldom expects to see any more of it. Those different habits naturally affect their temper and disposition in every sort of business. A merchant is commonly a bold; a country gentleman, a timid undertaker. The one is not afraid to layout at once a large capital upon the improvement of his land, when he has a probable prospect of raising the value of it in proportion to the expense. The other, if he has any capital, which is not always the case, seldom ventures to employ it in this manner. If he improves at all, it is commonly not with a capital, but with what he can save out of his annual revenue. Whoever has had the fortune to live in a mercantile town situated in an unimproved country, must have frequently observed how much more spirited the operations of merchants were in this way, than those of mere country gentlemen. The habits, besides, of order, economy and attention, to which mercantile business naturally forms a merchant, render him much fitter to execute, with profit and success, any project of improvement.

Thirdly, and lastly, commerce and manufactures gradually introduced order and good government, and with them, the liberty and security of individuals, among the inhabitants of the country, who had before lived almost in a continual state of war with their neighbours, and of servile dependency upon their superiors. This, though it has been the least observed, is by far the most important of all their effects. Mr Hume is the only writer who, so far as I know, has hitherto taken notice of it....

BOOK IV
Of Systems of Political Economy

Introduction

Political economy, considered as a branch of the science of a statesman or legislator, proposes two distinct objects; first, to provide a plentiful revenue or subsistence for the people, or more properly to enable them to provide such a revenue or subsistence for themselves; and secondly, to supply the state or commonwealth with a revenue sufficient for the public services. It proposes to enrich both the people and the sovereign.

The different progress of opulence in different ages and nations, has given occasion to two different systems of political economy, with regard to enriching the people. The one may be called the system of commerce, the other that of agriculture. I shall endeavour to explain both as fully and distinctly as I can, and shall begin with the system of commerce. It is the modern system, and is best understood in our own country and in our own times.

Of the Principle of the Commercial, or Mercantile System

That wealth consists in money, or in gold and silver, is a popular notion which naturally arises from the double function of money, as the instrument of commerce, and as the measure of value. In consequence of its being the instrument of commerce, when we have money we can more readily obtain whatever else we have occasion for, than by means of any other commodity. The great affair, we always find, is to get money. When that is obtained there is no difficulty in making any subsequent purchase. In consequence of its being the measure of value, we estimate that of all other commodities by the quantity of money which they will exchange for. We say of a rich man that he is worth a great deal, and of a poor man that he is worth very little money. A frugal man, or a man eager to be rich, is said to love money; and a careless, a generous, or a profuse man, is said to be indifferent about it. To grow rich is to get money; and wealth and money, in short, are, in common language, considered as in every respect synonymous . . . .

The importation of gold and silver is not the principal, much less the sole benefit which a nation derives from its foreign trade. Between whatever places foreign trade is carried on, they all of them derive two distinct benefits from it. It carries out that surplus part of the produce of their land and labour for which there is no demand among them, and brings back in return for it something else for which there is a demand. It gives a value to their superfluities, by exchanging them for something else, which may satisfy a part of their wants, and increase their enjoyments. By means of it, the narrowness of the home market does not hinder the division of labour in any particular branch of art or manufacture from being carried to the highest perfection. By opening a more extensive market for whatever part of the produce of their labour may exceed the home consumption, it encourages them to improve its productive powers, and to augment its annual produce to the utmost, and thereby to increase the real revenue and wealth of the society. These great and important services foreign trade is continually occupied in performing, to all the different countries between which it is carried on. They all derive great benefit from it, though that in which the merchant resides generally derives the greatest, as he is generally more employed in supplying the wants, and carrying out the superfluities of his own, than of any other particular country. To import the gold and silver which may be wanted, into the countries which have no mines, is, no doubt, a part of the business of foreign commerce. It is, however, a most insignificant part of it. A country which carried on foreign trade merely upon this account, could scarce have occasion to freight a ship in a century.

It is not by the importation of gold and silver, that the discovery of America has enriched Europe. By the abundance of the American mines, those metals have become cheaper. . . . So far Europe has, no doubt, gained a real conveniency, though surely a very trifling one. The cheapness of gold and silver renders those metals rather less fit for the purposes of money than they were before. In order to make the same purchases, we must load ourselves with a greater quantity of them, and carry about a shilling in our pocket where a groat would have done before. It is difficult to say which is most trifling, this inconveniency, or the opposite conveniency. Neither the one nor the other could have made any very essential change in the state of Europe. The discovery of America, however, certainly made a most essential one. By opening a new and inexhaustible market to all the commodities of Europe, it gave occasion to new divisions of labour and improvements of art, which, in the narrow circle of the ancient commerce, could never have taken place for want of a market to take off the greater part of their produce. The productive powers of labour were improved, and its produce increased in all the different countries of Europe, and together with it the real revenue and wealth of the inhabitants. The commodities of Europe were almost all new to America, and many of those of America were new to Europe. A new set of exchanges, therefore, began to take place which had never been thought of before, and which should naturally have proved as advantageous to the new, as it certainly did to the old continent. The savage injustice of the Europeans rendered an event, which ought to have been beneficial to all, ruinous and destructive to several of those unfortunate countries . . . .

Of Restraints upon the Importation from Foreign Countries of Such Goods as Can be Produced at Home

By restraining, either by high duties, or by absolute prohibitions, the importation of such goods from foreign countries as can be produced at home, the monopoly of the home-market is more or less secured to the domestic industry employed in producing them. Thus the prohibition of importing either live cattle or salt provisions from foreign countries secures to the graziers of Great Britain the monopoly of the home-market for butchers-meat. The high duties upon the importation of corn, which in times of moderate plenty amount to a prohibition, give a like advantage to the growers of that commodity. The prohibition of the importation of foreign woollens is equally favourable to the woollen manufacturers. The silk manufacture, though altogether employed upon foreign materials, has lately obtained the same advantage. The linen manufacture has not yet obtained it, but is making great strides towards it. Many other sorts of manufacturers have, in the same manner, obtained in Great Britain, either altogether, or very nearly a monopoly against their countrymen. The variety of goods of which the importation into Great Britain is prohibited, either absolutely, or under certain circumstances, greatly exceeds what can easily be suspected by those who are not well acquainted with the laws of the customs.

That this monopoly of the home-market frequently gives great encouragement to that particular species of industry which enjoys it, and frequently turns towards that employment a greater share of both the labour and stock of the society than would otherwise have gone to it, cannot be doubted. But whether it tends either to increase the general industry of the society, or to give it the most advantageous direction, is not, perhaps, altogether so evident.

The general industry of the society never can exceed what the capital of the society can employ. As the number of workmen that can be kept in employment by any particular person must bear a certain proportion to his capital, so the number of those that can be continually employed by all the members of a great society, must bear a certain proportion to the whole capital of that society, and never can exceed that proportion. No regulation of commerce can increase the quantity of industry in any society beyond what its capital can maintain. It can only divert a part of it into a direction into which it might not otherwise have gone; and it is by no means certain that this artificial direction is likely to be more advantageous to the society than that into which it would have gone of its own accord.

Every individual is continually exerting himself to find out the most advantageous employment for whatever capital he can command. It is his own advantage, indeed, and not that of the society, which he has in view. But the study of his own advantage naturally, or rather necessarily leads him to prefer that employment which is most advantageous to the society.

First, every individual endeavours to employ his capital as near home as he can, and consequently as much as he can in the support of domestic industry; provided always that he can thereby obtain the ordinary, or not a great deal less than the ordinary profits of stock.

Thus upon equal or nearly equal profits, every wholesale merchant naturally prefers the home-trade to the foreign trade of consumption, and the foreign trade of consumption to the carrying trade. In the home-trade his capital is never so long out of his sight as it frequently is in the foreign trade of consumption. He can know better the character and situation of the persons whom he trusts, and if he should happen to be deceived, he knows better the laws of the country from which he must seek redress. In the carrying trade, the capital of the merchant is, as it were, divided between two foreign countries, and no part of it is ever necessarily brought home, or placed under his own immediate view and command. . . . The merchant, in order to save a second loading and unloading, endeavours always to sell in the home-market as much of the goods of all those different countries as he can, and thus, so far as he can, to convert his carrying trade into a foreign trade of consumption. A merchant, in the same manner, who is engaged in the foreign trade of consumption, when he collects goods for foreign markets, will always be glad, upon equal or nearly equal profits, to sell as great a part of them at home as he can. He saves himself the risk and trouble of exportation, when, so far as he can, he thus converts his foreign trade of consumption into a home-trade. Home is in this manner the centre, if I may say so, round which the capitals of the inhabitants of every country are continually circulating, and towards which they are always tending, though by particular causes they may sometimes be driven off and repelled from it towards more distant employments. But a capital employed in the home-trade, it has already been shown, necessarily puts into motion a greater quantity of domestic industry, and gives revenue and employment to a greater number of the inhabitants of the country, than an equal capital employed in the foreign trade of consumption: and one employed in the foreign trade of consumption has the same advantage over an equal capital employed in the carrying trade. Upon equal, or only nearly equal profits, therefore, every individual naturally inclines to employ his capital in the manner in which it is likely to afford the greatest support to domestic industry, and to give revenue and employment to the greatest number of people of his own country.

Secondly, every individual who employs his capital in the support of domestic industry, necessarily endeavours so to direct that industry, that its produce may be of the greatest possible value.

The produce of industry is what it adds to the subject or materials upon which it is employed. In proportion as the value of this produce is great or small, so will likewise be the profits of the employer. But it is only for the sake of profit that any man employs a capital in the support of industry; and he will always, therefore, endeavour to employ it in the support of that industry of which the produce is likely to be of the greatest value, or to exchange for the greatest quantity either of money or of other goods.

But the annual revenue of every society is always precisely equal to the exchangeable value of the whole annual produce of its industry, or rather is precisely the same thing with that exchangeable value. As every individual, therefore, endeavours as much as he can both to employ his capital in the support of domestic industry, and so to direct that industry that its produce may be of the greatest value; every individual necessarily labours to render the annual revenue of the society as great as he can. He generally, indeed, neither intends to promote the public interest, nor knows how much he is promoting it. By preferring the support of domestic to that of foreign industry, he intends only his own security; and by directing that industry in such a manner as its produce may be of the greatest value, he intends only his own gain, and he is in this, as in many other cases, led by an invisible hand to promote an end which was no part of his intention. Nor is it always the worse for the society that it was no part of it. By pursuing his own interest he frequently promotes that of the society more effectually than when he really intends to promote it. I have never known much good done by those who affected to trade for the public good. It is an affectation, indeed, not very common among merchants, and very few words need be employed in dissuading them from it.

What is the species of domestic industry which his capital can employ, and of which the produce is likely to be of the greatest value, every individual, it is evident, can, in his local situation, judge much better than any statesman or lawgiver can do for him. The statesman, who should attempt to direct private people in what manner they ought to employ their capitals, would not only load himself with a most unnecessary attention, but assume an authority which could safely be trusted, not only to no single person but to no council or senate whatever, and which would nowhere be dangerous as in the hands of a man who had folly and presumption enough to fancy himself fit to exercise it.

To give the monopoly of the home-market to the produce of domestic industry, in any particular art or manufacture, is in some measure to direct private people in what manner they ought to employ their capitals, and must, in almost all cases, be either a useless or a hurtful regulation. If this produce of domestic can be brought there as cheap as that of foreign industry, the regulation is evidently useless. If it cannot, it must generally be hurtful. It is the maxim of every prudent master of a family, never to attempt to make at home what it will cost him more to make than to buy. The tailor does not attempt to make his own shoes, but buys them of the shoemaker. The shoemaker does not attempt to make his own clothes, but employs a tailor. The farmer attempts to make neither the one nor the other, but employs those different artificers. All of them find it for their interest to employ their whole industry in a way in which they have some advantage over their neighbours, and to purchase with a part of its produce, or what is the same thing, with the price of a part of it, whatever else they have occasion for.

What is prudence in the conduct of every private family, can scarce be folly in that of a great kingdom. If a foreign country can supply us with a commodity cheaper than we ourselves can make it, better buy it of them with some part of the produce of our own industry, employed in a way in which we have some advantage. The general industry of the country, being always in proportion to the capital which employs it, will not thereby be diminished, no more than that of the above-mentioned artificers; but only left to find out the way in which it can be employed with the greatest advantage. It is certainly not employed to the greatest advantage, when it is thus directed towards an object which it can buy cheaper than it can make. The value of its annual produce is certainly more or less diminished, when it is thus turned away from producing commodities evidently of more value than the commodity which it is directed to produce. According to the supposition, that commodity could be purchased from foreign countries cheaper than it can be made at home. It could, therefore, have been purchased with a part only of the commodities, or, what is the same thing, with a part only of the price of the commodities, which the industry employed by an equal capital, would have produced at home, had it been left to follow its natural course. The industry of the country, therefore, is thus turned away from a more, to a less advantageous employment, and the exchangeable value of its annual produce, instead of being increased, according to the intention of the lawgiver, must necessarily be diminished by every such regulation . . . .

The case in which it may sometimes be a matter of deliberation, how far, or in what manner it is proper to restore the free importation of foreign goods, after it has been for some time interrupted, is, when particular manufactures, by means of high duties or prohibitions upon all foreign goods which can come into competition with them, have been so far extended as to employ a great multitude of hands. Humanity may in this case require that the freedom of trade should be restored only by slow gradations, and with a good deal of reserve and circumspection. Were those high duties and prohibitions taken away all at once, cheaper foreign goods of the same kind might be poured so fast into the home market, as to deprive all at once many thousands of our people of their ordinary employment and means of subsistence. The disorder which this would occasion might no doubt be very considerable. It would in all probability, however, be much less than is commonly imagined, for the two following reasons:

First, all those manufactures, of which any part is commonly exported to other European countries without a bounty, could be very little affected by the freest importation of foreign goods. Such manufactures must be sold as cheap abroad as any other foreign goods of the same quality and kind, and consequently must be sold cheaper at home. They would still, therefore, keep possession of the home market, and though a capricious man of fashion might sometimes prefer foreign wares, merely because they were foreign, to cheaper and better goods of the same kind that were made at home, this folly could, from the nature of things, extend to so few, that it could make no sensible impression upon the general employment of the people. But a great part of all the different branches of our woollen manufacture, of our tanned leather, and of our hardware, are annually exported to other European countries without any bounty, and these are the manufactures which employ the greatest number of hands. The silk, perhaps, is the manufacture which would suffer the most by this freedom of trade, and after it the linen, though the latter much less than the former.

Secondly, though a great number of people should, by thus restoring the freedom of trade, be thrown all at once out of their ordinary employment and common method of subsistence, it would by no means follow that they would thereby be deprived either of employment or subsistence. By the reduction of the army and navy at the end of the late war more than a hundred thousand soldiers and seamen, a number equal to what is employed in the greatest manufactures, were all at once thrown out of their ordinary employment; but, though they no doubt suffered some inconveniency, they were not thereby deprived of all employment and subsistence. The greater part of the seamen, it is probable, gradually betook themselves to the merchant-service as they could find occasion, and in the mean time both they and the soldiers were absorbed in the great mass of the people, and employed in a great variety of occupations. Not only no great convulsion, but no sensible disorder arose from so great a change in the situation of more than a hundred thousand men, all accustomed to the use of arms, and many of them to rapine and plunder. The number of vagrants was scarce anywhere sensibly increased by it, even the wages of labour were not reduced by it in any occupation, so far as I have been able to learn, except in that of seamen in the merchant-service. But if we compare together the habits of a soldier and of any sort of manufacturer, we shall find that those of the latter do not tend so much to disqualify him from being employed in a new trade, as those of the former from being employed in any. The manufacturer has always been accustomed to look for his subsistence from his labour only: the soldier to expect it from his pay. Application and industry have been familiar to the one; idleness and dissipation to the other. But it is surely much easier to change the direction of industry from one sort of labour to another, than to turn idleness and dissipation to any. To the greater part of manufactures besides, it has already been observed, there are other collateral manufactures of so similar a nature, that a workman can easily transfer his industry from one of them to another. The greater part of such workmen too are occasionally employed in country labour. The stock which employed them in a particular manufacture before, will still remain in the country to employ an equal number of people in some other way. The capital of the country remaining the same, the demand for labour will likewise be the same, or very nearly the same, though it may be exerted in different places and for different occupations. Soldiers and seamen, indeed, when discharged from the king's service, are at liberty to exercise any trade, within any town or place of Great Britain or Ireland. Let the same natural liberty of exercising what species of industry they please be restored to all his majesty's subjects, in the same manner as to soldiers and seamen; that is, break down the exclusive privileges of corporations, and repeal the statute of apprenticeship, both which are real encroachments upon natural liberty, and add to these the repeal of the law of settlements, so that a poor workman, when thrown out of employment either in one trade or in one place, may seek for it in another trade or in another place, without the fear either of a prosecution or of a removal, and neither the public nor the individuals will suffer much more from the occasional disbanding some particular classes of manufacturers, than from that of soldiers. Our manufacturers have no doubt great merit with their country, but they cannot have more than those who defend it with their blood, nor deserve to be treated with more delicacy.

To expect, indeed, that the freedom of trade should ever be entirely restored in Great Britain, is as absurd as to expect that an Oceana or Utopia should ever be established in it. Not only the prejudices of the public, but what is much more unconquerable, the private interests of many individuals, irresistibly oppose it. Were the officers of the army to oppose with the same zeal and unanimity any reduction in the number of forces, with which master manufacturers set themselves against every law that is likely to increase the number of their rivals in the home market; were the former to animate their soldiers, in the same manner as the latter enflame their workmen, to attack with violence and outrage the proposers of any such regulation; to attempt to reduce the army would be as dangerous as it has now become to attempt to diminish in any respect the monopoly which our manufacturers have obtained against us. This monopoly has so much increased the number of some particular tribes of them, that, like an overgrown standing army, they have become formidable to the government, and upon many occasions intimidate the legislature. The member of parliament who supports every proposal for strengthening this monopoly, is sure to acquire not only the reputation of understanding trade, but great popularity and influence with an order of men whose numbers and wealth render them of great importance. If he opposes them, on the contrary, and still more if he has authority enough to be able to thwart them, neither the most acknowledged probity, nor the highest rank, nor the greatest public services can protect him from the most infamous abuse and detraction, from personal insults, nor sometimes from real danger, arising from the insolent outrage of furious and disappointed monopolists.

The undertaker of a great manufacture who, by the home markets being suddenly laid open to the competition of foreigners, should be obliged to abandon his trade, would no doubt suffer very considerably. That part of his capital which had usually been employed in purchasing materials and in paying his workmen, might, without much difficulty, perhaps, find another employment. But that part of it which was fixed in workhouses, and in the instruments of trade, could scarce be disposed of without considerable loss. The equitable regard, therefore, to his interest requires that changes of this kind should never be introduced suddenly, but slowly, gradually, and after a very long warning. The legislature, were it possible that its deliberations could be always directed, not by the clamorous importunity of partial interests, but by an extensive view of the general good, ought upon this very account, perhaps, to be particularly careful neither to establish any new monopolies of this kind, nor to extend further those which are already established. Every such regulation introduces some degree of real disorder into the constitution of the state, which it will be difficult afterwards to cure without occasioning another disorder . . . .

Of the Extraordinary Restraints Upon the Importation of Goods of Almost All Kinds, From Those Countries with which the Balance is Supposed to be Disadvantageous

Part I: Of the Unreasonableness of those Restraints even upon the Principles of the Commercial System

To lay extraordinary restraints upon those particular countries with which the importation of goods of almost all kinds from balance of trade is supposed to be disadvantageous, is the second expedient by which the commercial system proposes to increase the quantity of gold and silver. Thus in Great Britain, Silesia lawns may be imported for home consumption upon paying certain duties. But French cambrics and lawns are prohibited to be imported, except into the port of London, there to be warehoused for exportation. Higher duties are imposed upon the wines of France than upon those of Portugal, or indeed of any other country. By what is called the impost 1692, a duty of five and twenty per cent of the rate or value was laid upon all French goods; while the goods of other nations were, the greater part of them, subjected to much lighter duties, seldom exceeding five per cent. The wine, brandy, salt and vinegar of France were indeed excepted; these commodities being subjected to other heavy duties, either by other laws, or by particular clauses of the same law. In 1696, a second duty of twenty-five per cent, the first not having been thought a sufficient discouragement, was imposed upon all French goods, except brandy; together with a new duty of five and twenty pounds upon the ton of French wine, and another of fifteen pounds upon the ton of French vinegar. French goods have never been omitted in any of those general subsidies, or duties of five per cent, which have been imposed upon all, or the greater part of the goods enumerated in the book of rates. If we count the one third and two third subsidies as making a complete subsidy between them, there have been five of these general subsidies; so that before the commencement of the present war seventy-five per cent may be considered as the lowest duty to which the greater part of the goods of the growth, produce, or manufacture of France were liable. But upon the greater part of goods, those duties are equivalent to a prohibition. The French in their turn have, I believe, treated our goods and manufactures just as hardly; though I am not so well acquainted with the particular hardships which they have imposed upon them. Those mutual restraints have put an end to almost all fair commerce between the two nations, and smugglers are now the principal importers, either of British goods into France, or of French goods into Great Britain. The principles which I have been examining in the foregoing chapter took their origin from private interest and the spirit of monopoly; those which I am going to examine in this, from national prejudice and animosity. They are, accordingly, as might well be expected, still more unreasonable. They are so, even upon the principles of the commercial system. . . .

Part II: Of the Unreasonableness of those Extraordinary Restraints upon other Principles

. . . Nothing, however, can be more absurd than this whole doctrine of the balance of trade, upon which, not only these restraints, but almost all the other regulations of commerce are founded. When two places trade with one another, this doctrine supposes that, if the balance be even, neither of them either loses or gains; but if it leans in any degree to one side, that one of them loses, and the other gains in proportion to its declension from the exact equilibrium. Both suppositions are false. A trade which is forced by means of bounties and monopolies, may be, and commonly is disadvantageous to the country in whose favour it is meant to be established, as I shall endeavour to show hereafter. But that trade which, without force or constraint, is naturally and regularly carried on between any two places, is always advantageous, though not always equally so, to both.

By advantage or gain, I understand, not the increase of the quantity of gold and silver, but that of the exchangeable value of the annual produce of the land and labour of the country, or the increase of the annual revenue of its inhabitants.

If the balance be even, and if the trade between the two places consist altogether in the exchange of their native commodities, they will, upon most occasions, not only both gain, but they will gain equally, or very near equally; each will in this case afford a market for a part of the surplus produce of the other: each will replace a capital which had been employed in raising and preparing for the market this part of the surplus produce of the other, and which had been distributed among, and given revenue and maintenance to a certain number of its inhabitants. Some part of the inhabitants of each, therefore, will indirectly derive their revenue and maintenance from the other. As the commodities exchanged too are supposed to be of equal value, so the two capitals employed in the trade will, upon most occasions, be equal, or very nearly equal; and both being employed in raising the native commodities of the two countries, the revenue and maintenance which their distribution will afford to the inhabitants of each will be equal, or very nearly equal. This revenue and maintenance, thus mutually afforded, will be greater or smaller in proportion to the extent of their dealings. If these should annually amount to an hundred thousand pounds, for example, or to a million on each side, each of them would afford an annual revenue, in the one case, of an hundred thousand pounds, in the other, of a million, to the inhabitants of the other . . . .

Of Treaties of Commerce

When a nation binds itself by treaty either to permit the entry of certain goods from one foreign country which it prohibits from all others, or to exempt the goods of one country from duties to which it subjects those of all others, the country, or at least the merchants and manufacturers of the country, whose commerce is so favoured, must necessarily derive great advantage from the treaty. Those merchants and manufacturers enjoy a sort of monopoly in the country which is so indulgent to them. That country becomes a market both more extensive and more advantageous for their goods: more extensive, because the goods of other nations being either excluded or subjected to heavier duties, it takes off a greater quantity of theirs: more advantageous, because the merchants of the favoured country, enjoying a sort of monopoly there, will often sell their goods for a better price than if exposed to the free competition of all other nations.

Such treaties, however, though they may be advantageous to the merchants and manufacturers of the favoured, are necessarily disadvantageous to those of the favouring country. A monopoly is thus granted against them to a foreign nation; and they must frequently buy the foreign goods they have occasion for, dearer than if the free competition of other nations was admitted. That part of its own produce with which such a nation purchases foreign goods, must consequently be sold cheaper, because when two things are exchanged for one another, the cheapness of the one is a necessary consequence, or rather is the same thing with the dearness of the other. The exchangeable value of its annual produce, therefore, is likely to be diminished by every such treaty. This diminution, however, can scarce amount to any positive loss, but only to a lessening of the gain which it might otherwise make. Though it sells its goods cheaper than it otherwise might do, it will not probably sell them for less than they cost; nor, as in the case of bounties, for a price which will not replace the capital employed in bringing them to market, together with the ordinary profits of stock. The trade could not go on long if it did. Even the favouring country, therefore, may still gain by the trade, though less than if there was a free competition . . . .

It is thus that every system which endeavours, either, by extraordinary encouragements, to draw towards a particular species of industry a greater share of the capital of the society than what would naturally go to it; or, by extraordinary restraints, to force from a particular species of industry some share of the capital which would otherwise be employed in it; is in reality subversive of the great purpose which it means to promote. It retards, instead of accelerating, the progress of the society towards real wealth and greatness; and diminishes, instead of increasing, the real value of the annual produce of its land and labour.

All systems either of preference or of restraint, therefore, being thus completely taken away, the obvious and simple system of natural liberty establishes itself of its own accord. Every man, as long as he does not violate the laws of justice, is left perfectly free to pursue his own interest his own way, and to bring both his industry and capital into competition with those of any other man, or order of men. The sovereign is completely discharged from a duty, in the attempting to perform which he must always be exposed to innumerable delusions, and for the proper performance of which no human wisdom or knowledge could ever be sufficient; the duty of superintending the industry of private people, and of directing it towards the employments most suitable to the interest of the society. According to the system of natural liberty, the sovereign has only three duties to attend to; three duties of great importance, indeed, but plain and intelligible to common understandings: first, the duty of protecting the society from the violence and invasion of other independent societies; secondly, the duty of protecting, as far as possible, every member of the society from the injustice or oppression of every other member of it, or the duty of establishing an exact administration of justice; and, thirdly, the duty of erecting and maintaining certain public works and certain public institutions, which it can never be for the interest of any individual, or small number of individuals, to erect and maintain; because the profit could never repay the expense to any individual or small number of individuals, though it may frequently do much more than repay it to a great society.

BOOK V

Of the Revenue of the Sovereign or Commonwealth

Of the Expenses of the Sovereign or Commonwealth

Part I: Of the Expense of Defence

The first duty of the sovereign, that of protecting the society from the violence and invasion of other independent societies, can be performed only by means of a military force. But the expense both of preparing this military force in time of peace, and of employing it in time of war, is very different in the different states of society, in the different periods of improvement.

Among nations of hunters, the lowest and rudest state of society, such as we find it among the native tribes of North America, every man is a warrior as well as a hunter. When he goes to war, either to defend his society, or to revenge the injuries which have been done to it by other societies, he maintains himself by his own labour, in the same manner as when he lives at home. His society, for in this state of things there is properly neither sovereign nor commonwealth, is at no sort of expense, either to prepare him for the field, or to maintain him while he is in it.

Among nations of shepherds, a more advanced state of society, such as we find it among the Tartars and Arabs, every man is, in the same manner, a warrior. Such nations have commonly no fixed habitation, but live, either in tents, or in a sort of covered wagons which are easily transported from place to place. The whole tribe or nation changes its situation according to the different seasons of the year, as well as according to other accidents. When its herds and flocks have consumed the forage of one part of the country, it removes to another, and from that to a third. In the dry season, it comes down to the banks of the rivers; in the wet season it retires to the upper country. When such a nation goes to war, the warriors will not trust their herds and flocks to the feeble defence of their old men, their women and children; and their old men, their women and children, will not be left behind without defence and without subsistence. The whole nation, besides, being accustomed to a wandering life, even in time of peace, easily takes the field in time of war. Whether it marches as an army, or moves about as a company of herdsmen, the way of life is nearly the same, though the object proposed by it be very different. They all go to war together, therefore, and everyone does as well as he can . . . .

An army of hunters can seldom exceed two or three hundred men. The precarious subsistence which the chance affords could seldom allow a greater number to keep together for any considerable time. An army of shepherds, on the contrary, may sometimes amount to two or three hundred thousand. As long as nothing stops their progress, as long as they can go on from one district, of which they have consumed the forage, to another which is yet entire; there seems to be scarce any limit to the number who can march on together. A nation of hunters can never be formidable to the civilized nations in their neighbourhood. A nation of shepherds may. Nothing can be more contemptible than an Indian war in North America. Nothing, on the contrary, can be more dreadful than a Tartar invasion has frequently been in Asia. The judgment of Thucydides, that both Europe and Asia could not resist the Scythians united, has been verified by the experience of all ages. The inhabitants of the extensive, but defenceless plains of Scythia or Tartary, have been frequently united under the dominion of the chief of some conquering horde or clan; and the havoc and devastation of Asia have always signalized their union. The inhabitants of the inhospitable deserts of Arabia, the other great nation of shepherds, have never been united but once; under Mahomet and his immediate successors. Their union, which was more the effect of religious enthusiasm than of conquest, was signalized in the same manner. If the hunting nations of America should ever become shepherds, their neighbourhood would be much more dangerous to the European colonies than it is at present.

In a yet more advanced state of society; among those nations of husbandmen who have little foreign commerce and no other manufactures, but those coarse and household ones which almost every private family prepares for its own use; every man, in the same manner, either is a warrior, or easily becomes such. They who live by agriculture generally pass the whole day in the open air, exposed to all the inclemencies of the seasons. The hardiness of their ordinary life prepares them for the fatigues of war, to some of which their necessary occupations bear a great analogy. The necessary occupation of a ditcher prepares him to work in the trenches, and to fortify a camp as well as to enclose a field. The ordinary pastimes of such husbandmen are the same as those of shepherds, and are in the same manner the images of war. But as husbandmen have less leisure than shepherds, they are not so frequently employed in those pastimes. They are soldiers, but soldiers not quite so much masters of their exercise. Such as they are, however, it seldom costs the sovereign or commonwealth any expense to prepare them for the field.

Agriculture, even in its rudest and lowest state, supposes a settlement; some sort of fixed habitation which cannot be abandoned without great loss. When a nation of mere husbandmen, therefore, goes to war, the whole people cannot take the field together. The old men, the women and children, at least, must remain at home to take care of the habitation. All the men of the military age, however, may take the field, and, in small nations of this kind, have frequently done so. In every nation the men of the military age are supposed to amount to about a fourth or a fifth part of the whole body of the people. If the campaign too should begin after seed-time, and end before harvest, both the husbandman and his principal labourers can be spared from the farm without much loss.

He trusts that the work which must be done in the meantime can be well enough executed by the old men, the women and the children. He is not unwilling, therefore, to serve without pay during a short campaign, and it frequently costs the sovereign or commonwealth as little to maintain him in the field as to prepare him for it . . . .

When the art of war too has gradually grown up to be a very intricate and complicated science, when the event of war ceases to be determined, as in the first ages of society, by a single irregular skirmish or battle, but when the contest is generally spun out through several different campaigns, each of which lasts during the greater part of the year; it becomes universally necessary that the public should maintain those who serve the public in war, at least while they are employed in that service. Whatever in time of peace might be the ordinary occupation of those who go to war, so very tedious and expensive a service would otherwise be by far too heavy a burden upon them . . . .

The art of war, however, as it is certainly the noblest of all arts, so in the progress of improvement it necessarily becomes one of the most complicated among them. The state of the mechanical, as well as of some other arts, with which it is necessarily connected, determines the degree of perfection to which it is capable of being carried at any particular time. But in order to carry it to this degree of perfection, it is necessary that it should become the sole or principal occupation of a particular class of citizens, and the division of labour is as necessary for the improvement of this, as of every other art. Into other arts the division of labour is naturally introduced by the prudence of individuals, who find that they promote their private interest better by confining themselves to a particular trade, than by exercising a great number. But it is the wisdom of the state only which can render the trade of a soldier a particular trade separate and distinct from all others. A private citizen who, in time of profound peace, and without any particular encouragement from the public, should spend the greater part of his time in military exercises, might, no doubt, both improve himself very much in them, and amuse himself very well; but he certainly would not promote his own interest. It is the wisdom of the state only which can render it for his interest to give up the greater part of his time to this peculiar occupation: and states have not always had this wisdom, even when their circumstances had become such, that the preservation of their existence required that they should have it.

A shepherd has a great deal of leisure; a husbandman, in the rude state of husbandry, has some; an artificer or manufacturer has none at all. The first may, without any loss, employ a great deal of his time in martial exercises; the second may employ some part of it; but the last cannot employ a single hour in them without some loss, and his attention to his own interest naturally leads him to neglect them altogether. These improvements in husbandry too, which the progress of arts and manufactures necessarily introduces, leave the husbandman as little leisure as the artificer. Military exercises come to be as much neglected by the inhabitants of the country as by those of the town, and the great body of the people becomes altogether unwarlike. That wealth, at the same time, which always follows the improvements of agriculture and manufactures, and which in reality is no more than the accumulated produce of those improvements, provokes the invasion of all their neighbours. An industrious, and upon that account a wealthy nation, is of all nations the most likely to be attacked; and unless the state takes some new measures for the public defence, the natural habits of the people render them altogether incapable of defending themselves.

In these circumstances, there seem to be but two methods, by which the state can make any tolerable provision for the public defence.

It may either, first, by means of a very rigorous police, and in spite of the whole bent of the interest, genius and inclinations of the people, enforce the practice of military exercises, and oblige either all the citizens of the military age, or a certain number of them, to join in some measure the trade of a soldier to whatever other trade or profession they may happen to carry on.

Or, secondly, by maintaining and employing a certain number of citizens in the constant practice of military exercises, it may render the trade of a soldier a particular trade, separate and distinct from all others.

If the state has recourse to the first of those two expedients, its military force is said to consist in a militia; if to the second, it is said to consist in a standing army. The practice of military exercises is the sole or principal occupation of the soldiers of a standing army, and the maintenance or pay which the state affords them is the principal and ordinary fund of their subsistence. The practice of military exercises is only the occasional occupation of the soldiers of a militia, and they derive the principal and ordinary fund of their subsistence from some other occupation. In a militia, the character of the labourer, artificer, or tradesman, predominates over that of the soldier: in a standing army, that of the soldier predominates over every other character; and in this distinction seems to consist the essential difference between those two different species of military force . . . .

Before the invention of firearms, that army was superior in which the soldiers had, each individually, the greatest skill and dexterity in the use of their arms. Strength and agility of body were of the highest consequence, and commonly determined the fate of battles. But this skill and dexterity in the use of their arms, could be acquired only, in the same manner as fencing is at present, by practising, not in great bodies, but each man separately, in a particular school, under a particular master, or with his own particular equals and companions. Since the invention of firearms, strength and agility of body, or even extraordinary dexterity and skill in the use of arms, though they are far from being of no consequence, are, however, of less consequence. The nature of the weapon, though it by no means puts the awkward upon a level with the skilful, puts him more nearly so than he ever was before. All the dexterity and skill, it is supposed, which are necessary for using it, can be well enough acquired by practising in great bodies.

Regularity, order, and prompt obedience to command, are qualities which, in modern armies, are of more importance towards determining the fate of battles, than the dexterity and skill of the soldiers in the use of their arms. But the noise of firearms, the smoke, and the invisible death to which every man feels himself every moment exposed, as soon as he comes within cannon-shot, and frequently a long time before the battle can be well said to be engaged, must render it very difficult to maintain any considerable degree of this regularity, order, and prompt obedience, even in the beginning of a modern battle. In an ancient battle there was no noise but what arose from the human voice; there was no smoke, there was no invisible cause of wounds or death. Every man, till some mortal weapon actually did approach him, saw clearly that no such weapon was near him. In these circumstances, and among troops who had some confidence in their own skill and dexterity in the use of their arms, it must have been a good deal less difficult to preserve some degree of regularity and order, not only in the beginning, but through the whole progress of an ancient battle, and till one of the two armies was fairly defeated. But the habits of regularity, order, and prompt obedience to command, can be acquired only by troops which are exercised in great bodies.

A militia, however, in whatever manner it may be either disciplined or exercised, must always be much inferior to a well disciplined and well exercised standing army.

The soldiers, who are exercised only once a week, or once a month, can never be so expert in the use of their arms, as those who are exercised every day, or every other day; and though this circumstance may not be of so much consequence in modern, as it was in ancient times, yet the acknowledged superiority of the Prussian troops, owing, it is said, very much to their superior expertness in their exercise, may satisfy us that it is, even at this day, of very considerable consequence.

The soldiers, who are bound to obey their officer only once a week or once a month, and who are at all other times at liberty to manage their own affairs their own way, without being in any respect accountable to him, can never be under the same awe in his presence, can never have the same disposition to ready obedience, with those whose whole life and conduct are every day directed by him, and who every day even rise and go to bed, or at least retire to their quarters, according to his orders. In what is called discipline, or in the habit of ready obedience, a militia must always be still more inferior to a standing army, than it may sometimes be in what is called the manual exercise, or in the management and use of its arms. But in modern war the habit of ready and instant obedience is of much greater consequence than a considerable superiority in the management of arms . . . .

A militia of any kind, it must be observed, however, which has served for several successive campaigns in the field, becomes in every respect a standing army. The soldiers are every day exercised in the use of their arms, and, being constantly under the command of their officers, are habituated to the same prompt obedience which takes place in standing armies. What they were before they took the field, is of little importance. They necessarily become in every respect a standing army, after they have passed a few campaigns in it. Should the war in America drag out through another campaign, the American militia may become in every respect a match for that standing army, of which the valour appeared, in the last war at least not inferior to that of the hardiest veterans of France and Spain.

This distinction being well understood, the history of all ages, it will be found, bears testimony to the irresistible superiority which a well-regulated standing army has over a militia . . . .

When a civilized nation depends for its defence upon a militia, it is at all times exposed to be conquered by any barbarous nation which happens to be in its neighbourhood. The frequent conquests of all the civilized countries in Asia by the Tartars, sufficiently demonstrates the natural superiority, which the militia of a barbarous, has over that of a civilized nation. A well-regulated standing army is superior to every militia. Such an army, as it can best be maintained by an opulent and civilized nation, so it can alone defend such a nation against the invasion of a poor and barbarous neighbour. It is only by means of a standing army, therefore, that the civilization of any country can be perpetuated, or even preserved for any considerable time.

As it is only by means of a well-regulated standing army that a civilized country can be defended; so it is only by means of it, that a barbarous country can be suddenly and tolerably civilized. A standing army establishes, with an irresistible force, the law of the sovereign through the remotest provinces of the empire, and maintains some degree of regular government in countries which could not otherwise admit of any. . . .

Men of republican principles have been jealous of a standing army as dangerous to liberty. It certainly is so, wherever the interest of the general and that of the principal officers are not necessarily connected with the support of the constitution of the state. The standing army of Caesar destroyed the Roman republic. The standing army of Cromwell turned the Long Parliament out of doors. But where the sovereign is himself the general, and the principal nobility and gentry of the country the chief officers of the army; where the military force is placed under the command of those who have the greatest interest in the support of the civil authority, because they have themselves the greatest share of that authority, a standing army can never be dangerous to liberty. On the contrary, it may in some cases be favourable to liberty. The security which it gives to the sovereign renders unnecessary that troublesome jealousy, which, in some modern republics, seems to watch over the minutest actions, and to be at all times ready to disturb the peace of every citizen. Where the security of the magistrate, though supported by the principal people of the country, is endangered by every popular discontent; where a small tumult is capable of bringing about in a few hours a great revolution, the whole authority of government must be employed to suppress and punish every murmur and complaint against it. To a sovereign, on the contrary, who feels himself supported, not only by the natural aristocracy of the country, but by a well regulated standing army, the rudest, the most groundless, and the most licentious remonstrances can give little disturbance. He can safely pardon or neglect them, and his consciousness of his own superiority naturally disposes him to do so. That degree of liberty which approaches to licentiousness can be tolerated only in countries where the sovereign is secured by a well-regulated standing army. It is in such countries only, that the public safety does not require, that the sovereign should be trusted with any discretionary power, for suppressing even the impertinent wantonness of this licentious liberty.

The first duty of the sovereign, therefore, that of defending the society from the violence and injustice of other independent societies, grows gradually more and more expensive, as the society advances in civilization. The military force of the society, which originally cost the sovereign no expense either in time of peace or in time of war, must, in the progress of improvement, first be maintained by him in time of war, and afterwards even in time of peace.

The great change introduced into the art of war by the invention of firearms, has enhanced still further both the expense of exercising and disciplining any particular number of soldiers in time of peace, and that of employing them in time of war. Both their arms and their ammunition are become more expensive. A musket is a more expensive machine than a javelin or a bow and arrows; a cannon or a mortar, than a ballista or a catapult. The powder, which is spent in a modern review, is lost irrecoverably, and occasions a very considerable expense. The javelins and arrows which were thrown or shot in an ancient one, could easily be picked up again, and were besides of very little value. The cannon and the mortar are, not only much dearer, but much heavier machines than the ballista or catapult, and require a greater expense, not only to prepare them for the field, but to carry them to it. As the superiority of the modern artillery too, over that of the ancients, is very great; it has become much more difficult, and consequently much more expensive, to fortify a town so as to resist even for a few weeks the attack of that superior artillery. In modern times many different causes contribute to render the defence of the society more expensive. The unavoidable effects of the natural progress of improvement have, in this respect, been a good deal enhanced by a great revolution in the art of war, to which a mere accident, the invention of gun-powder, seems to have given occasion.

In modern war the great expense of fire-arms gives an evident advantage to the nation which can best afford that expense; and consequently, to an opulent and civilized, over a poor and barbarous nation. In ancient times the opulent and civilized found it difficult to defend themselves against the poor and barbarous nations. In modern times the poor and barbarous find it difficult to defend themselves against the opulent and civilized. The invention of firearms, an invention which at first sight appears to be so pernicious, is certainly favourable both to the permanency and to the extension of civilization.

Part II: Of the Expense of Justice

The second duty of the sovereign, that of protecting, as far as possible, every member of the society from the injustice or oppression of every other member of it, or the duty of establishing an exact administration of justice, requires too very different degrees of expense in the different periods of society.

Among nations of hunters, as there is scarce any property, or at least none that exceeds the value of two or three days labour; so there is seldom any established magistrate or any regular administration of justice. Men who have no property can injure one another only in their persons or reputations. But when one man kills, wounds, beats, or defames another, though he to whom the injury is done suffers, he who does it receives no benefit. It is otherwise with the injuries to property. The benefit of the person who does the injury is often equal to the loss of him who suffers it. Envy, malice, or resentment, are the only passions which can prompt one man to injure another in his person or reputation. But the greater part of men are not very frequently under the influence of those passions; and the very worst men are so only occasionally. As their gratification too, how agreeable soever it may be to certain characters, is not attended with any real or permanent advantage, it is in the greater part of men commonly restrained by prudential considerations. Men may live together in society with some tolerable degree of security, though there is no civil magistrate to protect them from the injustice of those passions. But avarice and ambition in the rich, in the poor the hatred of labour and the love of present ease and enjoyment, are the passions which prompt to invade property, passions much more steady in their operation, and much more universal in their influence. Wherever there is great property, there is great inequality. For one very rich man, there must be at least five hundred poor, and the affluence of the few supposes the indigence of the many. The affluence of the rich excites the indignation of the poor, who are often both driven by want, and prompted by envy, to invade his possessions. It is only under the shelter of the civil magistrate that the owner of that valuable property, which is acquired by the labour of many years, or perhaps of many successive generations, can sleep a single night in security. He is at all times surrounded by unknown enemies, whom, though he never provoked, he can never appease, and from whose injustice he can be protected only by the powerful arm of the civil magistrate continually held up to chastise it. The acquisition of valuable and extensive property, therefore, necessarily requires the establishment of civil government. Where there is no property, or at least none that exceeds the value of two or three days labour, civil government is not so necessary.

Civil government supposes a certain subordination. But as the necessity of civil government gradually grows up with the acquisition of valuable property, so the principal causes which naturally introduce subordination gradually grow up with the growth of that valuable property . . . .

It is in the age of shepherds, in the second period of society, that the inequality of fortune first begins to take place, and introduces among men a degree of authority and subordination which could not possibly exist before. It thereby introduces some degree of that civil government which is indispensably necessary for its own preservation: and it seems to do this naturally, and even independent of the consideration of that necessity. The consideration of that necessity comes no doubt afterwards to contribute very much to maintain and secure that authority and subordination. The rich, in particular, are necessarily interested to support that order of things, which can alone secure them in the possession of their own advantages. Men of inferior wealth combine to defend those of superior wealth in the possession of their property, in order that men of superior wealth may combine to defend them in the possession of theirs. All the inferior shepherds and herdsmen feel that the security of their own herds and flocks depends upon the security of those of the great shepherd or herdsman; that the maintenance of their lesser authority depends upon that of his greater authority, and that upon their subordination to him depends his power of keeping their inferiors in subordination to them. They constitute a sort of little nobility, who feel themselves interested to defend the property and to support the authority of their own little sovereign, in order that he may be able to defend their property and to support their authority. Civil government, so far as it is instituted for the security of property, is in reality instituted for the defence of the rich against the poor, or of those who have some property against those who have none at all.

The judicial authority of such a sovereign, however, far from being a cause of expense, was for a long time a source of revenue to him. The persons who applied to him for justice were always willing to pay for it, and a present never failed to accompany a petition. After the authority of the sovereign too was thoroughly established, the person found guilty, over and above the satisfaction which he was obliged to make to the party, was likewise forced to pay an amercement to the sovereign. He had given trouble, he had disturbed, he had broke the peace of his lord the king, and for those offences an amercement was thought due. . . .

This scheme of making the administration of justice subservient to the purposes of revenue, could scarce fail to be productive of several very gross abuses. The person, who applied for justice with a large present in his hand, was likely to get something more than justice; while he, who applied for it with a small one, was likely to get something less. Justice too might frequently be delayed, in order that this present might be repeated. The amercement, besides, of the person complained of, might frequently suggest a very strong reason for finding him in the wrong, even when he had not really been so. That such abuses were far from being uncommon, the ancient history of every country in Europe bears witness . . . .

But when from different causes, chiefly from the continually increasing expense of defending the nation against the invasion of other nations, the private estate of the sovereign had become altogether insufficient for defraying the expense of the sovereignty; and when it had become necessary that the people should, for their own security, contribute towards this expense by taxes of different kinds, it seems to have been very commonly stipulated that no present for the administration of justice should, under any pretence, be accepted either by the sovereign, or by his bailiffs and substitutes, the judges. Those presents, it seems to have been supposed, could more easily be abolished altogether, than effectually regulated and ascertained. Fixed salaries were appointed to the judges which were supposed to compensate to them the loss of whatever might have been their share of the ancient emoluments of justice; as the taxes more than compensated to the sovereign the loss of his. Justice was then said to be administered gratis.

Justice, however, never was in reality administered gratis in any country. Lawyers and attorneys, at least, must always be paid by the parties; and, if they were not, they would perform their duty still worse than they actually perform it. The fees annually paid to lawyers and attorneys amount, in every court, to a much greater sum than the salaries of the judges. The circumstance of those salaries being paid by the crown, can nowhere much diminish the necessary expense of a law-suit. But it was not so much to diminish the expense, as to prevent the corruption of justice, that the judges were prohibited from receiving any present or fee from the parties . . . .

The whole expense of justice too might easily be defrayed by the fees of court; and, without exposing the administration of justice to any real hazard of corruption, the public revenue might thus be entirely discharged from a certain, though, perhaps, but a small encumbrance. It is difficult to regulate the fees of court effectually, where a person so powerful as the sovereign is to share in them, and to derive any considerable part of his revenue from them. It is very easy, where the judge is the principal person who can reap any benefit from them. The law can very easily oblige the judge to respect the regulation, though it might not always be able to make the sovereign respect it. Where the fees of court are precisely regulated and ascertained, where they are paid all at once, at a certain period of every process, into the hands of a cashier or receiver, to be by him distributed in certain known proportions among the different judges after the process is decided, and not till it is decided, there seems to be no more danger of corruption than where such fees are prohibited altogether. Those fees, without occasioning any considerable increase in the expense of a law-suit, might be rendered fully sufficient for defraying the whole expense of justice. By not being paid to the judges till the process was determined, they might be some incitement to the diligence of the court in examining and deciding it. In courts which consisted of a considerable number of judges, by proportioning the share of each judge to the number of hours and days which he had employed in examining the process, either in the court or in a committee by order of the court, those fees might give some encouragement to the diligence of each particular judge. Public services are never better performed than when their reward comes only in consequence of their being performed, and is proportioned to the diligence employed in performing them . . . .

The separation of the judicial from the executive power seems originally to have arisen from the increasing business of the society, in consequence of its increasing improvement. The administration of justice became so laborious and so complicated a duty as to require the undivided attention of the persons to whom it was entrusted. The person entrusted with the executive power, not having leisure to attend to the decision of private causes himself, a deputy was appointed to decide them in his stead . . . .

When the judicial is united to the executive power, it is scarce possible that justice should not frequently be sacrificed to, what is vulgarly called, politics. The persons entrusted with the great interests of the state may, even without any corrupt views, sometimes imagine it necessary to sacrifice to those interests the rights of a private man. But upon the impartial administration of justice depends the liberty of every individual, the sense which he has of his own security. In order to make every individual feel himself perfectly secure in the possession of every right which belongs to him, it is not only necessary that the judicial should be separated from the executive power, but that it should be rendered as much as possible independent of that power. The judge should not be liable to be removed from his office according to the caprice of that power. The regular payment of his salary should not depend upon the good-will, or even upon the good economy of that power.

Part III: Of the Expense of Public Works and Public Institutions

The third and last duty of the sovereign or commonwealth is that of erecting and maintaining those public institutions and those public works, which, though they may be in the highest degree advantageous to a great society, are, however, of such a nature, that the profit could never repay the expense to any individual or small number of individuals, and which it, therefore, cannot be expected that any individual or small number of individuals should erect or maintain. The performance of this duty requires too very different degrees of expense in the different periods of society.

After the public institutions and public works necessary for the defence of the society, and for the administration of justice, both of which have already been mentioned, the other works and institutions of this kind are chiefly those for facilitating the commerce of the society, and those for promoting the instruction of the people. The institutions for instruction are of two kinds; those for the education of the youth, and those for the instruction of people of all ages. The consideration of the manner in which the expense of those different sorts of public works and institutions may be most properly defrayed, will divide this third part of the present chapter into three different articles.

Article I: Of the Public Works and Institutions for Facilitating the Commerce of the Society

That the erection and maintenance of the public works which facilitate the commerce of any country, such as good roads, bridges, navigable canals, harbours, etc. must require very different degrees of expense in the different periods of society, is evident without any proof. The expense of making and maintaining the public roads of any country must evidently increase with the annual produce of the land and labour of that country, or with the quantity and weight of the goods which it becomes necessary to fetch and carry upon those roads. The strength of a bridge must be suited to the number and weight of the carriages, which are likely to pass over it. The depth and the supply of water for a navigable canal must be proportioned to the number and tonnage of the lighters, which are likely to carry goods upon it; the extent of a harbour to the number of the shipping which are likely to take shelter in it.

It does not seem necessary that the expense of those public works should be defrayed from that public revenue, as it is commonly called, of which the collection and application is in most countries assigned to the executive power. The greater part of such public works may easily be so managed, as to afford a particular revenue sufficient for defraying their own expense, without bringing any burden upon the general revenue of the society.

A highway, a bridge, a navigable canal, for example, may in most cases be both made and maintained by a small toll upon the carriages which make use of them: a harbour, by a moderate port-duty upon the tonnage of the shipping which load or unload in it. The coinage, another institution for facilitating commerce, in many countries, not only defrays its own expense, but affords a small revenue or seignorage to the sovereign. The post-office, another institution for the same purpose, over and above defraying its own expense, affords in almost all countries a very considerable revenue to the sovereign.

When the carriages which pass over a highway or a bridge, and the lighters which sail upon a navigable canal, pay toll in proportion to their weight or their tonnage, they pay for the maintenance of those public works exactly in proportion to the wear and tear which they occasion of them. It seems scarce possible to invent a more equitable way of maintaining such works. This tax or toll too, though it is advanced by the carrier, is finally paid by the consumer, to whom it must always be charged in the price of the goods. As the expense of carriage, however, is very much reduced by means of such public works, the goods, notwithstanding the toll, come cheaper to the consumer than they could otherwise have done; their price not being so much raised by the toll, as it is lowered by the cheapness of the carriage. The person who finally pays this tax, therefore, gains by the application, more than he loses by the payment of it. His payment is exactly in proportion to his gain. It is in reality no more than a part of that gain which he is obliged to give up in order to get the rest. It seems impossible to imagine a more equitable method of raising a tax . . . .

The tolls for the maintenance of a high road, cannot with any safety be made the property of private persons. A high road, though entirely neglected, does not become altogether impassable, though a canal does. The proprietors of the tolls upon a high road, therefore, might neglect altogether the repair of the road, and yet continue to levy very nearly the same tolls. It is proper, therefore, that the tolls for the maintenance of such a work should be put under the management of commissioners or trustees . . . .

Even those public works which are of such a nature that they cannot afford any revenue for maintaining themselves, but of which the conveniency is nearly confined to some particular place or district, are always better maintained by a local or provincial revenue, under the management of a local and provincial administration, than by the general revenue of the state, of which the executive power must always have the management. Were the streets of London to be lighted and paved at the expense of the treasury, is there any probability that they would be so well lighted and paved as they are at present, or even at so small an expense? The expense, besides, instead of being raised by a local tax upon the inhabitants of each particular street, parish, or district in London, would, in this case, be defrayed out of the general revenue of the state, and would consequently be raised by a tax upon all the inhabitants of the kingdom, of whom the greater part derive no sort of benefit from the lighting and paving of the streets of London.

The abuses which sometimes creep into the local and provincial administration of a local and provincial revenue, how enormous so ever they may appear, are in reality, however, almost always very trifling, in comparison of those which commonly take place in the administration and expenditure of the revenue of a great empire. They are, besides, much more easily corrected . . . .

Article II: Of the Expense of the Institutions for the Education of Youth

The institutions for the education of the youth may, in the same manner, furnish a revenue sufficient for defraying their own expense. The fee or honorary which the scholar pays to the master naturally constitutes a revenue of this kind.

Even where the reward of the master does not arise altogether from this natural revenue, it still is not necessary that it should be derived from that general revenue of the society, of which the collection and application is, in most countries, assigned to the executive power. Through the greater part of Europe, accordingly, the endowment of schools and colleges makes either no charge upon that general revenue, or but a very small one. It everywhere arises chiefly from some local or provincial revenue, from the rent of some landed estate, or from the interest of some sum of money allotted and put under the management of trustees for this particular purpose, sometimes by the sovereign himself, and sometimes by some private donor.

Have those public endowments contributed in general to promote the end of their institution? Have they contributed to encourage the diligence, and to improve the abilities of the teachers? Have they directed the course of education towards objects more useful, both to the individual and to the public, than those to which it would naturally have gone of its own accord? It should not seem very difficult to give at least a probable answer to each of those questions.

In every profession, the exertion of the greater part of those who exercise it, is always in proportion to the necessity they are under of making that exertion. This necessity is greatest with those to whom the emoluments of their profession are the only source from which they expect their fortune, or even their ordinary revenue and subsistence. In order to acquire this fortune, or even to get this subsistence, they must, in the course of a year, execute a certain quantity of work of a known value; and, where the competition is free, the rivalship of competitors, who are all endeavouring to justle one another out of employment, obliges every man to endeavour to execute his work with a certain degree of exactness. The greatness of the objects which are to be acquired by success in some particular professions may, no doubt, sometimes animate the exertion of a few men of extraordinary spirit and ambition. Great objects, however, are evidently not necessary in order to occasion the greatest exertions. Rivalship and emulation render excellency, even in mean professions, an object of ambition, and frequently occasion the very greatest exertions. Great objects, on the contrary, alone and unsupported by the necessity of application, have seldom been sufficient to occasion any considerable exertion. . . .

The endowments of schools and colleges have necessarily diminished more or less the necessity of application in the teachers. Their subsistence, so far as it arises from their salaries, is evidently derived from a fund altogether independent of their success and reputation in their particular professions.

In some universities the salary makes but a part, and frequently but a small part of the emoluments of the teacher, of which the greater part arises from the honoraries or fees of his pupils. The necessity of application, though always more or less diminished, is not in this case entirely taken away. Reputation in his profession is still of some importance to him, and he still has some dependency upon the affection, gratitude, and favourable report of those who have attended upon his instructions; and these favourable sentiments he is likely to gain in no way so well as by deserving them, that is, by the abilities and diligence with which he discharges every part of his duty.

In other universities the teacher is prohibited from receiving any honorary or fee from his pupils, and his salary constitutes the whole of the revenue which he derives from his office. His interest is, in this case, set as directly in opposition to his duty as it is possible to set it. It is the interest of every man to live as much at his ease as he can; and if his emoluments are to be precisely the same, whether he does, or does not perform some very laborious duty, it is certainly his interest, at least as interest is vulgarly understood, either to neglect it altogether, or, if he is subject to some authority which will not suffer him to do this, to perform it in as careless and slovenly a manner as that authority will permit. If he is naturally active and a lover of labour, it is his interest to employ that activity in any way, from which he can derive some advantage, rather than in the performance of his duty, from which he can derive none.

If the authority to which he is subject resides in the body corporate, the college, or university, of which he himself is a member, and in which the greater part of the other members are, like himself, persons who either are, or ought to be teachers; they are likely to make a common cause, to be all very indulgent to one another, and every man to consent that his neighbour may neglect his duty, provided he himself is allowed to neglect his own. In the university of Oxford, the greater part of the public professors have, for these many years, given up altogether even the pretence of teaching . . . .

If in each college the tutor or teacher, who was to instruct each student in all arts and sciences, should not be voluntarily chosen by the student, but appointed by the head of the college; and if, in case of neglect, inability, or bad usage, the student should not be allowed to change him for another, without leave first asked and obtained; such a regulation would not only tend very much to extinguish all emulation among the different tutors of the same college, but to diminish very much in all of them the necessity of diligence and of attention to their respective pupils. Such teachers, though very well paid by their students, might be as much disposed to neglect them, as those who are not paid by them at all, or who have no other recompense but their salary.

If the teacher happens to be a man of sense, it must be an unpleasant thing to him to be conscious, while he is lecturing his students, that he is either speaking or reading nonsense, or what is very little better than nonsense. It must too be unpleasant to him to observe that the greater part of his students desert his lectures; or perhaps attend upon them with plain enough marks of neglect, contempt, and derision. If he is obliged, therefore, to give a certain number of lectures, these motives alone, without any other interest, might dispose him to take some pains to give tolerably good ones. Several different expedients, however, may be fallen upon which will effectually blunt the edge of all those incitements to diligence. The teacher, instead of explaining to his pupils himself, the science in which he proposes to instruct them, may read some book upon it; and if this book is written in a foreign and dead language, by interpreting it to them into their own; or, what would give him still less trouble, by making them interpret it to him, and by now and then making an occasional remark upon it, he may flatter himself that he is giving a lecture. The slightest degree of knowledge and application will enable him to do this without exposing himself to contempt or derision, or saying anything that is really foolish, absurd, or ridiculous. The discipline of the college, at the same time, may enable him to force all his pupils to the most regular attendance upon this sham-lecture, and to maintain the most decent and respectful behaviour during the whole time of the performance.

The discipline of colleges and universities is in general contrived, not for the benefit of the students, but for the interest, or more properly speaking, for the ease of the masters. Its object is, in all cases, to maintain the authority of the master, and whether he neglects or performs his duty, to oblige the students in all cases to behave to him as if he performed it with the greatest diligence and ability. It seems to presume perfect wisdom and virtue in the one order, and the greatest weakness and folly in the other. Where the masters, however, really perform their duty, there are no examples, I believe, that the greater part of the students ever neglect theirs. No discipline is ever requisite to force attendance upon lectures which are really worth the attending, as is well known wherever any such lectures are given. Force and restraint may, no doubt, be in some degree requisite in order to oblige children, or very young boys, to attend to those parts of education which it is thought necessary for them to acquire during that early period of life; but after twelve or thirteen years of age, provided the master does his duty, force or restraint can scarce ever be necessary to carry on any part of education. Such is the generosity of the greater part of young men, that, so far from being disposed to neglect or despise the instructions of their master, provided he shows some serious intention of being of use to them, they are generally inclined to pardon a great deal of incorrectness in the performance of his duty, and sometimes even to conceal from the public a good deal of gross negligence.

Those parts of education, it is to be observed, for the teaching of which there are no public institutions, are generally the best taught. When a young man goes to a fencing or a dancing school, he does not, indeed, always learn to fence or to dance very well; but he seldom fails of learning to fence or to dance. The good effects of the riding school are not commonly so evident. The expense of a riding school is so great, that in most places it is a public institution. The three most essential parts of literary education, to read, write, and account, it still continues to be more common to acquire in private than in public schools; and it very seldom happens that anybody fails of acquiring them to the degree in which it is necessary to acquire them . . . .

Were there no public institutions for education, no system, no science would be taught for which there was not some demand; or which the circumstances of the times did not render it, either necessary, or convenient, or at least fashionable to learn. A private teacher could never find his account in teaching, either an exploded and antiquated system of a science acknowledged to be useful, or a science universally believed to be a mere useless and pedantic heap of sophistry and nonsense. Such systems, such sciences, can subsist nowhere, but in those incorporated societies for education whose prosperity and revenue are in a great measure independent of their reputation, and altogether independent of their industry. Were there no public institutions for education, a gentleman, after going through, with application and abilities, the most complete course of education, which the circumstances of the times were supposed to afford, could not come into the world completely ignorant of every thing which is the common subject of conversation among gentlemen and men of the world.

There are no public institutions for the education of women, and there is accordingly nothing useless, absurd, or fantastical in the common course of their education. They are taught what their parents or guardians judge it necessary or useful for them to learn; and they are taught nothing else. Every part of their education tends evidently to some useful purpose; either to improve the natural attractions of their person, or to form their mind to reserve, to modesty, to chastity, and to economy: to render them both likely to become the mistresses of a family, and to behave properly when they have become such. In every part of her life a woman feels some conveniency or advantage from every part of her education. It seldom happens that a man, in any part of his life, derives any conveniency or advantage from some of the most laborious and troublesome parts of his education.

Ought the public, therefore, to give no attention, it may be asked, to the education of the people? Or if it ought to give any, what are the different parts of education which it ought to attend to in the different orders of the people? And in what manner ought it to attend to them?

In some cases the state of the society necessarily places the greater part of individuals in such situations as naturally form in them, without any attention of government, almost all the abilities and virtues which that state requires, or perhaps can admit of. In other cases the state of the society does not place the greater part of individuals in such situations, and some attention of government is necessary in order to prevent the almost entire corruption and degeneracy of the great body of the people.

In the progress of the division of labour, the employment of the far greater part of those who live by labour, that is, of the great body of the people, comes to be confined to a few very simple operations; frequently to one or two. But the understandings of the greater part of men are necessarily formed by their ordinary employments. The man whose whole life is spent in performing a few simple operations, of which the effects too are, perhaps, always the same, or very nearly the same, has no occasion to exert his understanding, or to exercise his invention in finding out expedients for removing difficulties which never occur. He naturally loses, therefore, the habit of such exertion, and generally becomes as stupid and ignorant as it is possible for a human creature to become. The torpor of his mind renders him, not only incapable of relishing or bearing a part in any rational conversation, but of conceiving any generous, noble, or tender sentiment, and consequently of forming any just judgment concerning many even of the ordinary duties of private life. Of the great and extensive interests of his country, he is altogether incapable of judging; and unless very particular pains have been taken to render him otherwise, he is equally incapable of defending his country in war. The uniformity of his stationary life naturally corrupts the courage of his mind, and makes him regard with abhorrence the irregular, uncertain, and adventurous life of a soldier. It corrupts even the activity of his body, and renders him incapable of exerting his strength with vigour and perseverance, in any other employment than that to which he has been bred. His dexterity at his own particular trade seems, in this manner, to be acquired at the expense of his intellectual, social, and martial virtues. But in every improved and civilized society this is the state into which the labouring poor, that is, the great body of the people, must necessarily fall, unless government takes some pains to prevent it . . . .

The education of the common people requires, perhaps, in a civilized and commercial society, the attention of the public more than that of people of some rank and fortune. People of some rank and fortune are generally eighteen or nineteen years of age before they enter upon that particular business, profession, or trade, by which they propose to distinguish themselves in the world. They have before that full time to acquire, or at least to fit themselves for afterwards acquiring, every accomplishment which can recommend them to the public esteem, or render them worthy of it. Their parents or guardians are generally sufficiently anxious that they should be so accomplished, and are, in most cases, willing enough to layout the expense which is necessary for that purpose. If they are not always properly educated, it is seldom from the want of expense laid out upon their education; but from the improper application of that expense. It is seldom from the want of masters; but from the negligence and incapacity of the masters who are to be had, and from the difficulty, or rather from the impossibility which there is, in the present state of things, of finding any better. The employments too in which people of some rank or fortune spend the greater part of their lives, are not, like those of the common people, simple and uniform. They are almost all of them extremely complicated, and such as exercise the head more than the hands. The understandings of those who are engaged in such employments can seldom grow torpid for want of exercise. The employments of people of some rank and fortune, besides, are seldom such as harass them from morning to night. They generally have a good deal of leisure, during which they may perfect themselves in every branch either of useful or ornamental knowledge of which they may have laid the foundation, or for which they may have acquired some taste in the earlier part of life.

It is otherwise with the common people. They have little time to spare for education. Their parents can scarce afford to maintain them even in infancy. As soon as they are able to work, they must apply to some trade by which they can earn their subsistence. That trade too is generally so simple and uniform as to give little exercise to the understanding; while, at the same time, their labour is both so constant and so severe, that it leaves them little leisure and less inclination to apply to, or even to think of anything else.

But though the common people cannot, in any civilized society, be so well instructed as people of some rank and fortune, the most essential parts of education, however, to read, write, and account, can be acquired at so early a period of life, that the greater part even of those who are to be bred to the lowest occupations, have time to acquire them before they can be employed in those occupations. For a very small expense the public can facilitate, can encourage, and can even impose upon almost the whole body of the people, the necessity of acquiring those most essential parts of education.

The public can facilitate this acquisition by establishing in every parish or district a little school, where children may be taught for a reward so moderate, that even a common labourer may afford it; the master being partly, but not wholly paid by the public; because if he was wholly, or even principally paid by it, he would soon learn to neglect his business. In Scotland the establishment of such parish schools has taught almost the whole common people to read, and a very great proportion of them to write and account. In England the establishment of charity schools has had an effect of the same kind, though not so universally, because the establishment is not so universal. If in those little schools the books, by which the children are taught to read, were a little more instructive than they commonly are: and if, instead of a little smattering of Latin; which the children of the common people are sometimes taught there, and which can scarce ever be of any use to them: they were instructed in the elementary parts of geometry and mechanics, the literary education of this rank of people would perhaps be as complete as it can be. There is scarce a common trade which does not afford some opportunities of applying to it the principles of geometry and mechanics, and which would not therefore gradually exercise and improve the common people in those principles, the necessary introduction to the most sublime as well as to the most useful sciences.

The public can encourage the acquisition of those most essential parts of education by giving small premiums, and little badges of distinction, to the children of the common people who excel in them.

The public can impose upon almost the whole body of the people the necessity of acquiring those most essential parts of education, by obliging every man to undergo an examination or probation in them before he can obtain the freedom in any corporation, or be allowed to set up any trade either in a village or town corporate . . . .

The ancient institutions of Greece and Rome seem to have been much more effectual, for maintaining the martial spirit of the great body of the people, than the establishment of what are called the militias of modern times. They were much more simple. When they were once established, they executed themselves, and it required little or no attention from government to maintain them in the most perfect vigour. Whereas to maintain even in tolerable execution the complex regulations of any modern militia, requires the continual and painful attention of government, without which they are constantly falling into total neglect and disuse. The influence, besides, of the ancient institutions was much more universal. By means of them the whole body of the people was completely instructed in the use of arms. Whereas it is but a very small part of them who can ever be so instructed by the regulations of any modern militia; except, perhaps, that of Switzerland. But a coward, a man incapable either of defending or of revenging himself, evidently wants one of the most essential parts of the character of a man. He is as much mutilated and deformed in his mind, as another is in his body, who is either deprived of some of its most essential members, or has lost the use of them. He is evidently the more wretched and miserable of the two; because happiness and misery, which reside altogether in the mind, must necessarily depend more upon the healthful or unhealthful, the mutilated or entire state of the mind, than upon that of the body. Even though the martial spirit of the people were of no use towards the defence of the society, yet to prevent that sort of mental mutilation, deformity and wretchedness, which cowardice necessarily involves in it, from spreading themselves through the great body of the people, would still deserve the most serious attention of government; in the same manner as it would deserve its most serious attention to prevent a leprosy or any other loathsome and offensive disease, though neither mortal nor dangerous, from spreading itself among them; though, perhaps, no other public good might result from such attention besides the prevention of so great a public evil.

The same thing may be said of the gross ignorance and stupidity which, in a civilized society, seem so frequently to benumb the understandings of all the inferior ranks of people. A man, without the proper use of the intellectual faculties of a man, is, if possible, more contemptible than even a coward, and seems to be mutilated and deformed in a still more essential part of the character of human nature. Though the state was to derive no advantage from the instruction of the inferior ranks of people, it would still deserve its attention that they should not be altogether uninstructed. The state, however, derives no inconsiderable advantage from their instruction. The more they are instructed, the less liable they are to the delusions of enthusiasm and superstition, which, among ignorant nations, frequently occasion the most dreadful disorders. An instructed and intelligent people besides are always more decent and orderly than an ignorant and stupid one. They feel themselves, each individually, more respectable, and more likely to obtain the respect of their lawful superiors, and they are therefore more disposed to respect those superiors. They are more disposed to examine, and more capable of seeing through, the interested complaints of faction and sedition, and they are, upon that account, less apt to be misled into any wanton or unnecessary opposition to the measures of government. In free countries, where the safety of government depends very much upon the favourable judgment which the people may form of its conduct, it must surely be of the highest importance that they should not be disposed to judge rashly or capriciously concerning it.

Article III: Of the Expense of the Institutions for the Instruction of People of all Ages

The institutions for the instruction of people of all ages are chiefly those for religious instruction. This is a species of instruction of which the object is not so much to render the people good citizens in this world, as to prepare them for another and a better world in a life to come. The teachers of the doctrine which contains this instruction, in the same manner as other teachers, may either depend altogether for their subsistence upon the voluntary contributions of their hearers; or they may derive it from some other fund to which the law of their country may entitle them; such as a landed estate, a tithe or land tax, an established salary or stipend. Their exertion, their zeal and industry, are likely to be much greater in the former situation than in the latter. In this respect the teachers of new religions have always had a considerable advantage in attacking those ancient and established systems of which the clergy, reposing themselves upon their benefices, had neglected to keep up the fervour of faith and devotion in the great body of the people; and having given themselves up to indolence, were become altogether incapable of making any vigorous exertion in defence even of their own establishment. The clergy of an established and well-endowed religion frequently become men of learning and elegance, who possess all the virtues of gentlemen, or which can recommend them to the esteem of gentlemen; but they are apt gradually to lose the qualities, both good and bad, which gave them authority and influence with the inferior ranks of people, and which had perhaps been the original causes of the success and establishment of their religion. Such a clergy, when attacked by a set of popular and bold, though perhaps stupid and ignorant enthusiasts, feel themselves as perfectly defenceless as the indolent, effeminate, and full fed nations of the southern parts of Asia, when they were invaded by the active, hardy, and hungry Tartars of the North. Such a clergy, upon such an emergency, have commonly no other resource than to call upon the civil magistrate to persecute, destroy, or drive out their adversaries, as disturbers of the public peace. It was thus that the Roman catholic clergy called upon the civil magistrate to persecute the protestants; and the church of England, to persecute the dissenters; and that in general every religious sect, when it has once enjoyed for a century or two the security of a legal establishment, has found itself incapable of making any vigorous defence against any new sect which chose to attack its doctrine or discipline. Upon such occasions the advantage in point of learning and good writing may sometimes be on the side of the established church. But the arts of popularity, all the arts of gaining proselytes, are constantly on the side of its adversaries. In England those arts have been long neglected by the well-endowed clergy of the established church, and are at present chiefly cultivated by the dissenters and by the Methodists. The independent provisions, however, which in many places have been made for dissenting teachers, by means of voluntary subscriptions, of trust rights, and other evasions of the law, seem very much to have abated the zeal and activity of those teachers. They have many of them become very learned, ingenious, and respectable men; but they have in general ceased to be very popular preachers. The Methodists, without half the learning of the dissenters, are much more in vogue . . . .

But whatever may have been the good or bad effects of the independent provision of the clergy; it has, perhaps, been very seldom bestowed upon them from any view to those effects. Times of violent religious controversy have generally been times of equally violent political faction. Upon such occasions, each political party has either found it, or imagined it, for its interest, to league itself with some one or other of the contending religious sects. But this could be done only by adopting, or at least by favouring, the tenets of that particular sect. The sect which had the good fortune to be leagued with the conquering party, necessarily shared in the victory of its ally, by whose favour and protection it was soon enabled in some degree to silence and subdue all its adversaries. Those adversaries had generally leagued themselves with the enemies of the conquering party, and were therefore the enemies of that party. The clergy of this particular sect having thus become complete masters of the field, and their influence and authority with the great body of the people being in its highest vigour, they were powerful enough to over-awe the chiefs and leaders of their own party, and to oblige the civil magistrate to respect their opinions and inclinations. Their first demand was generally, that he should silence and subdue all their adversaries; and their second, that he should bestow an independent provision on themselves. As they had generally contributed a good deal to the victory, it seemed not unreasonable that they should have some share in the spoil. They were weary, besides, of humouring the people, and of depending upon their caprice for a subsistence. In making this demand therefore they consulted their own ease and comfort, without troubling themselves about the effect which it might have in future times upon the influence and authority of their order. The civil magistrate, who could comply with this demand only by giving them something which he would have chosen much rather to take, or to keep to himself, was seldom very forward to grant it. Necessity, however, always forced him to submit at last, though frequently not till after many delays, evasions, and affected excuses.

But if politics had never called in the aid of religion, had the conquering party never adopted the tenets of one sect more than those of another, when it had gained the victory, it would probably have dealt equally and impartially with all the different sects, and have allowed every man to choose his own priest and his own religion as he thought proper. There would in this case, no doubt, have been a great multitude of religious sects. Almost every different congregation might probably have made a little sect by itself, or have entertained some peculiar tenets of its own. Each teacher would no doubt have felt himself under the necessity of making the utmost exertion, and of using every art both to preserve and to increase the number of his disciples. But as every other teacher would have felt himself under the same necessity, the success of no one teacher, or sect of teachers, could have been very great. The interested and active zeal of religious teachers can be dangerous and troublesome only where there is, either but one sect tolerated in the society, or where the whole of a large society is divided into two or three great sects; the teachers of each acting by concert, and under a regular discipline and subordination. But that zeal must be altogether innocent where the society is divided into two or three hundred, or perhaps into as many thousand small sects, of which no one could be considerable enough to disturb the public tranquillity. The teachers of each sect, seeing themselves surrounded on all sides with more adversaries than friends, would be obliged to learn that candour and moderation which is so seldom to be found among the teachers of those great sects, whose tenets being supported by the civil magistrate, are held in veneration by almost all the inhabitants of extensive kingdoms and empires, and who therefore see nothing round them but followers, disciples, and humble admirers. The teachers of each little sect, finding themselves almost alone, would be obliged to respect those of almost every other sect, and the concessions which they would mutually find it both convenient and agreeable to make to one another, might in time probably reduce the doctrine of the greater part of them to that pure and rational religion, free from every mixture of absurdity, imposture, or fanaticism, such as wise men have in all ages of the world wished to see established; but such as positive law has perhaps never yet established, and probably never will establish in any country: because, with regard to religion, positive law always has been, and probably always will be, more or less influenced by popular superstition and enthusiasm. This plan of ecclesiastical government, or more properly of no ecclesiastical government, was what the sect called Independents, a sect no doubt of very wild enthusiasts, proposed to establish in England towards the end of the civil war. If it had been established, though of a very unphilosophical origin, it would probably by this time have been productive of the most philosophical good temper and moderation with regard to every sort of religious principle. It has been established in Pennsylvania, where, though the Quakers happen to be the most numerous, the law in reality favours no one sect more than another, and it is there said to have been productive of this philosophical good temper and moderation.

But though this equality of treatment should not be productive of this good temper and moderation in all, or even in the greater part of the religious sects of a particular country; yet provided those sects were sufficiently numerous, and each of them consequently too small to disturb the public tranquillity, the excessive zeal of each for its particular tenets could not well be productive of any very hurtful effects, but, on the contrary, of several good ones: and if the government was perfectly decided both to let them all alone, and to oblige them all to let alone one another, there is little danger that they would not of their own accord subdivide themselves fast enough, so as soon to become sufficiently numerous.

In every civilized society, in every society where the distinction of ranks has once been completely established, there have been always two different schemes or systems of morality current at the same time; of which the one may be called the strict or austere; the other the liberal, or, if you will, the loose system. The former is generally admired and revered by the common people: The latter is commonly more esteemed and adopted by what are called people of fashion. The degree of disapprobation with which we ought to mark the vices of levity, the vices which are apt to arise from great prosperity, and from the excess of gaiety and good humour, seems to constitute the principal distinction between those two opposite schemes or systems. In the liberal or loose system, luxury, wanton and even disorderly mirth, the pursuit of pleasure to some degree of intemperance, the breach of chastity, at least in one of the two sexes, etc. provided they are not accompanied with gross indecency, and do not lead to falsehood or injustice, are generally treated with a good deal of indulgence, and are easily either excused or pardoned altogether. In the austere system, on the contrary, those excesses are regarded with the utmost abhorrence and detestation. The vices of levity are always ruinous to the common people, and a single week's thoughtlessness and dissipation is often sufficient to undo a poor workman forever, and to drive him through despair upon committing the most enormous crimes. The wiser and better sort of the common people, therefore, have always the utmost abhorrence and detestation of such excesses, which their experience tells them are so immediately fatal to people of their condition. The disorder and extravagance of several years, on the contrary, will not always ruin a man of fashion, and people of that rank are very apt to consider the power of indulging in some degree of excess as one of the advantages of their fortune, and the liberty of doing so without censure or reproach, as one of the privileges which belong to their station. In people of their own station, therefore, they regard such excesses with but a small degree of disapprobation, and censure them either very slightly or not at all . . . .

There are two very easy and effectual remedies, however, by whose joint operation the state might, without violence, correct whatever was unsocial or disagreeably rigorous in the morals of all the little sects into which the country was divided.

The first of those remedies is the study of science and philosophy, which the state might render almost universal among all people of middling or more than middling rank and fortune; not by giving salaries to teachers in order to make them negligent and idle, but by instituting some sort of probation, even in the higher and more difficult sciences, to be undergone by every person before he was permitted to exercise any liberal profession, or before he could be received as a candidate for any honourable office of trust or profit. If the state imposed upon this order of men the necessity of learning, it would have no occasion to give itself any trouble about providing them with proper teachers. They would soon find better teachers for themselves than any whom the state could provide for them. Science is the great antidote to the poison of enthusiasm and superstition; and where all the superior ranks of people were secured from it, the inferior ranks could not be much exposed to it.

The second of those remedies is the frequency and gaiety of public diversions. The state, by encouraging, that is by giving entire liberty to all those who for their own interest would attempt, without scandal or indecency, to amuse and divert the people by painting, poetry, music, dancing; by all sorts of dramatic representations and exhibitions, would easily dissipate, in the greater part of them, that melancholy and gloomy humour which is almost always the nurse of popular superstition and enthusiasm. Public diversions have always been the objects of dread and hatred, to all the fanatical promoters of those popular frenzies. The gaiety and good humour which those diversions inspire were altogether inconsistent with that temper of mind, which was fittest for their purpose, or which they could best work upon. Dramatic representations besides, frequently exposing their artifices to public ridicule, and sometimes even to public execration, were upon that account, more than all other diversions, the objects of their peculiar abhorrence.

In a country where the law favoured the teachers of no one religion more than those of another, it would not be necessary that any of them should have any particular or immediate dependency upon the sovereign or executive power; or that he should have anything to do, either in appointing, or in dismissing them from their offices. In such a situation he would have no occasion to give himself any concern about them, further than to keep the peace among them, in the same manner as among the rest of his subjects; that is, to hinder them from persecuting, abusing, or oppressing one another. But it is quite otherwise in countries where there is an established or governing religion. The sovereign can in this case never be secure, unless he has the means of influencing in a considerable degree the greater part of the teachers of that religion . . . .

READING II:

JURISPRUDENCE

Or Notes from the Lectures on Justice, Police, Revenue, and Arms delivered in the University of Glasgow by Adam Smith Professor of Moral Philosophy[2]

Introduction

Jurisprudence is that science which inquires into the general principles which ought to be the foundation of the laws of all nations . . . . Jurisprudence is the theory of the general principles of law and government.

The four great objects of law are Justice, Police, Revenue, and Arms.

The object of Justice is the security from injury, and it is the foundation of civil government.

The objects of Police are the cheapness of commodities, public security, and cleanliness, if the two last were not too minute for a lecture of this kind. Under this head we will consider the opulence of a state.

[2] [What follows is students' notes from Smith's lectures. They are dated 1766, but they are more likely based on lectures delivered in 1762–3, Smith's final year at the University of Glasgow.]

It is likewise necessary that the magistrate who bestows his time and labour in the business of the state should be compensated for it. For this purpose and for defraying the expenses of government some fund must be raised. Hence the origin of revenue. The subject of consideration under this head will be the proper means of levying revenue, which must come from the people by taxes, duties, etc. In general whatever revenue can be raised most insensibly from the people ought to be preferred, and in the sequel it is proposed to be shown how far the laws of Britain and of other European nations are calculated for this purpose.

As the best police cannot give security unless the government can defend themselves from foreign injuries and attacks, the fourth thing appointed by law is for this purpose, and under this head will be shown the different species of arms with their advantages and disadvantages, the constitution of standing armies, militias, etc.

After these will be considered the laws of nations, under which are comprehended the demands which one independent society may have upon another, the privileges of aliens, and proper grounds for making war.

Of Justice

The end of justice is to secure from injury. A man may be injured in several respects.

1st, as a man

2ndly, as a member of a family

3rdly, as a member of a state.

As a man, he may be injured in his body, reputation, or estate.

As a member of a family, he may be injured as a father, as a son, as a husband or wife, as a master or servant, as a guardian or pupil. For the two last are to be considered in a family relation, till such time as the pupil can take care of himself.

As a member of a state, a magistrate may be injured by disobedience or a subject by oppression, etc.

A man may be injured 1st, in his body by wounding, maiming, murdering, or by infringing his liberty.

2ndly, in his reputation, either by falsely representing him as a proper object of resentment or punishment as by calling him a thief or robber, or by depreciating his real worth, and endeavouring to degrade him below the level of his profession. A physician's character is injured when we endeavour to persuade the world he kills his patients instead of curing them, for by such a report he loses his business. We do not however injure a man when we do not give him all the praise that is due to his merit. We do not injure Sir Isaac Newton or Mr Pope,[3] when we say that Sir Isaac was no better philosopher than Descartes or that Mr Pope was

[3] [Alexander Pope (1688–1744).]

no better poet than the ordinary ones of his own time. By these expressions we do not bestow on them all the praise that they deserve, yet we do them no injury, for we do not throw them below the ordinary rank of men in their own professions.

These rights which a man has to the preservation of his body and reputation from injury are called natural. Or as the civilians express them *iura hominum naturalia*.

3rdly, a man may be injured in his estate. His rights to his estate are called acquired or *iura adventitia* and are of two kinds, real and personal.

A real right is that whose object is a real thing and which can be claimed *a quocumque possessore*. Such are all possessions, houses, furniture.

Personal rights are such as can be claimed by a law-suit from a particular person, but not *a quocumque possessore*. Such are all debts and contracts, the payment or performance of which can be demanded only from one person. If I buy a horse and have him delivered to me, though the former owner sell him to another, I can claim him *a quocumque possessore;* but if he was not delivered to me, I can only pursue the seller.

Real rights are of four kinds, Property, Servitudes, Pledges, and Exclusive Privileges.

Property is our possessions of every kind which if any way lost, or taken from us by stealth or violence, may be redemanded *a quocumque possessore*.

Servitudes are burdens upon the property of another. Thus I may have a liberty of passing through a field belonging to another which lies between me and the highway, or if my neighbour have plenty of water in his fields and I have none in mine for my cattle, I may have a right to drive them to his. Such burdens on the property of another are called servitudes. These rights were originally personal, but the trouble and expense of numerous lawsuits in order to get possession of them, when the adjacent property which was burdened with them passed through a number of hands, induced legislators to make them real, and claimable *a quocumque possessore*. Afterwards the property was transferred with these servitudes upon it.

Pledges, which include all pawns and mortgages, are securities for something else to which we have a right. The laws of most civilized nations have considered them as real rights, and give a liberty to claim them as such.

Exclusive privileges are such as that of a book-seller to vend a book for a certain number of years, and to hinder any other person from doing it during that period. These rights are for the most part creatures of the civil law, though some few of them are natural, as in a state of hunters even before the origin of civil government if a man has started a hare and pursued her for sometime, he has an exclusive privilege to hunt her, by which he can hinder any other to come in upon her with a fresh pack of hounds.

An heir has also an exclusive privilege of hindering any person to take possession of the inheritance left him while he is deliberating whither or not it will be for his interest to take possession of it and payoff the debts with which it is burdened.

Personal rights are of three kinds as they arise from Contract, Quasi Contract, or Delinquency.

The foundation of contract is the reasonable expectation which the person who promises raises in the person to whom he binds himself; of which the satisfaction may be extorted by force.

Quasi Contract is the right which one has to a compensation for necessary trouble and expense about another man's affairs. If a person finds a watch in the highway he has a claim to a reward and to the defraying of his expences in finding out the owner. If a man lend me a sum of money he has a right not only to the sum, but to interest also.

Delinquency is founded upon damage done to any person, whither through malice or culpable negligence. A person has a right to claim these only from a certain person.

The objects of these seven rights make up the whole of a man's estate.

The origin of natural rights is quite evident. That a person has a right to have his body free from injury, and his liberty free from infringement unless there be a proper cause, no body doubts. But acquired rights such as property require more explanation. Property and civil government very much depend on one another. The preservation of property and the inequality of possession first formed it, and the state of property must always vary with the form of government. The civilians begin with considering government and then treat of property and other rights. Others who have written on this subject begin with the latter and then consider family and civil government. There are several advantages peculiar to each of these methods, though that of the civil law seems upon the whole preferable.

Of Public Jurisprudence

There are two principles which induce men to enter into a civil society, which we shall call the principles of authority and utility. At the head of every small society or association of men we find a person of superior abilities; in a warlike society he is a man of superior strength, and in a polished one of superior mental capacity. Age and a long possession of power have also a tendency to strengthen authority. Age is naturally in our imagination connected with wisdom and experience; and a continuance in power bestows a kind of right to the exercise of it. But superior wealth still more than any of these qualities contributes to confer authority. This proceeds not from any dependence that the poor have upon the rich, for in general the poor are independent, and support themselves by their labour, yet though they expect no benefit from them they have a strong propensity to pay them respect. This principle is fully explained in the *Theory of Moral Sentiments,* where it is shown that it arises from our sympathy with our superiors being greater than that with our equals or inferiors: we admire their happy situation, enter into it with pleasure, and endeavour to promote it.

Among the great, as superior abilities of body and mind are not so easily judged of by others, it is more convenient, as it is more common, to give the preference to riches. It is evident that an old family, that is, one which has been long distinguished, by its wealth has more authority than any other. An upstart is always disagreeable; we envy his superiority over us and think ourselves [as] well entitled to wealth as he. If I am told that a man's grandfather was very poor and dependent on my family, I will grudge very much to see his grandson in a station above me and will not be much disposed to submit to his authority. Superior age, superior abilities of body and of mind, ancient family, and superior wealth seem to be the four things that give one man authority over another.

The second principle which induces men to obey the civil magistrate is utility. Everyone is sensible of the necessity of this principle to preserve justice and peace in the society. By civil institutions, the poorest may get redress of injuries from the wealthiest and most powerful, and though there may be some irregularities in particular cases, as undoubtedly there are, yet we submit to them to avoid greater evils. It is the sense of public utility, more than of private, which influences men to obedience. It may sometimes be for my interest to disobey, and to wish government overturned. But I am sensible that other men are of a different opinion from me and would not assist me in the enterprise. I therefore submit to its decision for the good of the whole.

If government has been of a long standing in a country and if it be supported by proper revenues, and be at the same time in the hands of a man of great abilities, authority is then in perfection.

In all governments both these principles take place in some degree, but in a monarchy the principle of authority prevails, and in a democracy that of utility. In Britain, which is a mixed government, the faction's formed sometime ago under the names of Whig and Tory were influenced by these principles; the former submitted to government on account of it's utility and the advantages which they derived from it, while the latter pretended that it was of divine institution, and to offend against it was equally criminal as for a child to rebel against its parent. Men in general follow these principles according to their natural dispositions. In a man of a bold, daring, and bustling turn the principle of utility is predominant, and a peaceable, easy turn of mind usually is pleased with a tame submission to superiority.

It has been a common doctrine in this country that contract is the foundation of allegiance to the civil magistrate. But that this is not the case will appear from the following reasons.

In the first place, the doctrine of an original contract is peculiar to Great Britain, yet government takes place where it was never thought of, which is even the case with the greater part of people in this country. Ask a common porter or day-labourer why he obeys the civil magistrate, he will tell you that it is right to do so, that he sees others do it, that he would be punished if he refused to do it, or perhaps that it is a sin against God not to do it. But you will never hear him mention a contract as the foundation of his obedience.

2ndly, when certain powers of government were at first entrusted to certain persons upon certain conditions, it is true that the obedience of these who entrusted it might be founded on a contract, but their posterity have nothing to do with it, they are not conscious of it, and therefore cannot be bound by it. It may indeed be said that by remaining in the country you tacitly consent to the contract and are bound by it. But how can you avoid staying in it? You were not consulted whether you should be born in it or not. And how can you get out of it? Most people know no other language nor country, are poor, and obliged to stay not far from the place where they were born to labour for a subsistence. They cannot therefore be said to give any consent to a contract, though they may have the strongest sense of obedience. To say that by staying in a country a man agrees to a contract of obedience to government, is just the same with carrying a man into a ship and after he is at a distance from land to tell him that by being in the ship he has contracted to obey the master. The foundation of a duty cannot be a principle with which mankind is entirely unacquainted. They must have some idea however confused of the principle upon which they act.

But again, upon the supposition of an original contract, by leaving the state you expressly declare that you will no longer continue a subject of it and are freed from the obligation which you owed it, yet every state claims its own subjects and punishes them for such practices, which would be the highest injustice if their living in the country implies a consent to a former agreement. Again, if there be such a thing as an original contract, aliens who come into a country preferring it to others give the most express consent to it, yet a state always suspects aliens as retaining a prejudice in favour of their mother country, and they are never so much depended upon as freeborn subjects. So much is the English law influenced by this principle, that no alien can hold a place under the government, even though he should be naturalized by Act of Parliament. Besides if such a contract were supposed, why should the state require an oath of allegiance whenever a man enters on any office, for if they supposed a previous contract, what occasion is there for renewing it. Breach of allegiance or high treason is a much greater crime and more severely punished in all nations than breach of contract, in which no more but fulfilment is required. They must therefore be on a different footing. The less can by no means involve in it the greater contract. Contract is not therefore the principle of obedience to civil government, but the principles of authority and utility formerly explained.

We shall now endeavour to explain the nature of government, its different forms, what circumstances gave occasion for it, and by what it is maintained.

The forms of government however various may not improperly be reduced to these three, Monarchical, Aristocratical, and Democratical. These may be blended in a great number of ways, and we usually denominate the government from that one which prevails.

Monarchical government is where the supreme power and authority is vested in one, who can do what he pleases, make peace and war, impose taxes, and the like.

Aristocratical government is where a certain order of people in the state, either of the richest, or of certain families, have it in their power to choose magistrates, who are to have the management of the state.

Democratical government is where the management of affairs belongs to the whole body of the people together.

These two last forms may be called republican, and then the division of government is into monarchical and republican.

To acquire proper notions of government it is necessary to consider the first form of it, and observe how the other forms arose out of it.

In a nation of hunters there is properly no government at all. The society consists of a few independent families, who live in the same village and speak the same language, and have agreed among themselves to keep together for their mutual safety. But they have no authority one over another. The whole society interests itself in any offence. If possible they make it up between the parties, if not they banish from their society, kill, or deliver up to the resentment of the injured, him who has committed the crime. But this is no regular government. For though there may be some among them who are much respected, and have great influence in their determinations, yet he never can do anything without the consent of the whole.

Thus among hunters there is no regular government; they live according to the laws of nature.

The appropriation of herds and flocks, which introduced an inequality of fortune, was that which first gave rise to regular government. Till there be property there can be no government, the very end of which is to secure wealth, and to defend the rich from the poor. In this age of shepherds if one man possessed 500 oxen, and another had none at all, unless there were some government to secure them to him, he would not be allowed to possess them. This inequality of fortune, making a distinction between the rich and the poor, gave the former much influence over the latter, for they who had no flocks or herds must have depended on those who had them, because they could not now gain a subsistence from hunting as the rich had made the game, now become tame, their own property. They therefore who had appropriated a number of flocks and herds, necessarily came to have great influence over the rest; and accordingly we find in the Old Testament that Abraham, Lot, and the other patriarchs were like little petty princes. It is to [be] observed that this inequality of fortune in a nation of shepherds occasioned greater influence than in any period after that. Even at present, a man may spend a great estate and yet acquire no dependents. Arts and manufactures are increased by it, but it may make very few persons dependent. In a nation of shepherds it is quite otherways. They have no possible means of spending their property, having no domestic luxury, but by giving it in presents to the poor, and by this means they attain such influence over them as to make them in a manner their slaves . . . .

We shall now consider the different powers which naturally belong to government, how they are distributed, and what is their progress in the first periods of society.

The powers of government are three, to wit, the Legislative, which makes laws for the public good. The Judicial, or that which obliges private persons to obey these laws, and punishes those who disobey. The Executive, or as some call it, the Federal power, to which belongs the making war and peace.

All these powers in the original form of government belonged to the whole body of the people. It was indeed long before the legislative power was introduced, as it is the highest exertion of government to make laws and lay down rules to bind not only ourselves, but also our posterity, and those who never gave any consent to the making them. As for the judicial power, when two persons quarrelled between themselves the whole society naturally interposed, and when they could not make up matters turned them out of the society. During this early age crimes were few, and it was long before the punishment was made equal to the crime.

Cowardice and treason were the first crimes punished. For cowardice among hunters is considered as treason, because when they went out in small numbers, if their enemy attacked them, and some of their party deserted them, the rest might suffer by it, and therefore they who deserted were punished for treason.

The priest generally inflicted the punishment as it were by the command of the gods, so weak at that time was government. The power of making peace and war in like manner belonged to the people, and all the heads of families were consulted about it.

Though the judicial power which concerns individuals was long precarious, the society first interposing as friends, and then as arbitrators, the executive power came very soon to be exerted absolutely. When any private quarrel happens concerning the property of this cow, or of that ox, society is not immediately concerned. But it is deeply interested in making peace and war. In the age of shepherds this power is absolutely exerted. In Great Britain we can observe vestiges of the precariousness of the judicial power, but none of the executive. When a criminal was brought to trial, he was asked how he would choose that his cause should be decided, whither by combat, the ordeal trial, or the laws of his country. The society only obliged him not to disturb them in the decision. In England the question still remains, though the answer is not now arbitrary. It was very common in the ruder ages to demand a trial by dipping their hand in boiling water, by means of which almost everyone was found innocent, though now scarce anyone would escape by this means. When people were constantly exposed to the weather boiling water could have little effect upon them, though now, when we are quite covered, it must have a contrary effect. This choice of trial shows the weakness of the judicial laws. We find that the judicial combat continued in England as late as the days of Q. Elizabeth. It has now worn out gradually and insensibly, without so much as a law or a rule of court made against it.

In the periods of hunters and fishers and in that of shepherds, as was before observed, crimes are few; small crimes passed without any notice. In these ages no controversies arose from interpretations of testaments, settlements, contracts, which render our law-suits so numerous. For these were unknown among them. When these took place and difficult trades began to be practiced controversies became more frequent. But as men were generally employed in some branch of trade or another, without great detriment to themselves they could not spare time to wait upon them. All causes must be left undecided, which would be productive of every inconvenience, or they must fall upon some other method more suitable to the several members of society. The natural means they would fall upon would be to choose some of their number to whom all causes should be referred. The chieftain who was before this distinguished by his superior influence, when this comes to be the case would preserve his wonted precedence and would naturally be one of those who were chosen for this purpose. A certain number would be chosen to sit along with him, and in the first ages of society this number was always considerable. They would be afraid to trust matters of importance to a few, and accordingly we find that at Athens there were 500 judges at the same time. By this means the chieftain would still further increase his authority, and the government would appear in some degree monarchical. But this is only in appearance, for the final decision is still in the whole body of the people, and the government is really democratical.

The power of making peace and war, as was before observed, was at first lodged in the whole body of the people. But when society advanced, towns were fortified, magazines prepared, stocks of money got together, generals and officers appointed, the whole body of the people could not attend to deliberations of this kind. This province would either fall to the court of justice, or there would be another set of people appointed for this purpose, though it would naturally at first fall to the court of justice. This is properly called the senatorial power, which at Rome took care of the public revenue, public buildings, and the like. But afterwards at Rome the court of justice and the senatorial one became quite distinct. The same may be said of the areopagite court at Athens . . . .

We have shown how republics arose, and how they again became democratical; we are next to show how this liberty was lost, and monarchy or something like it was introduced.

Considering these states in the situation above described, as possessed of their towns and a small territory in the adjacent country, they must either confine themselves within their ancient boundaries, or enlarge their territory by conquest: they must either be what may not improperly be called a defensive republic or a conquering one. The Grecian states are a good example of the former and Rome and Carthage of the latter. We are to show how each of these lost their liberty, and first how the defensive states lost theirs.

When a country arrives at a certain degree of refinement it becomes less fit for war. When the arts arrive at a certain degree of improvement, the number of the people increases, yet that of fighting men becomes less. In a state of shepherds the whole nation can go out to war, and even when it becomes more refined, and the division of labour takes place, and everyone is possessed of a small farm, they can send out a great number. In such an age their campaigns are always in summer, and from seedtime till harvest their young men have nothing to do but to serve in them. The whole business at home can be performed by the old men and women, and even these have sometimes beat the enemy in the absence of their soldiers. In a state where arts are carried on, and which consists chiefly of manufacturers, there cannot be sent out such numbers, because if a weaver or tailor be called away nothing is done in his absence. Scarce one in an hundred can be spared from Britain and Holland. Of an hundred inhabitants fifty are women, and of fifty men, twenty five are unfit for war . . . .

Thus we have seen how small republics, whether conquering or defensive, came at length to a dissolution, from the improvements in mechanics arts, commerce, and the arts of war. We are next to consider what form of government succeeded the republican.

When small republics were conquered by another state, monarchy, or whatever other government pleased the conquerors, was established, though they generally followed the model of their own country. The Athenians always established democracy, and the Spartans aristocracy. The Romans indeed more prudently divided their conquests into provinces, which were governed pretty absolutely by persons appointed by [the] Senate for that purpose. The case is somewhat different when a state is conquered by its own subjects. Both the nature of the action and the instruments by which it is performed require a military monarchy, or a monarchy supported by military force, because it is as necessary to keep them in awe as to conquer them. This was the form of government that was established in Rome during the time of the emperors; these emperors took the whole executive power into their own hands, they made peace and war as 'they thought proper, and even named the magistrates, either immediately themselves, or by means of a Senate of their own appointment. They did not however alter any institutions of the civil law. Right and wrong were decided as formerly. Cromwell did the same in our own country: he kept the state in awe by an insignificant army, but he allowed the judge to determine right and wrong as formerly. Nay, he made such improvements in the civil law, by taking away wardships, etc., that the first thing the Parliament of Charles II did was to confirm many of Cromwell's laws.

The Roman authors tell us that justice was never better administered than under the worst of the emperors, Domitian[4] and Nero. It is the interest of all new administrators to make few alterations in what the generality of people are much concerned and have been long accustomed to. They will more easily go into anything else, when they are indulged in this. It was particularly the interest of the emperors to keep up the ancient system of laws, and accordingly we find that all consuls who misbehaved in their respective provinces were severely punished. It was not so under the Republic; the most scandalous crimes were committed by governors, as we learn from Cicero's Orations.

A military government allows the strictest administration of justice. Nobody indeed can have a fair trial where the emperor is immediately concerned, then he will do as he pleases. But where he is in no way interested, it is his interest to adhere to the ancient laws . . . .

In consequence of this arose the allodial government, which introduced an inequality of fortune. All these chieftains held their lands allodially without any burden of cess, wardship, etc. One of these great lords was possessed of almost a county, but as he was unable himself to reap any advantage from so much of it he found it necessary to parcel it out among vassals, who either paid a certain annuity, attended him in war, or performed some service of this nature. By this means his incomes became so great that, as there was then no domestic luxury, he could not consume them in any way but by maintaining a great number of retainers about his house. These were another species of dependants, who increased his authority and secured domestic peace. For they kept the tenants in awe, and were kept in awe by the tenants. So great was the authority of these lords, that if anyone claimed a debt from any of their vassals, the king had no power to send a messenger into the lord's dominions to force payment. He could only apply to the lord, and desire him to do justice. To them also lay the last resort in judging of all manner of property under their own jurisdiction, the power of life and death, of coining money, and of making bye laws and regulations in their own territories. But besides this power of government which in a great measure

[4] [Titus Flavius Domitianus, English name Domitian (AD51–96), Roman emperor 81–96.]

was betwixt the king and the great lords, if there had been no other the balance would not have been properly kept. But besides the allodial lords there was a great number of free people, who were allowed to consult about justice in their own spheres. Every county was divided into hundreds, and subdivided into tens. Each of these had their respective court, *viz.* the decemary court, the hundred court. Over those was placed the *Wittenagemot* or assembly of the whole people. Appeals were brought from the ten to the hundred, and from it to [the] county court. An appeal could be brought to the king's court in case the inferior court denied justice by refusing to hear a cause, or if it was protracted by unreasonable delays. Appeals were also sometimes carried to the *Wittenagemot,* which was made up of the king, allodial lords, aldermen or earls, bishops, abbots, etc. This was the first form of government in the west of Europe, after the downfall of the Roman Empire.

We are next to show how the allodial government was overturned, and the feudal system introduced.

As these great lords were continually making war upon one another, in order to secure the attendance of their tenants they gave them leases of the lands which they possessed from year to year, which afterwards for the same reasons came to be held for life. When they were about to engage in any very hazardous enterprise, that, in case of the worst consequences, the families of their vassals who went along with them might not be left destitute and that they might still be more encouraged to follow them, they extended this right to the life of the son and grandson; as it was thought cruel to turn out an old possessor, the right became at last hereditary, and called feudal. The feudal tenant was bound to certain offices, but service in war was the chief thing required, and if the heir was not able to perform it he was obliged to appoint one in his place. It was in this manner that wardships were introduced. When the heir female succeeded, the feudal baron had a right to marry her to whomever he pleased, because it was thought reasonable that he should have a vassal of his own choosing. The *prima seizin* was another emolument of the master. When the father died the son had no right to the estate till he publicly declared his willingness to accept of it. And on this account the lord sometimes had the estate in his own hand and enjoyed the profits of it for sometime. The heir paid a sum to get it back, which was called relief. There was still another emolument belonging to the lord, called *escheat,* that is, after the estate became hereditary, if there was no heir of the family to succeed, it returned to the lord. The same thing happened if the heir failed of performing the services for which he had the tenure. There were besides these some small sums due to the superior on redeeming his son when taken prisoner, or on knighting him, and on the marriage of his daughter and some such occasions. The same causes that made allodial lords give away their lands to their vassals on leases which afterwards became hereditary, made the king give away the greater part of his lands to be held feudally, and what a tenant possessed *in feu* was much the same with real property. They were indeed subject to the above mentioned emoluments, but they possessed their lands for themselves and posterity. Feudal property may in some respects be inferior to allodial, but the difference is so inconsiderable that allodial lordships soon came to be held feudally. About the tenth century all estates came to be held feudally, and the allodial lords, that they might enjoy the king's protection, exchanged their rights for a feudal tenure.

It is to be observed that these historians who give an account of the origin of feudal laws from the usurpation of the nobility are quite mistaken. They say that the nobility wanted to have these lands which they held at pleasure of the king to be hereditary, that it might not be in his power to turn them out, and that the feudal law was introduced on account of the diminution of the king's power. But it was actually the contrary; it was on account of the increase of his power, and it required great influence in the king to make the lords hold their lands feudally. The best proof of this is that William the Conqueror changed all the allodial lordships in England into feudal tenures and Malcolm Kenmure did the same in Scotland.

The introduction of the feudal system into all Europe took away everything like popular government. The popular courts were all removed. Neither decemary, hundred, nor county courts were allowed. All public affairs were managed by the king and the great feudal lords. No commoners, none but hereditary lords had a right to sit in Parliament. These great lords who held immediately of the king were considered as his companions, *pares convivii comites*. They advised concerning public affairs and nothing of importance could be done without them. The consent of the majority was to be obtained before any law could be passed, and it was necessary to have them called together. The barons or inferior lords observed the same method in their jurisdictions, and they who held of [them] were called *pares curiae baronis*. It was likewise necessary that they should be consulted, as they too were in arms. The baron could neither go to war nor make a law without the consent of the majority. Nothing could be done in the kingdom without almost universal consent, and thus they fell into a kind of aristocracy with the king at the head of it . . . .

We have now shown how the government of England turned absolute; we shall next consider how liberty was restored, and what security the British have for the possession of it. The Act of Henry VII allowing the nobility to dispose of their estates had already placed them entirely on a level with the Commons. Elizabeth, who always affected popularity, was continually unwilling to impose taxes on her subjects. In order to supply her exigencies she sold the royal demesnes, as she knew that none of her offspring was to succeed her. Her successors therefore standing in need of frequent supplies were obliged to make application to Parliament. The Commons were now become very considerable, as they represented the whole body of the people, and as they knew the king could not want, they never granted him anything without in some degree infringing his privileges. At one time they obtained freedom of speech, at another they got it enacted that their concurrence should be necessary to every law. The king, on account of his urgent necessities, was forced to grant whatever they asked and thus the authority of the Parliament established itself. A peculiar advantage which Britain enjoyed after the accession of James I was that as the dominions of Britain were every way bounded by the sea, there was no need for a standing army and consequently the king had no power by which he could overawe either people or Parliament. The £120,000 a year which was settled upon the king at that time might have secured his independency, had not the bad economy of Charles II rendered him as indigent as any of his predecessors. His successor was still more dependant and was forced to quit the throne and the kingdom altogether. This brought a new family which as the royal demesnes were entirely alienated depended wholly upon taxes, and were obliged to court the people for them. Ever since, the king's revenue though much greater than it was then depends so much on the concurrence of the Parliament that it never can endanger the liberty of the nation. The revenue at present consists chiefly of three branches, to *wit. 1st*, the Civil List, which is entirely consumed in the maintenance of the royal family and can give the king no influence, nor hurt the liberty of the subject. *2ndly,* the annual land and malt taxes, which depend entirely on the Parliament. *3rdly*, the funds mortgaged for paying of the public debts, such as the taxes on salt, beer, malt, etc., levied by the officers of custom and excise. These the king can by no means touch; they are paid to the Court of Exchequer, which is generally managed by people of interest and integrity who possess their offices for life and are quite independent of the king. Even they can pay nothing but to those appointed by Parliament, and must have the discharge of the public creditor. The surplus of the mortgages goes into what is called the sinking fund for paying the public debt [which] secures the government in the present family, because if a revolution were to happen the public creditors, who are men of interest, would lose both principal and interest. Thus the nation is quite secure in the management of the public revenue, and in this manner a rational system of liberty has been introduced into Britain. The Parliament consists of about 200 peers and 500 commoners. The Commons in a great measure manage all public affairs, as no money bill can take its rise except in that House. Here is a happy mixture of all the different forms of government properly restrained and a perfect security to liberty and property.

There are still some other securities to liberty. The judges appointed for the administration of justice are fixed for life, and quite independent of the king. Again, the king's ministers are liable to impeachment by the House of Commons for maladministration and the king cannot pardon them. The Habeas Corpus Act, by which the arbitrary measures of the king to detain a person in prison as long as he pleased is restrained, and by which the judge who refuses to bring a prisoner to his trial if desired within forty days is rendered incapable of any office, is another security to the liberty of the subject. The method of election, and placing the power of judging concerning all elections in the hands of the Commons, are also securities to liberty. All these established customs render it impossible for the king to attempt anything absolute . . . .

It will be proper when we are treating of courts to enquire into the origin of juries. In the beginning of the allodial government, when the several courts had arrived at a very small degree of improvement and before they had experience to examine thoroughly into matters, when any person was brought before them on an action depending on his oath he was obliged to bring twelve compurgators to swear that the oath was just. There are remains of this at present in actions of debt, where if the person can bring in a certain number of persons to swear that his oath is just he gains the suit. It is to be observed that the imperfection of this way of trying was one of the great causes that gave origin to the judicial combat. A nobleman, or indeed any man of spirit, who was eluded of his right by a set of perjured fellows, would rather choose to combat it in the field and appeal to the judgment of God than leave his cause to them. Henry II first instituted that the sheriff and a certain number of persons who had opportunity to be best acquainted with the crime should have the whole affair laid before them, and that the person should be judged by their sentence. The law of England, always the friend of liberty, deserves praise in no instance more than in the careful provision of impartial juries. They who are chosen must be near the place where the crime was committed, that they may have an opportunity of being acquainted with it. A great part of the jury may be laid aside by the panel. He can lay aside thirty of their number, and he can challenge them either per capita, that is, any single juryman, or any number of them, if he suspect the sheriff of partiality. There may be many small causes for suspicion of partiality, and of the relevancy of these the court is judge. Nothing can be a greater security for life, liberty, and property than this institution. The judges are men of integrity, quite independent, holding their offices for life, but are tied down by the law. The jurymen are your neighbours who are to judge of a fact upon which your life depends. They too can be laid aside for several reasons. The laws of England with regard to juries are only defective in one point, in which they differ from the laws of Scotland. In England the whole jury must be unanimous, which renders the office of a juryman a very disagreeable service. A case may appear to you more clear than it does to me, and may really be different from what it appears to either of us, and yet there is a necessity for our agreement, and of consequence a necessity that one of us should swear contrary to our conscience. In criminal causes there is little danger; people are generally disposed to favour innocence and to preserve life. But in civil cases people are not so much troubled; they are not so much disposed to favour, and many of them are exceedingly doubtful.

People of fashion are not fond of meddling in a jury attended with such inconveniences, and therefore only the meaner sort of people attend the judge. A great man would not choose to be so often called and returned, and perhaps treated in such a manner as no gentleman would choose to be.

In this case the law providing for security has done too much. In this country, where unanimity is not required, the service is not so disagreeable. Though a person differ from the majority, he may stand by his opinion and is not forced to comply, and the people of the highest rank are willing to be jurors. In the actions which come before the Court of Chancery no jury is required, and the Court of Session in Scotland has taken them away in civil causes.

Three

Languages and Criticism

READING I

Considerations Concerning the First Formation of Languages, and the Different Genius of Original and Compounded Languages[1]

The assignation of particular names, to denote particular objects, that is, the institution of nouns substantive, would probably be one of the first steps towards the formation of language. Two savages, who had never been taught to speak, but had been bred up remote from the societies of men, would naturally begin to form that language by which they would endeavour to make their mutual wants intelligible to each other, by uttering certain sounds, whenever they meant to denote certain objects. Those objects only which were most familiar to them, and which they had most frequent occasion to mention, would have particular names assigned to them. The particular cave whose covering sheltered them from the weather, the particular tree whose fruit relieved their hunger, the particular fountain whose water allayed their thirst, would first be denominated by the words *cave, tree, fountain,* or by whatever other appellations they might think proper, in that primitive jargon, to mark them. Afterwards, when the more enlarged experience of these savages had led them to observe, and their necessary occasions obliged them to make mention of other caves, and other trees, and other fountains, they would naturally bestow, upon each of those new objects, the same name, by which they had been accustomed to express the similar object they were first acquainted with. The new objects had none of them any name of its own, but each of them exactly resembled another object, which had such an appellation. It was impossible that those savages could behold the new objects, without recollecting the old ones; and the name of the old ones, to which the new bore so close a resemblance. When they had occasion, therefore, to mention, or to point out to each other, any of the new objects, they would naturally utter the name of the

[1] This essay appeared in *The Philological Miscellany* in 1761.

correspondent old one, of which the idea could not fail, at that instant, to present itself to their memory in the strongest and liveliest manner. And thus, those words, which were originally the proper names of individuals, would each of them insensibly become the common name of a multitude. A child that is just learning to speak, calls every person who comes to the house its papa or its mama; and thus bestows upon the whole species those names which it had been taught to apply to two individuals. I have known a clown, who did not know the proper name of the river which ran by his own door. It was *the river,* he said, and he never heard any other name for it. His experience, it seems, had not led him to observe any other river. The general word *river,* therefore, was, it is evident, in his acceptance of it, a proper name, signifying an individual object. If this person had been carried to another river, would he not readily have called it a river? Could we suppose any person living on the banks of the Thames so ignorant, as not to know the general word *river,* but to be acquainted only with the particular word *Thames,* if he was brought to any other river, would he not readily call it *a Thames?* This, in reality, is no more than what they, who are well acquainted with the general word, are very apt to do. An Englishman, describing any great river which he may have seen in some foreign country, naturally says, that it is another Thames. The Spaniards, when they first arrived upon the coast of Mexico, and observed the wealth, populousness, and habitations of that fine country, so much superior to the savage nations which they had been visiting for some time before, cried out, that it was another Spain. Hence it was called New Spain; and this name has stuck to that unfortunate country ever since. We say, in the same manner, of a hero, that he is an Alexander; of an orator, that he is a Cicero; of a philosopher, that he is a Newton. This way of speaking, which the grammarians call an Antonomasia, and which is still extremely common, though now not at all necessary, demonstrates how much mankind are naturally disposed to give to one object the name of any other, which nearly resembles it, and thus to denominate a multitude, by what originally was intended to express an individual.

It is this application of the name (of an individual to a great multitude of objects, whose resemblance naturally recalls the idea of that individual, and of the name which expresses it, that seems originally to have given occasion to the formation of those classes and assortments, which, in the schools, are called genera and species, and of which the ingenious and eloquent M. Rousseau of Geneva[2] finds himself so much at a loss to account for the origin. What constitutes a species is merely a number of objects, bearing a certain degree of resemblance to one another, and on that account denominated by a single appellation, which may be applied to express any one of them.

[2] [Jean-Jacques Rousseau (1712–78).]

When the greater part of objects had thus been arranged under their proper classes and assortments, distinguished by such general names, it was impossible that the greater part of that almost infinite number of individuals, comprehended under each particular assortment or species, could have any peculiar or proper names of their own, distinct from the general name of the species. When there was occasion, therefore, to mention any particular object, it often became necessary to distinguish it from the other objects comprehended under the same general name, either, first, by its peculiar qualities; or, secondly, by the peculiar relation which it stood in to some other things. Hence the necessary origin of two other sets of words, of which the one should express quality; the other, relation.

Nouns adjective are the words which express quality considered as qualifying, or, as the schoolmen say, in concrete with, some particular subject. Thus the word *green* expresses a certain quality considered as qualifying, or as in concrete with, the particular subject to which it may be applied. Words of this kind, it is evident, may serve to distinguish particular objects from others comprehended under the same general appellation. The words *green tree,* for example, might serve to distinguish a particular tree from others that were withered or blasted.

Prepositions are the words which express relation considered, in the same manner, in concrete with the co-relative object. Thus the prepositions *of, to, for, with, by, above, below,* etc. denote some relation subsisting between the objects expressed by the words between which the prepositions are placed; and they denote that this relation is considered in concrete with the co-relative object. Words of this kind serve to distinguish particular objects from others of the same species, when those particular objects cannot be so properly marked out by any peculiar qualities of their own. When we say, *the green tree of the meadow,* for example, we distinguish a particular tree, not only by the quality which belongs to it, but by the relation which it stands in to another object.

As neither quality nor relation can exist in abstract, it is natural to suppose that the words which denote them considered in concrete, the way in which we always see them subsist, would be of much earlier invention than those which express them considered in abstract, the way in which we never see them subsist. The words *green* and *blue* would, in all probability, be sooner invented than the words *greenness* and *blueness;* the words *above* and *below,* than the words *superiority* and *inferiority.* To invent words of the latter kind requires a much greater effort of abstraction than to invent those of the former. It is probable, therefore, that such abstract terms would be of much later institution. Accordingly, their etymologies generally show that they are so, they being generally derived from others that are concrete.

But though the invention of nouns adjective be much more natural than that of the abstract nouns substantive derived from them, it would still, however, require a considerable degree of abstraction and generalization. Those, for example, who first invented the words *green, blue, red,* and the other names of colours, must have observed and compared together a great number of objects, must have remarked their resemblances and dissimilitudes in respect of the quality of colour, and must have arranged them, in their own minds, into different classes and assortments, according to those resemblances and dissimilitudes. An adjective is by nature a general, and in some measure an abstract word, and necessarily presupposes the idea of a certain species or assortment of things, to all of which it is equally applicable. The word *green* could not, as we were supposing might be the case of the word *cave,* have been originally the name of an individual, and afterwards have become, by what grammarians call an Antonomasia, the name of a species. The word *green* denoting, not the name of a substance, but the peculiar quality of a substance, must from the very first have been a general word, and considered as equally applicable to any other substance possessed of the same quality. The man who first distinguished a particular object by the epithet of *green,* must have observed other objects that were not *green,* from which he meant to separate it by this appellation. The institution of this name, therefore, supposes comparison. It likewise supposes some degree of abstraction. The person who first invented this appellation must have distinguished the quality from the object to which it belonged, and must have conceived the object as capable of subsisting without the quality. The invention, therefore, even of the simplest nouns adjective, must have required more metaphysics than we are apt to be aware of. The different mental operations, of arrangement or classing, of comparison, and of abstraction, must all have been employed, before even the names of the different colours, the least metaphysical of all nouns adjective, could be instituted. From all which I infer, that when languages were beginning to be formed, nouns adjective would by no means be the words of the earliest invention.

There is another expedient for denoting the different qualities of different substances, which as it requires no abstraction, nor any conceived separation of the quality from the subject, seems more natural than the invention of nouns adjective, and which, upon this account, could hardly fail, in the first formation of language, to be thought of before them. This expedient is to make some variation upon the noun substantive itself, according to the different qualities which it is endowed with. Thus, in many languages, the qualities both of sex and of the want of sex, are expressed by different terminations in the nouns substantive, which denote objects so qualified. In Latin, for example, *lupus, lupa; equus, equa; juvencus, juvenca; Julius, Julia; Lucretius, Lucretia,* etc. denote the qualities of male and female in the animals and persons to whom such appellations belong, without needing the addition of any adjective for this purpose. On the other hand, the words *forum, pratum, Plaustrum,* denote by their peculiar termination the total absence of sex in the different substances which they stand for. Both sex, and the want of all sex, being naturally considered as qualities modifying and inseparable from the particular substances to which they belong, it was natural to express them rather by a modification in the noun substantive, than by any general and abstract word expressive of this particular species of quality. The expression bears, it is evident, in this way, a much more exact analogy to the idea or object which it denotes, than in the other. The quality appears, in nature, as a modification of the substance, and as it is thus expressed, in language, by a modification of the noun substantive, which denotes that substance, the quality and the subject are, in this case, blended together, if I may say so, in the expression, in the same manner as they appear to be in the object and in the idea. Hence the origin of the masculine, feminine, and neutral genders, in all the ancient languages. By means of these, the most important of all distinctions, that of substances into animated and inanimated, and that of animals into male and female, seem to have been sufficiently marked without the assistance of adjectives, or of any general names denoting this most extensive species of qualifications . . . .

It was impossible, however, that nouns substantive could, without losing altogether their original form, undergo so great a number of variations, as would be sufficient to express that almost infinite variety of qualities, by which it might, upon different occasions, be necessary to specify and distinguish them. Though the different formation of nouns substantive, therefore, might, for some time, forestall the necessity of inventing nouns adjective, it was impossible that this necessity could be forestalled altogether. When nouns adjective came to be invented, it was natural that they should be formed with some similarity to the substantives, to which they were to serve as epithets or qualifications. Men would naturally give them the same terminations with the substantives to which they were first applied, and from that love of similarity of sound, from that delight in the returns of the same syllables, which is the foundation of analogy in all languages, they would be apt to vary the termination of the same adjective, according as they had occasion to apply it to a masculine, to a feminine, or to a neutral substantive. They would say, *magnus lupus, magna lupa, magnum pratum,* when they meant to express a great *he wolf,* a great *she wolf,* a great *meadow.*

This variation, in the termination of the noun adjective, according to the gender of the substantive, which takes place in all the ancient languages, seems to have been introduced chiefly for the sake of a certain similarity of sound, of a certain species of rhyme, which is naturally so very agreeable to the human ear. Gender, it is to be observed, cannot properly belong to a noun adjective, the signification of which is always precisely the same, to whatever species of substantives it is applied. When we say, *a great man, a great woman,* the word *great* has precisely the same meaning in both cases, and the difference of the sex in the subjects to which it may be applied, makes no sort of difference in its signification. *Magnus, magna, magnum,* in the same manner, are words which express precisely the same quality, and the change of the termination is accompanied with no sort of variation in the meaning. Sex and gender are qualities which belong to substances, but cannot belong to the qualities of substances. In general, no quality, when considered in concrete, or as qualifying some particular subject, can itself be conceived as the subject of any other quality; though when considered in abstract it may. No adjective therefore can qualify any other adjective. A *great good man*, means a man who is both *great* and *good*. Both the adjectives qualify the substantive; they do not qualify one another. On the other hand, when we say, the *great goodness* of the man, the word *goodness* denoting a quality considered in abstract, which may itself be the subject of other qualities, is upon that account capable of being qualified by the word *great*.

If the original invention of nouns adjective would be attended with so much difficulty, that of prepositions would be accompanied with yet more. Every preposition, as I have already observed, denotes some relation considered in concrete with the co-relative object. The preposition *above*, for example, denotes the relation of superiority, not in abstract, as it is expressed by the word *superiority*, but in concrete with some co-relative object. In this phrase, for example, *the tree above the cave*, the word *above* expresses a certain relation between the *tree* and the *cave*, and it expresses this relation in concrete with the co-relative object, *the cave*. A preposition always requires, in order to complete the sense, some other word to come after it; as may be observed in this particular instance. Now, I say, the original invention of such words would require a yet greater effort of abstraction and generalization, than that of nouns adjective. First of all, a relation is, in itself, a more metaphysical object than a quality. Nobody can be at a loss to explain what is meant by a quality; but few people will find themselves able to express, very distinctly, what is understood by a relation. Qualities are almost always the objects of our external senses; relations never are. No wonder, therefore, that the one set of objects should be so much more comprehensible than the other. Secondly, though prepositions always express the relation which they stand for, in concrete with the co-relative object, they could not have originally been formed without a considerable effort of abstraction. A preposition denotes a relation, and nothing but a relation. But before men could institute a word, which signified a relation, and nothing but a relation, they must have been able, in some measure, to consider this relation abstractedly from the related objects; since the idea of those objects does not, in any respect, enter into the signification of the preposition. The invention of such a word, therefore, must have required a considerable degree of abstraction. Thirdly, a preposition is from its nature a general word, which, from its very first institution, must have been considered as equally applicable to denote any other similar relation. The man who first invented the word *above*, must not only have distinguished, in some measure, the relation of *superiority* from the objects which were so related, but he must also have distinguished this relation from other relations, such as, from the relation of *inferiority* denoted by the word *below,* from the relation of *juxtaposition,* expressed by the word *beside,* and the like. He must have conceived this word, therefore, as expressive of a particular sort or species of relation, distinct from every other, which could not be done without a considerable effort of comparison and generalization.

Whatever were the difficulties, therefore, which embarrassed the first invention of nouns adjective, the same, and many more, must have embarrassed that of prepositions. If mankind, therefore, in the first formation of languages, seem to have, for some time, evaded the necessity of nouns adjective, by varying the termination of the names of substances, according as these varied in some of their most important qualities, they would much more find themselves under the necessity of evading, by some similar contrivance, the yet more difficult invention of prepositions. The different cases in the ancient languages is a contrivance of precisely the same kind. The genitive and dative cases, in Greek and Latin, evidently supply the place of the prepositions; and by a variation in the noun substantive, which stands for the co-relative term, express the relation which subsists between what is denoted by that noun substantive, and what is expressed by some other word in the sentence. In these expressions, for example, *fructus arboris, the fruit of the tree; sacer Herculi, sacred to Hercules;* the variations made in the co-relative words, *arbor* and *Hercules,* express the same relations which are expressed in English by the prepositions *of* and *to*.

To express a relation in this manner, did not require any effort of abstraction. It was not here expressed by a peculiar word denoting relation and nothing but relation, but by a variation upon the co-relative term. It was expressed here, as it appears in nature, not as something separated and detached, but as thoroughly mixed and blended with the co-relative object.

To express relation in this manner, did not require any effort of generalization. The words *arboris* and *Herculi,* while they involve in their signification the same relation expressed by the English prepositions *of* and *to,* are not, like those prepositions, general words, which can be applied to express the same relation between whatever other objects it might be observed to subsist.

To express relation in this manner did not require any effort of comparison. The words *arboris* and *Herculi* are not general words intended to denote a particular species of relations which the inventors of those expressions meant, in consequence of some sort of comparison, to separate and distinguish from every other sort of relation. The example, indeed, of this contrivance would soon probably be followed, and whoever had occasion to express a similar relation between any other objects would be very apt to do it by making a similar variation on the name of the co-relative object. This, I say, would probably, or rather certainly happen; but it would happen without any intention or foresight in those who first set the example, and who never meant to establish any general rule. The general rule would establish itself insensibly, and by slow degrees, in consequence of that love of analogy and similarity of sound, which is the foundation of by far the greater part of the rules of grammar.

To express relation, therefore, by a variation in the name of the co-relative object, requiring neither abstraction, nor generalization, nor comparison of any kind, would, at first, be much more natural and easy, than to express it by those general words called prepositions, of which the first invention must have demanded some degree of all those operations . . . .

It is, perhaps, worth while to observe that those prepositions, which in modern languages hold the place of the ancient cases, are, of all others, the most general, and abstract, and metaphysical; and of consequence, would probably be the last invented. Ask any man of common acuteness, What relation is expressed by the preposition *above?* He will readily answer, that of *superiority*. By the preposition *below?* He will as quickly reply, that of *inferiority*. But ask him, what relation is expressed by the preposition *of,* and, if he has not beforehand employed his thoughts a good deal upon these subjects, you may safely allow him a week to consider of his answer. The prepositions *above* and *below* do not denote any of the relations expressed by the cases in the ancient languages. But the preposition *of,* denotes the same relation, which is in them expressed by the genitive case; and which, it is easy to observe, is of a very metaphysical nature. The preposition *of,* denotes relation in general, considered in concrete with the co-relative object. It marks that the noun substantive which goes before it, is somehow or other related to that which comes after it, but without in any respect ascertaining, as is done by the preposition *above,* what is the peculiar nature of that relation. We often apply it, therefore, to express the most opposite relations; because, the most opposite relations agree so far that each of them comprehends in it the general idea or nature of a relation. We say, *the father of the son,* and *the son of the father; the fir-trees of the forest,* and the *forest of the fir-trees.* The relation in which the father stands to the son, is, it is evident, a quite opposite relation to that in which the son stands to the father; that in which the parts stand to the whole, is quite opposite to that in which the whole stands to the parts. The word *of,* however, serves very well to denote all those relations, because in itself it denotes no particular relation, but only relation in general; and so far as any particular relation is collected from such expressions, it is inferred by the mind, not from the preposition itself, but from the nature and arrangement of the substantives, between which the preposition is placed . . . .

As men have frequently occasion to make mention of multitudes as well as of single objects, it became necessary that they should have some method of expressing number. Number may be expressed either by a particular word, expressing number in general, such as the words *many, more,* etc. or by some variation upon the words which express the things numbered. It is this last expedient which mankind would probably have recourse to, in the infancy of language. Number, considered in general, without relation to any particular set of objects numbered, is one of the most abstract and metaphysical ideas, which the mind of man is capable of forming; and, consequently, is not an idea, which would readily occur to rude mortals, who were just beginning to form a language. They would naturally, therefore, distinguish when they talked of a single, and when they talked of a multitude of objects, not by any metaphysical adjectives, such as the English *a, an, many,* but by a variation upon the termination of the word which signified the objects numbered. Hence the origin of the singular and plural numbers, in all the ancient languages; and the same distinction has likewise been retained in all the modern languages, at least, in the greater part of words . . . .

If the declensions of the ancient languages are so very complex, their conjugations are infinitely more so. And the complexness of the one is founded upon the same principle with that of the other, the difficulty of forming, in the beginnings of language, abstract and general terms.

Verbs must necessarily have been coeval with the very first attempts towards the formation of language. No affirmation can be expressed without the assistance of some verb. We never speak but in order to express our opinion that something either is or is not. But the word denoting this event, or this matter of fact, which is the subject of our affirmation, must always be a verb.

Impersonal verbs, which express in one word a complete event, which preserve in the expression that perfect simplicity and unity, which there always is in the object and in the idea, and which suppose no abstraction, or metaphysical division of the event into its several constituent members of subject and attribute, would, in all probability, be the species of verbs first invented. The verbs *pluit, it rains; ningit, it snows; tonat, it thunders; lucet, it is day; turbatur, there is a confusion,* etc. each of them express a complete affirmation, the whole of an event, with that perfect simplicity and unity with which the mind conceives it in nature. On the contrary, the phrases, *Alexander ambulat, Alexander walks; Petrus sedet, Peter sits,* divide the event, as it were, into two parts, the person or subject, and the attribute, or matter of fact, affirmed of that subject. But in nature, the idea or conception of Alexander walking, is as perfectly and completely one simple conception, as that of Alexander not walking. The division of this event, therefore, into two parts, is altogether artificial, and is the effect of the imperfection of language, which, upon this, as upon many other occasions, supplies, by a number of words, the want of one, which could express at once the whole matter of fact that was meant to be affirmed. Everybody must observe how much more simplicity there is in the natural expression, *pluit,* than in the more artificial expressions, *imber decidit, the rain falls,* or *tempestas est pluvia, the weather is rainy.* In these two last expressions, the simple event, or matter of fact, is artificially split and divided in the one, into two; in the other, into three parts.

In each of them it is expressed by a sort of grammatical circumlocution, of which the significancy is founded upon a certain metaphysical analysis of the component parts of the idea expressed by the word *pluit.* The first verbs, therefore, perhaps even the first words, made use of in the beginnings of language, would in all probability be such impersonal verbs. It is observed accordingly, I am told, by the Hebrew grammarians, that the radical words of their language, from which all the others are derived, are all of them verbs, and impersonal verbs.

It is easy to conceive how, in the progress of language, those impersonal verbs should become personal. Let us suppose, for example, that the word *venit, it comes,* was originally an impersonal verb, and that it denoted, not the coming of something in general, as at present, but the coming of a particular object, such as *the Lion.* The first savage inventors of language, we shall suppose, when they observed the approach of this terrible animal, were accustomed to cry out to one another, *venit,* that is, *the lion comes;* and that this word thus expressed a complete event, without the assistance of any other. Afterwards, when, on the further progress of language, they had begun to give names to particular substances, whenever they observed the approach of any other terrible object, they would naturally join the name of that object to the word *venit,* and cry out, *venit ursus, venit lupus.* By degrees the word *venit* would thus come to signify the coming of any terrible object, and not merely the coming of the lion. It would now, therefore, express, not the coming of a particular object, but the coming of an object of a particular kind. Having become more general in its signification, it could no longer represent any particular distinct event by itself, without the assistance of a noun substantive, which might serve to ascertain and determine its signification. It would now, therefore, have become a personal, instead of an impersonal verb. We may easily conceive how, in the further progress of society, it might still grow more general in its signification, and come to signify, as at present, the approach of anything whatever, whether good, bad, or indifferent.

It is probably in some such manner as this, that almost all verbs have become personal, and that mankind have learned by degrees to split and divide almost every event into a great number of metaphysical parts, expressed by the different parts of speech, variously combined in the different members of every phrase and sentence. The same sort of progress seems to have been made in the art of speaking as in the art of writing. When mankind first began to attempt to express their ideas by writing, every character represented a whole word. But the number of words being almost infinite, the memory found itself quite loaded and oppressed by the multitude of characters which it was obliged to retain. Necessity taught them, therefore, to divide words into their elements, and to invent characters which should represent, not the words themselves, but the elements of which they were composed. In consequence of this invention, every particular word came to be represented, not by one character, but by a multitude of characters; and the expression of it in writing became much more intricate and complex than before. But though particular words were thus represented by a greater number of characters, the whole language was expressed by a much smaller number, and about four and twenty letters were found capable of supplying the place of that immense multitude of characters, which were requisite before. In the same manner, in the beginnings of language, men seem to have attempted to express every particular event, which they had occasion to take notice of, by a particular word, which expressed at once the whole of that event. But as the number of words must, in this case, have become really infinite, in consequence of the really infinite variety of events, men found themselves partly compelled by necessity, and partly conducted by nature, to divide every event into what may be called its metaphysical elements, and to institute words, which should denote not so much the events, as the elements of which they were composed. The expression of every particular event, became in this manner more intricate and complex, but the whole system of the language became more coherent, more connected, more easily retained and comprehended.

When verbs, from being originally impersonal, had thus, by the division of the event into its metaphysical elements, become personal, it is natural to suppose that they would first be made use of in the third person singular. No verb is ever used impersonally in our language, nor, so far as I know, in any other modern tongue. But in the ancient languages, whenever any verb is used impersonally, it is always in the third person singular. The termination of those verbs, which are still always impersonal, is constantly the same with that of the third person singular of personal verbs. The consideration of these circumstances, joined to the naturalness of the thing itself, may serve to convince us that verbs first became personal in what is now called the third person singular.

But as the event, or matter of fact, which is expressed by a verb, may be affirmed either of the person who speaks, or of the person who is spoken to, as well as of some third person or object, it became necessary to fall upon some method of expressing these two peculiar relations of the event. In the English language this is commonly done, by prefixing, what are called the personal pronouns, to the general word which expresses the event affirmed. *I came, you came, he* or *it came;* in these phrases the event of having come is, in the first, affirmed of the speaker; in the second, of the person spoken to; in the third, of some other person, or object. The first formers of language, it may be imagined, might have done the same thing, and prefixing in the same manner the two first personal pronouns to the same termination of the verb, which expressed the third person singular, might have said *ego venit, tu venit,* as well as *ille* or *illud venit.* And I make no doubt but they would have done so, if at the time when they had first occasion to express these relations of the verb, there had been any such words as either *ego* or *tu* in their language. But in this early period of the language, which we are now endeavouring to describe, it is extremely improbable that any such words would be known. Though custom has now rendered them familiar to us, they, both of them, express ideas extremely metaphysical and abstract. The word *I,* for example, is a word of a very particular species. Whatever speaks may denote itself by this personal pronoun. The word *I,* therefore, is a general word, capable of being predicated, as the logicians say, of an infinite variety of objects. It differs, however, from all other general words in this respect; that the objects of which it may be predicated, do not form any particular species of objects distinguished from all others. The word *I,* does not, like the word *man,* denote a particular class of objects, separated from all others by peculiar qualities of their own. It is far from being the name of a species, but, on the contrary, whenever it is made use of, it always denotes a precise individual, the particular person who then speaks. It may be said to be, at once, both what the logicians call, a singular, and what they call, a common term; and to join in its signification the seemingly opposite qualities of the most precise individuality, and the most extensive generalization. This word, therefore, expressing so very abstract and metaphysical an idea, would not easily or readily occur to the first formers of language. What are called the personal pronouns, it may be observed, are among the last words of which children learn to make use. A child, speaking of itself, says, *Billy walks, Billy sits,* instead of *I walk, I sit.* As in the beginnings of language, therefore, mankind seem to have evaded the invention of at least the more abstract prepositions, and to have expressed the same relations which these *now* stand for, by varying the termination of the co-relative term, so they likewise would naturally attempt to evade the necessity of inventing those more abstract pronouns by varying the termination of the verb, according as the event which it expressed was intended to be affirmed of the first, second, or third person. This seems, accordingly, to be the universal practice of all the ancient languages. In Latin, *veni, venisti, venit,* sufficiently denote, without any other addition, the different events expressed by the English phrases, *I came, you came, he* or *it came.* The verb would, for the same reason, vary its termination, according as the event was intended to be affirmed of the first, second, or third persons plural; and what is expressed by the English phrases, *we came, ye came, they came,* would be denoted by the Latin words, *venimus, venistis, venerunt.* Those primitive languages, too, which, upon account of the difficulty of inventing numeral names, had introduced a dual, as well as a plural number, into the declension of their nouns substantive, would probably, from analogy, do the same thing in the conjugations of their verbs. And thus in all those original languages, we might expect to find, at least six, if not eight or nine variations, in the termination of every verb, according as the event which it denoted was meant to be affirmed of the first, second, or third persons singular, dual, or plural. These variations again being repeated, along with others, through all its different tenses, through all its different modes, and through all its different voices, must necessarily have rendered their conjugations still more intricate and complex than their declensions.

Language would probably have continued upon this footing in all countries, nor would ever have grown more simple in its declensions and conjugations, had it not become more complex in its composition, in consequence of the mixture of several languages with one another, occasioned by the mixture of different nations. As long as any language was spoke by those only who learned it in their infancy, the intricacy of its declensions and conjugations could occasion no great embarrassment. The far greater part of those who had occasion to speak it, had acquired it at so very early a period of their lives, so insensibly and by such slow degrees, that they were scarce ever sensible of the difficulty. But when two nations came to be mixed with one another, either by conquest or migration, the case would be very different. Each nation, in order to make itself intelligible to those with whom it was under the necessity of conversing; would be obliged to learn the language of the other. The greater part of individuals too, learning the new language, not by art or by remounting to its rudiments and first principles, but by rote, and by what they commonly heard in conversation, would be extremely perplexed by the intricacy of its declensions and conjugations. They would endeavour, therefore, to supply their ignorance of these, by whatever shift the language could afford them. Their ignorance of the declensions they would naturally supply by the use of prepositions; and a Lombard, who was attempting to speak Latin, and wanted to express that such a person was a citizen of Rome, or a benefactor to Rome, if he happened not to be acquainted with the genitive and dative cases of the word *Roma,* would naturally express himself by prefixing the prepositions *ad* and *de* to the nominative; and, instead of *Roma,* would say, *ad Roma,* and *de Roma. Al Roma* and *di Roma,* accordingly, is the manner in which the present Italians, the descendants of the ancient Lombards and Romans, express this and all other similar relations. And in this manner prepositions seem to have been introduced, in the room of the ancient declensions. . . .

A similar expedient enables men, in the situation above mentioned, to get rid of almost the whole intricacy of their conjugations. There is in every language a verb, known by the name of the substantive verb; in Latin, *sum;* in English, *I am.* This verb denotes not the existence of any particular event, but existence in general. It is, upon this account, the most abstract and metaphysical of all verbs; and, consequently, could by no means be a word of early invention. When it came to be invented, however, as it had all the tenses and modes of any other verb, by being joined with the passive participle, it was capable of supplying the place of the whole passive voice, and of rendering this part of their conjugations as simple and uniform, as the use of prepositions had rendered their declensions. A Lombard, who wanted to say, *I am loved,* but could not recollect the word *amor,* naturally endeavoured to supply his ignorance, by saying, *ego sum amatus. Io sono amato,* is at this day the Italian expression, which corresponds to the English phrase above mentioned . . . .

In general it may be laid down for a maxim, that the more simple any language is in its composition the more complex it must be in its declensions and conjugations; and, on the contrary, the more simple it is in its declensions and conjugations, the more complex it must be in its composition . . . .

The English is compounded of the French and the ancient Saxon languages. The French was introduced into Britain by the Norman conquest, and continued, till the time of Edward III to be the sole language of the law as well as the principal language of the court. The English, which came to be spoken afterwards, and which continues to be spoken now, is a mixture of the ancient Saxon and this Norman French. As the English language, therefore, is more complex in its composition than either the French or the Italian, so is it likewise more simple in its declensions and conjugations. Those two languages retain, at least, a part of the distinction of genders, and their adjectives vary their termination according as they are applied to a masculine or to a feminine substantive. But there is no such distinction in the English language, whose adjectives admit of no variety of termination. The French and Italian languages have, both of them, the remains of a conjugation; and all those tenses of the active voice, which cannot be expressed by the possessive verb joined to the passive participle, as well as many of those which can, are, in those languages, marked by varying the termination of the principal verb. But almost all those other tenses are in the English eked out by other auxiliary verbs, so that there is in this language scarce even the remains of a conjugation. *I love, I loved, loving,* are all the varieties of termination which the greater part of English verbs admit of. All the different modifications of meaning, which cannot be expressed by any of those three terminations, must be made out by different auxiliary verbs joined to some one or other of them. Two auxiliary verbs supply all the deficiencies of the French and Italian conjugations; it requires more than half a dozen to supply those of the English, which, besides the substantive and possessive verbs, makes use of *do, did; will, would; shall, should; can, could; may, might.*

It is in this manner that language becomes more simple in its rudiments and principles, just in proportion as it grows more complex in its composition, and the same thing has happened in it, which commonly happens with regard to mechanical engines. All machines are generally, when first invented, extremely complex in their principles, and there is often a particular principle of motion for every particular movement which it is intended they should perform. Succeeding improvers observe, that one principle may be so applied as to produce several of those movements; and thus the machine becomes gradually more and more simple, and produces its effects with fewer wheels, and fewer principles of motion. In language, in the same manner, every case of every noun, and every tense of every verb, was originally expressed by a particular distinct word, which served for this purpose and for no other. But succeeding observation discovered, that one set of words was capable of supplying the place of all that infinite number, and that four or five prepositions, and half a dozen auxiliary verbs, were capable of answering the end of all the declensions, and of all the conjugations in the ancient languages.

But this simplification of languages, though it arises, perhaps, from similar causes, has by no means similar effects with the correspondent simplification of machines. The simplification of machines renders them more and more perfect, but this simplification of the rudiments of languages renders them more and more imperfect, and less proper for many of the purposes of language: and this for the following reasons.

First of all, languages are by this simplification rendered more prolix, several words having become necessary to express what could have been expressed by a single word before. Thus the words, *Dei* and *Deo,* in the Latin, sufficiently show, without any addition, what relation the object signified is understood to stand in to the objects expressed by the other words in the sentence. But to express the same relation in English, and in all other modern languages, we must make use of, at least, two words, and say, *of God, to God.* So far as the declensions are concerned, therefore, the modern languages are much more prolix than the ancient. The difference is still greater with regard to the conjugations. What a Roman expressed by the single word, *amavissem,* an Englishman is obliged to express by four different words, *I should have loved.* It is unnecessary to take any pains to show how much this prolixness must enervate the eloquence of all modern languages. How much the beauty of any expression depends upon its conciseness, is well known to those who have any experience in composition.

Secondly, this simplification of the principles of languages renders them less agreeable to the ear. The variety of termination in the Greek and Latin, occasioned by their declensions and conjugations, gives a sweetness to their language altogether unknown to ours, and a variety unknown to any other modern language. In point of sweetness, the Italian, perhaps, may surpass the Latin, and almost equal the Greek; but in point of variety, it is greatly inferior to both.

Thirdly, this simplification, not only renders the sounds of our language less agreeable to the ear, but it also restrains us from disposing such sounds as we have, in the manner that might be most agreeable. It ties down many words to a particular situation, though they might often be placed in another with much more beauty. In the Greek and Latin, though the adjective and substantive were separated from one another, the correspondence of their terminations still showed their mutual reference, and the separation did not necessarily occasion any sort of confusion. Thus in the first line of Virgil,

> Tityre tu patulæ recubans sub tegmine fagi;

we easily see that *tu* refers to *recubans,* and *patulæ* to *fagi;* though the related words are separated from one another by the intervention of several others; because the terminations, showing the correspondence of their cases, determine their mutual reference. But if we were to translate this line literally into English, and say, *Tityrus, thou of spreading reclining under the shade beech.* Oedipus himself could not make sense of it; because there is here no difference of termination, to determine which substantive each adjective belongs to. It is the same case with regard to verbs. In Latin the verb may often be placed, without any inconveniency or ambiguity, in any part of the sentence. But in English its place is almost always precisely determined. It must follow the subjective and precede the objective member of the phrase in almost all cases. Thus in Latin whether you say, *Joannem verberavit Robertus,* or *Robertus verberavit Joannem,* the meaning is precisely the same, and the termination fixes John to be the sufferer in both cases. But in English *John beat Robert,* and *Robert beat John,* have by no means the same signification. The place therefore of the three principal members of the phrase is in the English, and for the same reason in the French and Italian languages, almost always precisely determined; whereas in the ancient languages a greater latitude is allowed, and the place of those members is often, in a great measure, indifferent. We must have recourse to Horace, in order to interpret some parts of Milton's literal translation;

> Who now enjoys thee credulous all gold,
> Who always vacant, always amiable
> Hopes thee; of flattering gales
> Unmindful —

are verses which it is impossible to interpret by any rules of our language. There are no rules in our language, by which any man could discover, that, in the first line, *credulous* referred to *who,* and not to *thee;* or that *all gold* referred to any thing; or, that in the fourth line, *unmindful,* referred to *who,* in the second, and not to *thee* in the third; or, on the contrary, that, in the second line, *always vacant, always amiable,* referred to *thee* in the third, and not to *who* in the same line with it. In the Latin, indeed, all this is abundantly plain.

> Qui nunc te fruitur credulus aurea,
> Qui semper vacuam, semper amabilem
> Sperat te; nescius auræ fallacis.

Because the terminations in the Latin determine the reference of each adjective to its proper substantive, which it is impossible for any thing in the English to do: How much this power of transposing the order of their words must have facilitated the composition of the ancients, both in verse and prose, can hardly be imagined. That it must greatly have facilitated their versification it is needless to observe; and in prose, whatever beauty depends upon the arrangement and construction of the several members of the period, must to them have been acquirable with much more ease, and to much greater perfection, than it can be to those whose expression is constantly confined by the prolixness, constraint, and monotony of modern languages.

READING II

A Letter to the Authors of *The Edinburgh Review*[3]

Gentlemen,

It gives me pleasure to see a work so generally useful, as that which you have undertaken, likely to be so well executed in this country. I am afraid, however, you will find it impossible to support it with any degree of spirit, while you confine yourselves almost entirely to an account of the books published in Scotland. This country, which is but just beginning to attempt figuring in the learned world, produces as yet so few works of reputation, that it is scarce possible a paper which criticizes upon them chiefly, should interest the public for any considerable time. The singular absurdity of some performances which you have so well represented in your first number, might divert your readers for once: But no eloquence could support a paper which consisted chiefly of accounts of such performances.

It is upon this account, that I take upon me, in the name of several of your readers, to propose to you, that you should enlarge your plan; that you should still continue to take notice, with the same humanity and candour, of every Scotch production that is tolerably decent. But that you should observe with regard to Europe in general the same plan which you followed with regard to England, examining such performances only, as, though they may not go down to the remotest posterity, have yet a chance of being remembered for thirty or forty years to come, and seem in the meantime to add something to that stock of literary amusement with which the world is at present provided. You will thus be able to give all proper encouragement to such efforts as this country is likely to make towards acquiring a reputation in the learned world, which I imagine it was the well-natured design of your work to support; and you will oblige the public much more, by giving them an account of such books as are worthy of their regard, than by filling your paper with all the insignificant literary news of the times, of which not an article in a hundred is likely to be thought of a fortnight after the publication of the work that gave occasion to it.

Nor will this task be so very laborious as at first one might be apt to imagine. For though learning is cultivated in some degree in almost

[3] [This letter appeared in the March 1756 edition of the *Edinburgh Review*.]

every part of Europe, it is in France and England only that it is cultivated with such success or reputation as to excite the attention of foreign nations. In Italy, the country in which it was first revived, it has been almost totally extinguished. In Spain, the country in which, after Italy, the first dawnings of modern genius appeared, it has been extinguished altogether. Even the art of printing seems to have been almost neglected in those two countries, from the little demand, I suppose, which there was for books: and though it has of late been revived in Italy, yet the expensive editions which have been published there of the Italian classics are plainly calculated for the libraries of Princes and monasteries, not to answer the demand of private persons. The Germans have never cultivated their own language; and while the learned accustom themselves to think and write in a language different from their own, it is scarce possible that they should either think or write, upon any delicate or nice subject, with happiness and precision. In medicine, chemistry, astronomy, and mathematics, sciences which require only plain judgment joined to labour and assiduity, without demanding a great deal of what is called either taste or genius; the Germans have been, and still continue to be successful. The works of the Academies, indeed, both in Germany and Italy, and even in Russia, are the objects of some curiosity everywhere; but it is seldom that the works of any particular man are inquired for out of his own country. On the contrary, the works of many particular men both in France and England are more inquired for among foreign nations than those of any of their academies.

If we may pass any general judgment concerning the literary merit of those two great rivals in learning, trade, government and war: Imagination, genius and invention, seem to be the talents of the English; taste, judgment, propriety and order, of the French. In the old English poets, in Shakespeare, Spencer and Milton, there often appears, amidst some irregularities and extravagancies, a strength of imagination so vast, so gigantic and supernatural, as astonishes and confounds their reader into that admiration of their genius, which makes him despise, as mean and insignificant, all criticism upon the inequalities in their writings. In the eminent French writers, such sallies of genius are more rarely to be met with; but instead of them, a just arrangement, an exact propriety and decorum, joined to an equal and studied elegance of sentiment and diction, which, as it never strikes the heart like those violent and momentary flashes of imagination, so it never revolts the judgment by any thing that is absurd or unnatural, nor ever wearies the attention by any gross inequality in the style, or want of connection in the method, but entertains the mind with a regular succession of agreeable, interesting and connected objects.

In natural philosophy, the science which in modern times has been most happily cultivated, almost all the great discoveries, which have not come from Italy or Germany, have been made in England. France has scarce produced anything very considerable in that way. When that science was first revived in Europe, a fanciful, an ingenious and elegant, though fallacious, system was generally embraced in that country: nor can we with reason wonder that it was so. It may well be said of the Cartesian philosophy,[4] now when it is almost universally exploded, that, in the simplicity, precision and perspicuity of its principles and conclusions, it had the same superiority over the Peripatetic system, which the Newtonian philosophy has over it. A philosophy, which, upon its first appearance, had so many advantages over its rival system, was regarded by the French with peculiar fondness and admiration, when they considered it as the production of their own countryman, whose renown added new glory to their nation; and their attachment to it seems among them to have retarded and encumbered the real advancement of the science of nature. They seem now however to be pretty generally disengaged from the enchantment of that illusive philosophy; and it is with pleasure that I observe in the new French Encyclopaedia the ideas of Bacon, Boyle,[5] and Newton, explained with that order, perspicuity and good judgment, which distinguish all the eminent writers of that nation. As, since the union, we are apt to regard ourselves in some measure as the countrymen of those great men, it flattered my vanity, as a Briton, to observe the superiority of the English philosophy thus acknowledged by their rival nation. The two principal authors of that vast collection of every sort of literature, Mr Diderot and Mr Alembert,[6] express everywhere the greatest passion for the science and learning of England, and insert into their work not only the discoveries and observations of those renowned philosophers I just now mentioned, but of many inferior English writers, whose names are now almost unknown, and whose works have been long disregarded in their own country. It mortified me, at the same time, to consider that posterity and foreign nations are more likely to be made acquainted with the English philosophy by the writings of others, than by those of the English themselves. It seems to be the peculiar talent of the French nation, to arrange every subject in that natural and simple order, which carries the attention, without any effort, along with it. The English seem to have employed themselves entirely in inventing, and to have disdained the more inglorious but not less useful labour of arranging and methodizing their discoveries, and of expressing them in the most simple and natural manner. There is not only no tolerable system of natural philosophy in the English language, but there is not even any tolerable system of any part of it. The Latin treatises of Keill and Gregory,[7] two Scotsmen, upon the principles of mechanics and astronomy, may be regarded as the best things that have been written in this way by any native of Great Britain, though in many

[4] [That is, of René Descartes (1596–1650).]
[5] [Francis Bacon (1561–1626) and Robert Boyle (1627–91).]
[6] [Denis Diderot (1713–84) and Jean le Rond d'Alembert (1717–83).]
[7] [John Keill (1671–1721) and David Gregory (1661–1708).]

respects confused, inaccurate and superficial. In Dr Smith's Optics,[8] all the great discoveries which had before been made in that science are very completely recorded, along with many considerable corrections and improvements by that Gentleman himself. But if, in the knowledge of his science, he appears much superior to the two Scotsmen above mentioned, he is inferior even to them, who are far from being perfect, in the order and disposition of his work. It will not I hope be imputed to any mean motive, that I take notice of this fault, which in these subjects is not of the highest importance, and which that Gentleman himself would, I dare say, be willing to acknowledge; for whose knowledge and capacity I have the highest esteem, whose book has every other quality to recommend it, and who is himself, along with Dr Bradley,[9] almost the only person now remaining in England to put us in mind of their illustrious predecessors. The learned world has been highly instructed by the labours and ingenuity of both these Gentlemen, and I will venture to say would have been much more so, if in their own country they had had more rivals and more judges. But the English of the present age, despairing perhaps to surpass the inventions, or to equal the renown of their forefathers, have disdained to hold the second place in a science in which they could not arrive at the first, and seem to have abandoned the study of it altogether.

The French work which I just now mentioned, promises to be the most complete of the kind which has ever been published or attempted in any language. It will consist of many volumes in folio, illustrated with above six hundred plates, which make two volumes apart. There are above twenty Gentlemen engaged in it, all of them very eminent in their several professions, and many of them already known to foreign nations by the valuable works which they have published, particularly Mr Alembert, Mr Diderot, Mr Daubenton,[10] Mr Rousseau of Geneva, Mr Formey Secretary to the academy at Berlin,[11] and many others. In the preliminary discourse, Mr Alembert gives an account of the connection of the different arts and sciences, their genealogy and filiation as he calls it; which, a few alterations and corrections excepted, is nearly the same with that of my Lord Bacon. In the body of the work, it is constantly marked, to what art or science, and to what branch of that art or science each particular article belongs. In the articles themselves, the reader will not find, as in other works of the same kind, a dry abstract of what is commonly known by the most superficial student of any science, but a complete, reasoned and even critical examination of each subject. Scarce anything seems to be omitted. Not only mathematics, natural philosophy and natural history, which commonly fill up the greater part of

[8] [Robert Smith (1689–1768).]
[9] [James Bradley (1693–1762).]
[10] [Louis-Jean-Marie Daubenton (1716–1800).]
[11] [Jean-Henri-Samuel Formey (1711–97).]

works of this kind, are completely treated of; but all the mechanical arts are fully described, with the several machines which they make use of. Theology, morals, metaphysics, the art of criticism, the history of the *belles lettres,* philosophy, the literary history of sects, opinions and systems of all kinds, the chief doctrines of ancient and modern jurisprudence, nay all the nicest subtleties of grammar, are explained in a detail that is altogether surprising. There are few men so learned in the science which they have peculiarly cultivated, as not to find in this work something even with regard to it which will both instruct and entertain them; and with regard to every other, they will seldom fail of finding all the satisfaction which they could desire. It promises indeed to be in every respect worthy of that magnificent eulogy which Mr Voltaire[12] bestows upon it, when, in the conclusion of his account of the artists who lived in the time of Louis the Fourteenth, he tells us, 'That the last age has put the present in which we live in a condition to assemble into one body, and to transmit to posterity, to be by them delivered down to remoter ages, the sacred repository of all the arts and all the sciences, all of them pushed as far as human industry can go'. This, continues he, 'is what a society of learned men, fraught with genius and knowledge, are now labouring upon: an immense and immortal work, which seems to accuse the shortness of human life'.

This work, which has several times been disagreeably interrupted by some jealousy either of the civil or of the ecclesiastical government of France, to neither of which however the authors seem to have given any just occasion of suspicion, is not yet finished. The volumes of it which are yet to be published, will deserve, as they successively appear, to be particularly taken notice of in your future periodical reviews. You will observe, that though none of the authors of this collection appear to be mean or contemptible, yet they are not all equal. That the style of some of them is more declamatory, than is proper for a Dictionary; in which not only declamation, but any loose composition, is, more than anywhere, out of its place. That they seem too to have inserted some articles which might have been left out, and of which the insertion can serve only to throw a ridicule upon a work calculated for the propagation of every part of useful knowledge. The article of *Amour,* for example, will tend little to the edification either of the learned or unlearned reader, and might, one should think, have been omitted even in an Encyclopaedia of all arts, sciences and trades. These censures however fall but upon a few articles, and those of no great importance. The remaining parts of the work may give occasion to many other observations of more consequence, upon the candour or partiality with which they represent the different systems of philosophy or theology, ancient or modern; the justness of their criticisms upon the celebrated authors of their own and of foreign nations; how far they have observed or neglected the just pro-

[12] [François-Marie Arouet, pen name Voltaire (1694–1778).]

portion betwixt the length of each article and the importance of the matter contained in it, and its fitness to be explained in a work of that kind; as well as many other observations of the same nature.

Nor is this the only great collection of science and literature at present carrying on in that country, to merit the attention of foreign nations. The description of the cabinet of the King, which promises to comprehend a complete system of natural history, is a work almost equally extensive. It was begun by the command of a minister whom France has long desired to see restored to the direction of the marine, and all Europe to that of the sciences, the Count de Maurepas. It is executed by two Gentlemen of most universally acknowledged merit, Mr Buffon[13] and Mr Daubenton. A small part only of this work is yet published. The reasoning and philosophical part concerning the formation of plants, the generation of animals, the formation of the foetus, the development of the senses *etc.* is by Mr Buffon. The system indeed of this Gentleman, it may be thought, is almost entirely hypothetical; and with regard to the causes of generation such, that it is scarce possible to form any very determinate idea of it. It must be acknowledged, however, that it is explained in an agreeable, copious, and natural eloquence, and that he has supported or connected it with many singular and curious observations and experiments of his own. The neatness, distinctness and propriety of all Mr Daubenton's descriptions, seem to leave no room for criticism upon his part, which, though the least pompous, is by far the most important of the work.

None of the sciences indeed seem to be cultivated in France with more eagerness than natural history. Perspicuous description and just arrangement constitute a great part of the merit of a natural historian; and this study is perhaps upon that account peculiarly suited to the genius of that nation. In Mr Reaumur's[14] history of insects, a work of which we are still to expect some volumes, your readers will find both these in the highest perfection, as well as the most attentive observation assisted by the most artful contrivances for inspecting into such things in the economy and management of those little animals, as one would have imagined it impossible that he ever should have discovered. Those who complain of his tediousness, have never entered regularly upon his work, but have contented themselves with dipping into some parts of it. As mean as the subject may appear, he never fails to carry our attention along with him, and we follow him through all his observations and experiments with the same innocent curiosity and simple-hearted pleasure with which he appears to have made them. It will surprise your readers to find, that this Gentleman, amidst many other laborious studies and occupations, while he was composing, from his own experiments too, many other curious and valuable works, could find time to fill eight volumes in quarto with his own observations upon this subject,

[13] [Georges-Louis Leclerc, Comte de Buffon (1707–78).]
[14] [René Antoine Ferchault de Réaumur (1683–1757).]

without ever once having recourse to the vain parade of erudition and quotation. These, and all other such works as these, which either seem to add something to the public stock of observations, if I may say so, or which collect more completely, or arrange in a better order, the observations that have already been made, the public will be pleased to see pointed out to them in your periodical *Review*, and will listen with attention to your criticisms upon the defects and perfections of what so well deserves to be criticized in general. As the works of all the academies in the different parts of Europe, are the objects of a pretty universal curiosity, though it would be impossible for you to give an account of everything that is contained in them; it will not be very difficult to point out what are the most considerable improvements and observations which those societies have communicated to the public during the six months which precede the publication of every *Review*.

The original and inventive genius of the English has not only discovered itself in natural philosophy, but in morals, metaphysics, and part of the abstract sciences. Whatever attempts have been made in modern times towards improvement in this contentious and unprosperous philosophy, beyond what the ancients have left us, have been made in England. The Meditations of Descartes excepted, I know nothing in French that aims at being original upon these subjects; for the philosophy of Mr Regis, as well as that of Father Malbranche,[15] are but refinements upon the Meditations of Descartes. But Mr Hobbes, Mr Locke, and Dr Mandeville, Lord Shaftsbury, Dr Butler, Dr Clarke, and Mr Hutcheson,[16] have all of them, according to their different and inconsistent systems, endeavoured at least to be, in some measure, original; and to add something to that stock of observations with which the world had been furnished before them. This branch of the English philosophy, which seems now to be entirely neglected by the English themselves, has of late been transported into France. I observe some traces of it, not only in the Encyclopaedia, but in the Theory of agreeable sentiments by Mr De Pouilly,[17] a work that is in many respects original; and above all, in the late Discourse upon the origin and foundation of the inequality amongst mankind by Mr Rousseau of Geneva.

Whoever reads this last work with attention, will observe, that the second volume of the *Fable of the Bees* has given occasion to the system of Mr Rousseau, in whom however the principles of the English author are softened, improved, and embellished, and stripped of all that tendency to corruption and licentiousness which has disgraced them in their original author. Dr Mandeville represents the primitive state of mankind as

[15] [Pierre-Sylvain Régis (1632–1707) and Nicolas Malebranche (1638–1715).]

[16] [Thomas Hobbes (1588–1679); John Locke (1632–1704); Bernard Mandeville (1670–1733); Anthony Ashley Cooper, Third Earl of Shaftesbury (1671–1713); Joseph Butler, Bishop of Durham (1692–1752); Samuel Clarke (1675–1729); and Francis Hutcheson (1694–1746).]

[17] [Lévesque de Pouilly (1692–1785).]

the most wretched and miserable that can be imagined: Mr. Rousseau, on the contrary, paints it as the happiest and most suitable to his nature. Both of them however suppose, that there is in man no powerful instinct which necessarily determines him to seek society for its own sake; but according to the one, the misery of his original state compelled him to have recourse to this otherwise disagreeable remedy; according to the other, some unfortunate accidents having given birth to the unnatural passions of ambition and the vain desire of superiority, to which he had before been a stranger, produced the same fatal effect. Both of them suppose the same slow progress and gradual development of all the talents, habits, and arts which fit men to live together in society, and they both describe this progress pretty much in the same manner. According to both, those laws of justice, which maintain the present inequality amongst mankind, were originally the inventions of the cunning and the powerful, in order to maintain or to acquire an unnatural and unjust superiority over the rest of their fellow-creatures. Mr Rousseau however criticizes upon Dr Mandeville: he observes, that *pity,* the only amiable principle which the English author allows to be natural to man, is capable of producing all those virtues, whose reality Dr Mandeville denies. Mr Rousseau at the same time seems to think, that this principle is in itself no virtue, but that it is possessed by savages and by the most profligate of the vulgar, in a greater degree of perfection than by those of the most polished and cultivated manners; in which he perfectly agrees with the English author.

The life of a savage, when we take a distant view of it, seems to be a life either of profound indolence, or of great and astonishing adventures; and both these qualities serve to render the description of it agreeable to the imagination. The passion of all young people for pastoral poetry, which describes the amusements of the indolent life of a shepherd; and for books of chivalry and romance, which describe the most dangerous and extravagant adventures, is the effect of this natural taste for these two seemingly inconsistent objects. In the descriptions of the manners of savages, we expect to meet with both these: and no author ever proposed to treat of this subject who did not excite the public curiosity. Mr Rousseau, intending to paint the savage life as the happiest of any, presents only the indolent side of it to view, which he exhibits indeed with the most beautiful and agreeable colours, in a style, which, though laboured and studiously elegant, is everywhere sufficiently nervous, and sometimes even sublime and pathetic. It is by the help of this style, together with a little philosophical chemistry, that the principles and ideas of the profligate Mandeville seem in him to have all the purity and sublimity of the morals of Plato, and to be only the true spirit of a republican carried a little too far. His work is divided into two parts: in the first, he describes the solitary state of mankind; in the second, the first beginnings and gradual progress of society. It would be to no purpose to give an analysis of either; for none could give any just idea of a work which consists almost entirely of rhetoric and description . . . .

I shall only add, that the dedication to the republic of Geneva, of which Mr Rousseau has the honour of being a citizen, is an agreeable, animated, and I believe too, a just panegyric; and expresses that ardent and passionate esteem which it becomes a good citizen to entertain for the government of his country and the character of his countrymen.

It is not my intention, you may believe, to confine you to an account of the philosophical works that are published either at home or abroad. Though the poets of the present age seem in general to be inferior to those of the last, there are not however wanting, in England, France, and even in Italy, several who represent not unworthily their more renowned predecessors. The works of Metastasio[18] are esteemed all over Europe; and Mr Voltaire, the most universal genius perhaps which France has ever produced, is acknowledged to be, in almost every species of writing, nearly upon a level with the greatest authors of the last age, who applied themselves chiefly to one. The original and inventive genius of that Gentleman never appeared more conspicuous than in his last tragedy, the orphan of China. It is both agreeable and surprising to observe how the atrocity, if I may say so, of Chinese virtue, and the rudeness of Tartar barbarity, have been introduced upon the French stage, without violating those nice decorums of which that nation are such delicate and scrupulous judges. In a letter to Mr Rousseau of Geneva, he denies that the history of the last war, which has been published under his name in Holland, is to be regarded as his in the state in which it has been printed. There are indeed in it a great number of very gross misrepresentations with regard to the share which Great Britain had in the last war, for which, Mr. Voltaire, as it was published without his consent, is not answerable, and which will certainly be corrected in the first genuine edition that is published with the consent of the author.

I am,
Your most humble Servant, etc.

---

[18] [Pietro Trapassi, assumed name Metastasio (1698–1782).]

Four

History and Philosophy of Science

The Principles which Lead and Direct Philosophical Enquiries; Illustrated by the History of Astronomy[1]

Wonder, Surprise, and Admiration, are words which, though often confounded, denote, in our language, sentiments that are indeed allied, but that are in some respects different also, and distinct from one another. What is new and singular, excites that sentiment which, in strict propriety, is called Wonder; what is unexpected, Surprise; and what is great or beautiful, Admiration.

We wonder at all extraordinary and uncommon objects, at all the rarer phenomena of nature, at meteors, comets, eclipses, at singular plants and animals, and at every thing, in short, with which we have before been either a little or not at all acquainted; and we still wonder, though forewarned of what we are to see.

We are surprised at those things which we have seen often, but which we least of all expected to meet with in the place where we find them; we are surprised at the sudden appearance of a friend, whom we have seen a thousand times, but whom we did not imagine we were to see then.

We admire the beauty of a plain or the greatness of a mountain, though we have seen both often before, and though nothing appears to us in either, but what we had expected with certainty to see.

Whether this criticism upon the precise meaning of these words be just, is of little importance. I imagine it is just, though I acknowledge, that the best writers in our language have not always made use of them according to it.... All that I contend for is, that the sentiments excited by what is new, by what is unexpected, and by what is great and beautiful,

[1] This essay was published posthumously together with several other of Smith's remaining unpublished essays in a collection entitled *Essays on Philosophical Subjects* (London and Edinburgh, 1795). Smith probably worked on this essay over a period of many years, beginning perhaps as early as the late 1740s.

are really different, however the words made use of to express them may sometimes be confounded. Even the admiration which is excited by beauty, is quite different (as will appear more fully hereafter) from that which is inspired by greatness, though we have but one word to denote them.

These sentiments, like all others when inspired by one and the same object, mutually support and enliven one another: an object with which we are quite familiar, and which we see every day, produces, though both great and beautiful, but a small effect upon us; because our admiration is not supported either by Wonder or by Surprise: and if we have heard a very accurate description of a monster, our Wonder will be the less when we see it; because our previous knowledge of it will in a great measure prevent our Surprise . . . .

Of the Effect of Unexpectedness, or of Surprise

When an object of any kind, which has been for some time expected and foreseen, presents itself, whatever be the emotion which it is by nature fitted to excite, the mind must have been prepared for it, and must have in some measure have conceived it before-hand; because the idea of the object having been so long present to it, must have before-hand excited some degree of the same emotion which the object itself would excite: the change, therefore, which its presence produces comes thus to be less considerable, and the emotion or passion which it excites glides gradually and easily into the heart, without violence, pain, or difficulty.

But the contrary of all this happens when the object is unexpected; the passion is then poured in all at once upon the heart, which is thrown, if it is a strong passion, into the most violent and convulsive emotions, such as sometimes cause immediate death; sometimes, by the suddenness of the ecstasy, so entirely disjoint the whole frame of the imagination, that it never after returns to its former tone and composure, but falls either into a frenzy or habitual lunacy; and such as almost always occasion a momentary loss of reason, or of that attention to other things which our situation or our duty requires.

How much we dread the effects of the more violent passions, when they come suddenly upon the mind, appears from those preparations which all men think necessary when going to inform any one of what is capable of exciting them. Who would choose all at once to inform his friend of an extraordinary calamity that had befallen him, without taking care before-hand, by alarming him with an uncertain fear, to announce, if one may say so, his misfortune, and thereby prepare and dispose him for receiving the tidings?

Those panic terrors which sometimes seize armies in the field, or great cities, when an enemy is in the neighbourhood, and which deprive for a time the most determined of all deliberate judgments, are never excited but by the sudden apprehension of unexpected danger. Such violent consternations, which at once confound whole multitudes, benumb their understandings, and agitate their hearts, with all agony of extravagant fear, can never be produced by any foreseen danger, how great forever. Fear, though naturally a very strong passion, never rises to such excesses, unless exasperated both by Wonder, from the uncertain nature of the danger, and by Surprise, from the suddenness of the apprehension.

Surprise, therefore, is not to be regarded as an original emotion of a species distinct from all others. The violent and sudden change produced upon the mind, when an emotion of any kind is brought suddenly upon it, constitutes the whole nature of Surprise.

But when not only a passion and a great passion comes all at once upon the mind, but when it comes upon it while the mind is in the mood most unfit for conceiving it, the Surprise is then the greatest. Surprises of joy when the mind is sunk into grief, or of grief when it is elated with joy, are therefore the most unsupportable. The change is in this case the greatest possible. Not only a strong passion is conceived all at once, but a strong passion the direct opposite of that which was before in possession of the soul. When a load of sorrow comes down upon the heart that is expanded and elated with gaiety and joy, it seems not only to damp and oppress it, but almost to crush and bruise it, as a real weight would crush and bruise the body. On the contrary, when from an unexpected change of fortune, a tide of gladness seems, if I may say so, to spring up all at once within it, when depressed and contracted with grief and sorrow, it feels as if suddenly extended and heaved up with violent and irresistible force, and is torn with pangs of all others most exquisite, and which almost always occasion faintings, deliriums, and sometimes instant death. For it may be worth while to observe, that though grief be a more violent passion than joy, as indeed all uneasy sensations seem naturally more pungent than the opposite agreeable ones, yet of the two, Surprises of joy are still more insupportable than Surprises of grief. We are told that after the battle of Thrasimenus, while a Roman lady, who had been informed that her son was slain in the action, was sitting alone bemoaning her misfortunes, the young man who escaped came suddenly into the room to her, and that she cried out and expired instantly in a transport of joy. Let us suppose the contrary of this to have happened, and that in the midst of domestic festivity and mirth, he had suddenly fallen down dead at her feet, is it likely that the effects would have been equally violent? I imagine not. The heart springs to joy with a sort of natural elasticity, it abandons itself to so agreeable an emotion, as soon as the object is presented; it seems to pant and leap forward to meet it, and the passion in its full force takes at once entire and complete possession of the soul. But it is otherways with grief; the heart recoils from, and resists the first approaches of that disagreeable passion, and it requires some time before the melancholy object can produce its full effect. Grief comes on slowly and gradually, nor ever rises at once to that height of agony to which it increased after a little time. But joy comes rushing upon us all at once like a torrent. The change produced therefore by a Surprise of joy is more sudden, and upon that account more violent and apt to have more fatal effects, than that which is occasioned by a Surprise of grief; there seems to be something in the nature of Surprise, which makes it unite more easily with the brisk and quick motion of joy, than with the slower and heavier movement of grief. Most men who can take the trouble to recollect, will find that they have heard of more people who died or became distracted with sudden joy, than with sudden grief. Yet from the nature of human affairs, the latter must be much more frequent than the former. A man may break his leg, or lose his son, though he has had no warning of either of these events, but he can hardly meet with an extraordinary piece of good fortune, without having had some foresight of what was to happen.

Not only grief and joy but all other passions, are more violent, when opposite extremes succeed each other. Is any resentment so keen as what follows the quarrels of lovers, or any love so passionate as what attends their reconcilement?

Even the objects of the external senses affect us in a more lively manner, when opposite extremes succeed to, or are placed beside each other. Moderate warmth seems intolerable heat if felt after extreme cold. What is bitter will seem more so when tasted after what is very sweet; a dirty white will seem bright and pure when placed by a jet black. The vivacity in short of every sensation, as well as of every sentiment, seems to be greater or less in proportion to the change made by the impression of either upon the situation of the mind or organ; but this change must necessarily be the greatest when opposite sentiments and sensations are contrasted, or succeed immediately to one another. Both sentiments and sensations are then the liveliest; and this superior vivacity proceeds from nothing but their being brought upon the mind or organ when in a state most unfit for conceiving them.

As the opposition of contrasted sentiments heightens their vivacity, so the resemblance of those which immediately succeed each other renders them more faint and languid. A parent who has lost several children immediately after one another, will be less affected with the death of the last than with that of the first, though the loss in itself be, in this case, undoubtedly greater; but his mind being altogether sunk into sorrow, the new misfortune seems to produce no other effect than a continuance of the same melancholy, and is by no means apt to occasion such transports of grief as are ordinarily excited by the first calamity of the kind; he receives it, though with great dejection, yet with some degree of calmness and composure, and without any thing of that anguish and agitation of mind which the novelty of the misfortune is apt to occasion. Those who have been unfortunate through the whole course of their lives are often indeed habitually melancholy, and sometimes peevish and splenetic, yet upon any fresh disappointment, though they are vexed and complain a little, they seldom fly out into any more violent passion, and never fall into those transports of rage and grief which often, upon the like occasions, distract the fortunate and successful.

Upon this are founded, in a great measure, some of the effects of habit and custom. It is well known that custom deadens the vivacity of both pain and pleasure, abates the grief we should feel for the one, and weakens the joy we should derive from the other. The pain is supported without agony, and pleasure enjoyed without rapture: because custom and the frequent repetition of any object comes at last to form and bend the mind or organ to that habitual mood and disposition which fits them to receive its impression, without undergoing any very violent change.

Of Wonder, or of the Effects of Novelty

It is evident that the mind takes pleasure in observing the resemblances that are discoverable betwixt different objects. It is by means of such observation that it endeavours to arrange and methodize all its ideas, and to reduce them into proper classes and assortments. Where it can observe but one single quality, that is common to a great variety of otherwise widely different objects, that single circumstance will be sufficient for it to connect them all together, to reduce them to one common class, and to call them by one general name. It is thus that all things endowed with a power of self-motion, beasts, birds, fishes, insects, are classed under the general name of Animal; that these again, along with those which want that power, are arranged under the still more general word Substance: and this is the origin of those assortments of objects and ideas which in the schools are called Genera and Species, and of those abstract and general names, which in all languages are made use of to express them.

The further we advance in knowledge and experience, the greater number of divisions and subdivisions of those Genera and Species we are both inclined and obliged to make. We observe a greater variety of particularities amongst those things which have a gross resemblance; and having made new divisions of them, according to those newly-observed particularities, we are then no longer to be satisfied with being able to refer an object to a remote genus, or very general class of things, to many of which it has but a loose and imperfect resemblance. A person, indeed, unacquainted with botany may expect to satisfy your curiosity, by telling you, that such a vegetable is a weed, or, perhaps in still more general terms, that it is a plant. But a botanist will neither give nor accept of such an answer. He has broke and divided that great class of objects into a number of inferior assortments, according to those varieties which his experience has discovered among them; and he wants to refer each individual plant to some tribe of vegetables, with all of which it may have a more exact resemblance, than with many things comprehended under the extensive genus of plants. A child imagines that it gives a satisfactory answer when it tells you, that an object whose name it knows not is a thing, and fancies that it informs you of something, when it thus ascertains to which of the two most obvious and comprehensive classes of objects a particular impression ought to be referred; to the class of realities or solid substances which it calls *things*, or to that of appearances which it calls *nothings*.

Whatever, in short, occurs to us we are fond of referring to some species or class of things, with all of which it has a nearly exact resemblance; and though we often know more about them than about it, yet we are apt to fancy that by being able to do so, we show ourselves to be better acquainted with it, and to have a more thorough insight into its nature. But when something quite new and singular is presented, we feel ourselves incapable of doing this. The memory cannot, from all its stores, cast up any image that nearly resembles this strange appearance. If by some of its qualities it seems to resemble, and to be connected with a species which we have before been acquainted with, it is by others separated and detached from that, and from all the other assortments of things we have hitherto been able to make. It stands alone and by itself in the imagination, and refuses to be grouped or confounded with any set of objects whatever. The imagination and memory exert themselves to no purpose, and in vain look around all their classes of ideas in order to find one under which it may be arranged. They fluctuate to no purpose from thought to thought, and we remain still uncertain and undetermined where to place it, or what to think of it. It is this fluctuation and vain recollection, together with the emotion or movement of spirits that they excite, which constitute the sentiment properly called *Wonder*, and which occasion that staring, and sometimes that rolling of the eyes, that suspension of the breath, and that swelling of the heart, which we may all observe, both in ourselves and others, when wondering at some new object, and which are the natural symptoms of uncertain and undetermined thought. What sort of thing can that be? What is that like? Are the questions which, upon such an occasion, we are all naturally disposed to ask. If we can recollect many such objects which exactly resemble this new appearance, and which present themselves to the imagination naturally, and as it were of their own accord, our Wonder is entirely at an end. If we can recollect but a few, and which it requires too some trouble to be able to call up, our Wonder is indeed diminished, but not quite destroyed. If we can recollect none, but are quite at a loss, it is the greatest possible.

With what curious attention does a naturalist examine a singular plant, or a singular fossil, that is presented to him? He is at no loss to refer it to the general genus of plants or fossils; but this does not satisfy him, and when he considers all the different tribes or species of either with which he has hitherto been acquainted, they all, he thinks, refuse to admit the new object among them. It stands alone in his imagination, and as it were detached from all the other species of that genus to which it belongs. He labours, however, to connect it with some one or other of them. Sometimes he thinks it may be placed in this, and sometimes in that other assortment; nor is he ever satisfied, till he has fallen upon one which, in most of its qualities, it resembles. When he cannot do this, rather than it should stand quite by itself, he will enlarge the precincts, if I may say so, of some species, in order to make room for it; or he will create a new species on purpose to receive it, and call it a Play of Nature, or give it some other appellation, under which he arranges all the oddities that he knows not what else to do with. But to some class or other of known objects he must refer it, and betwixt it and them he must find out some resemblance or other, before he can get rid of that Wonder, that uncertainty and anxious curiosity excited by its singular appearance, and by its dissimilitude with all the objects he had hitherto observed.

As single and individual objects thus excite our Wonder when, by their uncommon qualities and singular appearance, they make us uncertain to what species of things we ought to refer them; so a succession of objects which follow one another in an uncommon train or order, will produce the same effect, though there be nothing particular in any one of them taken by itself.

When one accustomed object appears after another, which it does not usually follow, it first excites, by its unexpectedness, the sentiment properly called Surprise, and afterwards, by the singularity of the succession, or order of its appearance, the sentiment properly called Wonder. We start and are surprised at seeing it there, and then wonder how it came there. The motion of a small piece of iron along a plain table is in itself no extraordinary object, yet the person who first saw it begin, without any visible impulse, in consequence of the motion of a loadstone at some little distance from it, could not behold it without the most extreme Surprise; and when that momentary emotion was over, he would still wonder how it came to be conjoined to an event with which, according to the ordinary train of things, he could have so little suspected it to have any connection.

When two objects, however unlike, have often been observed to follow each other, and have constantly presented themselves to the senses in that order, they come to be so connected together in the fancy, that the idea of the one seems, of its own accord, to call up and introduce that of the other. If the objects are still observed to succeed each other as before, this connection, or, as it has been called, this association of their ideas, becomes stricter and stricter, and the habit of the imagination to pass from the conception of the one to that of the other, grows more and more riveted and confirmed. As its ideas move more rapidly than external objects, it is continually running before them, and therefore anticipates, before it happens, every event which falls out according to this ordinary course of things. When objects succeed each other in the same train in which the ideas of the imagination have thus been accustomed to move, and in which, though not conducted by that chain of events presented to the senses, they have acquired a tendency to go on of their own accord, such objects appear all closely connected with one another, and the thought glides easily along them, without effort and without interruption. They fall in with the natural career of the imagination; and as the ideas which represented such a train of things would seem all mutually to introduce each other, every last thought to be called up by the foregoing, and to call up the succeeding; so when the objects themselves occur, every last event seems, in the same manner, to be introduced by the foregoing, and to introduce the succeeding. There is no break, no stop, no gap, no interval. The ideas excited by so coherent a chain of things seem, as it were, to float through the mind of their own accord, without obliging it to exert itself, or to make any effort in order to pass from one of them to another.

But if this customary connection be interrupted, if one or more objects appear in an order quite different from that to which the imagination has been accustomed, and for which it is prepared, the contrary of all this happens. We are at first surprised by the unexpectedness of the new appearance, and when that momentary emotion is over, we still wonder how it came to occur in that place. The imagination no longer feels the usual facility of passing from the event which goes before to that which comes after. It is an order or law of succession to which it has not been accustomed, and which it therefore finds some difficulty in following, or in attending to. The fancy is stopped and interrupted in that natural movement or career, according to which it was proceeding. Those two events seem to stand at a distance from each other; it endeavours to bring them together, but they refuse to unite; and it feels, or imagines it feels, something like a gap or interval betwixt them. It naturally hesitates, and, as it were, pauses upon the brink of this interval; it endeavours to find out something which may fill up the gap, which, like a bridge, may so far at least unite those seemingly distant objects, as to render the passage of the thought betwixt them smooth, and natural, and easy. The supposition of a chain of intermediate, though invisible, events, which succeed each other in a train similar to that in which the imagination can fill up this interval is the only bridge which, if one may say so, can smooth its passage from the one object to the other. Thus, when we observe the motion of the iron, in consequence of that of the loadstone, we gaze and hesitate, and feel a want of connection betwixt two events which follow one another in so unusual a train. But when, with Descartes, we imagine certain invisible effluvia to circulate round one of them, and by their repeated impulses to impel the other, both to move toward it, and to follow its motion, we fill up the interval betwixt them, we join them together by a sort of bridge, and thus take off that hesitation and difficulty which the imagination felt in passing from the one to the other. That the iron should move after the loadstone seems, upon this hypothesis, in some measure according to the ordinary course of things. Motion after impulse is an order of succession with which of all things we are the most familiar. Two objects which are so connected seem no longer to be disjoined, and the imagination flows smoothly and easily along them.

Such is the nature of this second species of Wonder, which arises from an unusual succession of things. The stop which is thereby given to the career of the imagination, the difficulty which it finds in passing along such disjointed objects, and the feeling of something like a gap or interval betwixt them, constitute the whole essence of this emotion. Upon the clear discovery of a connecting chain of intermediate events, it vanishes altogether. What obstructed the movement of the imagination is then removed. Who wonders at the machinery of the opera-house who has once been admitted behind the scenes? In the Wonders of nature, however, it rarely happens that we can discover so clearly this connecting chain. With regard to a few even of them, indeed, we seem to have been really admitted behind the scenes, and our Wonder accordingly is entirely at an end. Thus the eclipses of the sun and moon, which once, more than all the other appearances in the heavens, excited the terror and amazement of mankind, seem now no longer to be wonderful, since the connecting chain has been found out which joins them to the ordinary course of things. Nay, in those cases in which we have been less successful, even the vague hypotheses of Descartes, and the yet more indetermined notions of Aristotle, have, with their followers, contributed to give some coherence to the appearances of nature, and might diminish, though they could not destroy, their Wonder. If they did not completely fill up the interval betwixt the two disjointed objects, they bestowed upon them, however, some sort of loose connection which they wanted before.

That the imagination feels a real difficulty in passing along two events which follow one another in an uncommon order, may be confirmed by many obvious observations. If it attempts to attend beyond a certain time to a long series of this kind, the continual efforts it is obliged to make, in order to pass from one object to another, and thus follow the progress of the succession, soon fatigue it, and if repeated too often, disorder and disjoint its whole frame. It is thus that too severe an application to study sometimes brings on lunacy and frenzy, in those especially who are somewhat advanced in life, but whole imaginations, from being too late in applying, have not got those habits which dispose them to follow easily the reasonings in the abstract sciences. Every step of a demonstration, which to an old practitioner is quite natural and easy, requires from them the most intense application of thought. Spurred on, however, either by ambition, or by admiration for the subject, they still continue till they become, first confused, then giddy, and at last distracted. Could we conceive a person of the soundest judgment, who had grown up to maturity, and whose imagination had acquired those habits, and that mould, which the constitution of things in this world necessarily impress upon it, to be all at once transported alive to some other planet, where nature was governed by laws quite different from those which take place here; as he would be continually obliged to attend to events, which must to him appear in the highest degree jarring, irregular, and discordant, he would soon feel the same confusion and giddiness begin to come upon him, which would at last end in the same manner, in lunacy and distraction. Neither, to produce this effect, is it necessary that the objects should be either great or interesting, or even uncommon, in themselves. It is sufficient that they follow one another in an uncommon order. Let anyone attempt to look over even a game of cards, and to attend particularly to every single stroke, and if he is unacquainted with the nature and rules of the game; that is, with the laws which regulate the succession of the cards, he will soon feel the same confusion and giddiness begin to come upon him, which, were it to be continued for days and months, would end in the same manner, in lunacy and distraction. But if the mind be thus thrown into the most violent disorder, when it attends to a long series of events which follow one another in an uncommon train, it must feel some degree of the same disorder, when it observes even a single event fall out in this unusual manner: for the violent disorder can arise from nothing but the too frequent repetition of this smaller uneasiness.

That it is the unusualness alone of the succession which occasions this stop and interruption in the progress of the imagination, as well as the notion of an interval betwixt the two immediately succeeding objects, to be filled up by some chain of intermediate events, is not less evident. The same orders of succession, which to one set of men seem quite according to the natural course of things, and such as require no intermediate events to join them, shall to another appear altogether incoherent and disjointed, unless some such events be supposed: and this for no other reason, but because such orders of succession are familiar to the one, and strange to the other. When we enter the work-houses of the most common artisans, such as dyers, brewers, distillers, we observe a number of appearances, which present themselves in an order that seems to us very strange and wonderful. Our thought cannot easily follow it, we feel an interval betwixt every two of them, and require some chain of intermediate events, to fill it up, and link them together. But the artisan himself, who has been for many years familiar with the consequences of all the operations of his art, feels no such interval. They fall in with what custom has made the natural movement of his imagination: they no longer excite his wonder, and if he is not a genius superior to his profession, so as to be capable of making the very easy reflection, that those things, though familiar to him, may be strange to us, he will be disposed rather to laugh at, than sympathize with our Wonder. He cannot conceive what occasion there is for any connecting events to unite those appearances, which seem to him to succeed each other very naturally. It is their nature, he tells us, to follow one another in this order, and that accordingly they always do so. In the same manner bread has, since the world began, been the common nourishment of the human body, and men have long seen it, every day, converted into flesh and bones, substances in all respects so unlike it, that they have seldom had the curiosity to inquire by what process of intermediate events this change is brought about. Because the passage of the thought from the one object to the other is by custom become quite smooth and easy, almost without the supposition of any such process. Philosophers, indeed, who often look for a chain of invisible objects to join together two events that occur in an order familiar to all the world, have endeavoured to find out a chain of this kind betwixt the two events I have just now mentioned; in the same manner as they have endeavoured, by a like intermediate chain, to connect the gravity, the elasticity, and even the cohesion of natural bodies, with some of their other qualities. These, however, are all of them such combinations of events as give no stop to the imaginations of the bulk of mankind, as excite no Wonder, nor any apprehension that there is wanting the strictest connection between them. But as in those sounds, which to the greater part of men seem perfectly agreeable to measure and harmony, the nicer ear of a musician will discover a want, both of the most exact time, and of the most perfect coincidence: so the more practised thought of a philosopher, who has spent his whole life in the study of the connecting principles of nature, will often feel an interval betwixt two objects, which, to more careless observers, seem very strictly conjoined. By long attention to the connections which have ever been presented to his observation, by having often compared them with one another, he has, like the musician, acquired, if one may say so, a nicer ear, and a more delicate feeling with regard to things of this nature. And as to the one, that music seems dissonance which falls short of the most perfect harmony; so to the other, those events seem altogether separated and disjoined, which fall short of the strictest and most perfect connection.

Philosophy is the science of the connecting principles of nature. Nature, after the largest experience that common observation can acquire, seems to abound with events which appear solitary and incoherent with all that go before them; which therefore disturb the easy movement of the imagination; which make its ideas succeed each other, if one may say so, by irregular starts and sallies; and which thus tend, in some measure, to introduce those confusions and distractions we formerly mentioned. Philosophy, by representing the invisible chains which bind together all these disjointed objects, endeavours to introduce order into this chaos of jarring and discordant appearances, to allay this tumult of the imagination, and to restore it, when it surveys the great revolutions of the universe, to that tone of tranquillity and composure, which is both most agreeable in itself, and most suitable to its nature. Philosophy, therefore, may be regarded as one of those arts which address themselves to the imagination; and whose theory and history, upon that account, fall properly within the circumference of our subject. Let us endeavour to trace it, from its first origin, up to that summit of perfection to which it is at present supposed to have arrived, and to which, indeed, it has equally been supposed to have arrived in almost all former times. It is the most sublime of all the agreeable arts, and its revolutions have been the greatest, the most frequent, and the most distinguished of all those that have happened in the literary world. Its history, therefore, must, upon all accounts, be the most entertaining and the most instructive. Let us examine, therefore, all the different systems of nature, which, in these western parts of the world, the only parts of whose history we know any thing, have successively been adopted by the learned and ingenious; and, without regarding their absurdity or probability, their agreement or inconsistency with truth and reality, let us consider them only in that particular point of view which belongs to our subject; and content ourselves with inquiring how far each of them was fitted to sooth the imagination, and to render the theatre of nature a more coherent, and therefore a more magnificent spectacle, than otherwise it would have appeared to be. According as they have failed or succeeded in this, they have constantly failed or succeeded in gaining reputation and renown to their authors; and this will be found to be the clew that is most capable of conducting us through all the labyrinths of philosophical history: for, in the mean time, it will serve to confirm what has gone before, and to throw light upon what is to come after, that we observe, in general, that no system, how well soever in other respects supported, has ever been able to gain any general credit on the world, whose connecting principles were not such as were familiar to all mankind. Why has the chemical philosophy in all ages crept along in obscurity, and been so disregarded by the generality of mankind, while other systems, less useful, and not more agreeable to experience, have possessed universal admiration for whole centuries together? The connecting principles of the chemical philosophy are such as the generality of mankind know nothing about, have rarely seen, and have never been acquainted with; and which to them, therefore, are incapable of smoothing the passage of the imagination betwixt any two seemingly disjointed objects. Salts, sulphurs, and mercuries, acids, and alkalis, are principles which can smooth things to those only who live about the furnace; but whose most common operations seem, to the bulk of mankind, as disjointed as any two events which the chemists would connect together by them. Those artists, however, naturally explained things to themselves by principles that were familiar to themselves. As Aristotle observes, that the early Pythagoreans, who first studied arithmetic, explained all things by the properties of numbers; and Cicero tells us, that Aristoxenus, the musician, found the nature of the soul to consist in harmony. In the same manner, a learned physician lately gave a system of moral philosophy upon the principles of his own art, in which wisdom and virtue were the healthful state of the soul; the different vices and follies, the different diseases to which it was subject; in which the causes and symptoms of those diseases were ascertained; and, in the same medical strain, a proper method of cure prescribed. In the same manner also, others have written parallels of painting and poetry, of poetry and music, of music and architecture, of beauty and virtue, of all the fine arts; systems which have universally owed their origin to the lucubrations of those who were acquainted with the one art, but ignorant of the other; who therefore explained to themselves the phenomena, in that which was strange to them, by that which was familiar; and with whom, upon that account, the analogy, which in other writers gives occasion to a few ingenious similitudes, became the great hinge upon which every thing turned.

Of the Origin of Philosophy

Mankind, in the first ages of society, before the establishment of law, order, and security, have little curiosity to find out those hidden chains of events which bind together the seemingly disjointed appearances of nature. A savage, whose subsistence is precarious, whose life is every day exposed to the rudest dangers, has no inclination to amuse himself with searching out what, when discovered, seems to serve no other purpose than to render the theatre of nature a more connected spectacle to his imagination. Many of these smaller incoherences, which in the course of things perplex philosophers, entirely escape his attention. Those more magnificent irregularities, whose grandeur he cannot overlook, call forth his amazement. Comets, eclipses, thunder, lightning, and other meteors, by their greatness, naturally overawe him, and he views them with a reverence that approaches to fear. His inexperience and uncertainty with regard to everything about them, how they came, how they are to go, what went before, what is to come after them, exasperate his sentiment into terror and consternation. But our passions, as Father Malbranche observes, all justify themselves; that is, suggest to us opinions which justify them. As those appearances terrify him, therefore, he is disposed to believe everything about them which can render them still more the objects of his terror. That they proceed from some intelligent, though invisible causes, of whose vengeance and displeasure they are either the signs or the effects, is the notion of all others most capable of enhancing this passion, and is that, therefore, which he is most apt to entertain. To this too, that cowardice and pusillanimity, so natural to man in his uncivilized state, still more disposes him; unprotected by the laws of society, exposed, defenceless, he feels his weakness upon all occasions; his strength and security upon none.

But all the irregularities of nature are not of this awful or terrible kind. Some of them are perfectly beautiful and agreeable. These, therefore, from the same impotence of mind, would be beheld with love and complacency, and even with transports of gratitude; for whatever is the cause of pleasure naturally excites our gratitude. A child caresses the fruit that is agreeable to it, as it beats the stone that hurts it. The notions of a savage are not very different. The ancient Athenians, who solemnly punished the axe which had accidentally been the cause of the death of a man, erected altars, and offered sacrifices to the rainbow. Sentiments not unlike these, may sometimes, upon such occasions, begin to be felt even in the breasts of the most civilized, but are presently checked by the reflection, that the things are not their proper objects. But a savage, whose notions are guided altogether by wild nature and passion, waits for no other proof that a thing is the proper object of any sentiment, than that it excites it. The reverence and gratitude, with which some of the appearances of nature inspire him, convince him that they are the proper objects of reverence and gratitude, and therefore proceed from some intelligent beings, who take pleasure in the expressions of those sentiments. With him, therefore, every object of nature, which by its beauty or greatness, its utility or hurtfulness, is considerable enough to attract his attention, and whose operations are not perfectly regular, is supposed to act by the direction of some invisible and designing power. The sea is spread out into a calm, or heaved into a storm, according to the good pleasure of Neptune. Does the earth pour forth an exuberant harvest? It is owing to the indulgence of Ceres. Does the vine yield a plentiful vintage? It flows from the bounty of Bacchus. Do either refuse their presents? It is ascribed to the displeasure of those offended deities. The tree, which now flourishes, and now decays, is inhabited by a Dryad, upon whose health or sickness its various appearances depend. The fountain, which sometimes flows in a copious, and sometimes in a scanty stream, which appears sometimes clear and limpid, and at other times muddy and disturbed, is affected in all its changes by the Naiad who dwells within it. Hence the origin of Polytheism, and of that vulgar superstition which ascribes all the irregular events of nature to the favour or displeasure of intelligent, though invisible beings, to gods, daemons, witches, genii, fairies. For it may be observed, that in all Polytheistic religions, among savages, as well as in the early ages of Heathen antiquity, it is the irregular events of nature only that are ascribed to the agency and power of their gods. Fire burns, and water refreshes; heavy bodies descend, and lighter substances fly upwards, by the necessity of their own nature; nor was the invisible hand of Jupiter ever apprehended to be employed in those matters. But thunder and lightning, storms and sunshine, those more irregular events, were ascribed to his favour, or his anger. Man, the only designing power with which they were acquainted, never acts but either to stop, or to alter the course, which natural events would take, if left to themselves. Those other intelligent beings, whom they imagined, but knew not, were naturally supposed to act in the same manner; not to employ themselves in supporting the ordinary course of things, which went on of its own accord, but to stop, to thwart, and to disturb it. And thus, in the first ages of the world, the lowest and most pusillanimous superstition supplied the place of philosophy.

But when law has established order and security, and subsistence ceases to be precarious, the curiosity of mankind is increased, and their fears are diminished. The leisure which they then enjoy renders them more attentive to the appearances of nature, more observant of her smallest irregularities, and more desirous to know what is the chain which links them all together. That some such chain subsists betwixt all her seemingly disjointed phenomena, they are necessarily led to conceive; and that magnanimity, and cheerfulness, which all generous natures acquire who are bred in civilized societies, where they have so few occasions to feel their weakness, and so many to be conscious of their strength and security, renders them less disposed to employ, for this connecting chain, those invisible beings whom the fear and ignorance of their rude forefathers had engendered. Those of liberal fortunes, whose attention is not much occupied either with business or with pleasure, can fill up the void of their imagination, which is thus disengaged from the ordinary affairs of life, no other way than by attending to that train of events which passes around them. While the great objects of nature thus pass in review before them, many things occur in an order to which they have not been accustomed. Their imagination, which accompanies with ease and delight the regular progress of nature, is stopped and embarrassed by those seeming incoherences; they excite their wonder, and seem to require some chain of intermediate events, which, by connecting them with something that has gone before, may thus render the whole course of the universe consistent and of a piece. Wonder, therefore, and not any expectation of advantage from its discoveries, is the first principle which prompts mankind to the study of Philosophy, of that science which pretends to lay open the concealed connections that unite the various appearances of nature; and they pursue this study for its own sake, as an original pleasure or good in itself, without regarding its tendency to procure them the means of many other pleasures.

Greece, and the Greek colonies in Sicily, Italy, and the Lesser Asia, were the first countries which, in these western parts of the world, arrived at a state of civilized society. It was in them, therefore, that the first philosophers, of whose doctrine we have any distinct account, appeared. Law and order seem indeed to have been established in the great monarchies of Asia and Egypt, long before they had any footing in Greece: yet, after all that has been said concerning the learning of the Chaldeans and Egyptians, whether there ever was in those nations anything which deserved the name of science, or whether that despotism which is more destructive of security and leisure than anarchy itself, and which prevailed over all the East, prevented the growth of Philosophy, is a question which, for want of monuments, cannot be determined with any degree of precision.

The Greek colonies having been settled amid nations either altogether barbarous, or altogether unwarlike, over whom, therefore, they soon acquired a very great authority, seem, upon that account, to have arrived at a considerable degree of empire and opulence before any state in the parent country had surmounted that extreme poverty, which, by leaving no room for any evident distinction of ranks, is necessarily attended with the confusion and misrule which flows from a want of all regular subordination. The Greek islands being secure from the invasion of land armies, or from naval forces, which were in those days but little known, seem, upon that account too, to have got before the continent in all sorts of civility and improvement. The first philosophers, therefore, as well as the first poets, seem all to have been natives, either of their colonies, or of their islands. It was from thence that Homer, Archilochus, Stesichorus, Simonides, Sappho, Anacreon, derived their birth. Thales and Pythagoras, the founders of the two earliest sects of philosophy, arose, the one in an Asiatic colony, the other in an island; and neither of them established his school in the mother country.

What was the particular system of either of those two philosophers, or whether their doctrine was so methodized as to deserve the name of a system, the imperfection, as well as the uncertainty of all the traditions that have come down to us concerning them, makes it impossible to determine. The school of Pythagoras, however, seems to have advanced further in the study of the connecting principles of nature, than that of the Ionian philosopher. The accounts which are given of Anaximander, Anaximenes, Anaxagoras, Archelaus, the successors of Thales, represent the doctrines of those sages as full of the most inextricable confusion. Something, however, that approaches to a composed and orderly system, may be traced in what is delivered down to us concerning the doctrine of Empedocles, of Archytas, of Timaeus, and of Ocellus the Lucanian, the most renowned philosophers of the Italian school. The opinions of the two last coincide pretty much; the one, with those of Plato; the other, with those of Aristotle; nor do those of the two first seem to have been very different, of whom the one was the author of the doctrine of the Four Elements, the other the inventor of the Categories; who, therefore, may be regarded as the founders, the one, of the ancient Physics; the other, of the ancient Dialectic; and, how closely these were connected, will appear hereafter. It was in the school of Socrates, however, from Plato and Aristotle, that Philosophy first received that form, which introduced her, if one may say so, to the general acquaintance of the world. It is from them, therefore, that we shall begin to give her history in any detail. Whatever was valuable in the former systems, which was at all consistent with their general principles, they seem to have consolidated into their own. From the Ionian Philosophy, I have not been able to discover that they derived anything. From the Pythagorean school, both Plato and Aristotle seem to have derived the fundamental principles of almost all their doctrines. Plato, too, appears to have borrowed something from two other sects of philosophers, whose extreme obscurity seems to have prevented them from acquiring themselves any extensive reputation: the one was that of Cratylus and Heraclitus; the other was that of Xenophanes, Parmenides, Melissus, and Zeno. To pretend to rescue the system of any of those antesocratic sages, from that oblivion which at present covers them all, would be a vain and useless attempt. What seems, however, to have been borrowed from them, shall sometimes be marked as we go along.

There was still another school of philosophy, earlier than Plato, from which, however, he was so far from borrowing anything, that he seems to have bent the whole force of his reason to discredit and expose its principles. This was the Philosophy of Leucippus, Democritus, and Protagoras, which accordingly seems to have submitted to his eloquence, to have lain dormant, and to have been almost forgotten for some generations, till it was afterwards more successfully revived by Epicurus.

The History of Astronomy

Of all the phenomena of nature, the celestial appearances are, by their greatness and beauty, the most universal objects of the curiosity of mankind. Those who surveyed the heavens with the most careless attention, necessarily distinguished in them three different sorts of objects; the Sun, the Moon, and the Stars. These last, appearing always in the same situation, and at the same distance with regard to one another, and seeming to revolve every day round the earth in parallel circles, which widened gradually from the poles to the equator, were naturally thought to have all the marks of being fixed, like so many gems, in the concave side of the firmament, and of being carried round by the diurnal revolutions of that solid body: for the azure sky, in which the stars seem to float, was readily apprehended, upon account of the uniformity of their apparent motions, to be a solid body, the roof or outer wall of the universe, to whose inside all those little sparkling objects were attached . . . .

Systems in many respects resemble machines. A machine is a little system, created to perform, as well as to connect together, in reality, those different movements and effects which the artist has occasion for. A system is an imaginary machine invented to connect together in the fancy those different movements and effects which are already in reality performed. The machines that are first invented to perform any particular movement are always the most complex, and succeeding artists generally discover that, with fewer wheels, with fewer principles of motion, than had originally been employed, the same effects may be more easily produced. The first systems, in the same manner, are always the most complex, and a particular connecting chain, or principle, is generally thought necessary to unite every two seemingly disjointed appearances: but it often happens, that one great connecting principle is afterwards found to be sufficient to bind together all the discordant phenomena that occur in a whole species of things. How many wheels are necessary to carry on the movements of this imaginary machine, the system of Eccentric Spheres! The westward diurnal revolution of the Firmament, whose rapidity carries all the other heavenly bodies along with it, requires one. The periodical eastward revolutions of the Sun, Moon, and Five Planets, require, for each of those bodies, another. Their differently accelerated and retarded motions require, that those wheels, or circles, should neither be concentric with the Firmament, nor with one another; which, more than anything, seems to disturb the harmony of the universe. The retrograde and stationary appearance of the Five Planets, as well as the extreme inconstancy of the Moon's motion, require, for each of them, an Epicycle, another little wheel attached to the circumference of the great wheel, which still more interrupts the uniformity of the system. The motion of the apogeum of each of those bodies requires, in each of them, still another wheel, to carry the centres of their Eccentric Spheres round the centre of the Earth. And thus, this imaginary machine, though, perhaps, more simple, and certainly better adapted to the phenomena than the Fifty-six Planetary Spheres of Aristotle, was still too intricate and complex for the imagination to rest in it with complete tranquillity and satisfaction . . . .

But when the observations of Cassini[2] had established the authority of those laws, which Kepler[3] had first discovered in the system, the philosophy of Descartes, which could afford no reason, why such particular laws should be observed, might continue to amuse the learned in other sciences, but could no longer satisfy those that were skilled in Astronomy. Sir Isaac Newton first attempted to give a physical account of the motions of the Planets, which should accommodate itself to all the constant irregularities which astronomers had ever observed in their motions. The physical connection, by which Descartes had endeavoured to bind together the movements of the Planets, was the laws of impulse; of all the orders of succession, those which are most familiar to the imagination; as they all flow from the inertness of matter. After this quality, there is no other, with which we are so well acquainted, as that of gravity. We never act upon matter, but we have occasion to observe it. The superior genius and sagacity of Sir Isaac Newton, therefore, made the most happy, and, we may now say, the greatest and most admirable improvement that was ever made in philosophy, when he discovered, that he could join together the movements of the Planets by so familiar a principle of connection, which completely removed all the difficulties the imagination had hitherto felt in attending to them. He demonstrated, that, if the Planets were supposed to gravitate towards the Sun, and to one another, and at the same time to have had a projecting force originally impressed upon them, the primary ones might all described ellipses in one of the foci of which that great luminary was placed; and the secondary ones might describe figures of the same kind round their

[2] [Giovanni Domenico Cassini (1625–1712).

[3] [Johannes Kepler (1571–1630).]

respective primaries, without being disturbed by the continual motion of the centres of their revolutions. That if the force, which retained each of them in their orbits, was like that of gravity, and directed towards the Sun, they would, each of them, describe equal areas in equal times. That if this attractive power of the Sun, like all other qualities which are diffused in rays from a centre, diminished in the same proportion as the squares of the distances increased, their motions would be swiftest when nearest the Sun, and slowest when farthest off from him, in the same proportion in which, by observation, they are discovered to be; and that, upon the same supposition, of this gradual diminution of their respective gravities, their periodic times would bear the same proportion to their distances, which Kepler and Cassini had established betwixt them. Having thus shown, that gravity might be the connecting principle which joined together the movements of the Planets, he endeavoured next to prove that it really was so. Experience shows us, what is the power of gravity near the surface of the Earth. That it is such as to make a body fall, in the first second of its descent, through about fifteen Parisian feet. The Moon is about sixty semidiameters of the Earth distant from its surface. If gravity, therefore, was supposed to diminish, as the squares of the distance increase, a body, at the Moon, would fall towards the Earth in a minute; that is, in sixty seconds, through the same space, which it falls near its surface in one second. But the arch which the Moon describes in a minute, falls, by observation, about fifteen Parisian feet below the tangent drawn at the beginning of it. So far, therefore, the Moon may be conceived as constantly falling towards the Earth . . . .

But of all the attempts of the Newtonian Philosophy, that which would appear to be the most above the reach of human reason and experience, is the attempt to compute the weights and densities of the Sun, and of the Several Planets. An attempt, however, which was indispensably necessary to complete the coherence of the Newtonian system. The power of attraction which, according to the theory of gravity, each body possesses, is in proportion to the quantity of matter contained in that body. But the periodic time in which one body, at a given distance, revolves round another that attracts it, is shorter in proportion as this power is greater, and consequently as the quantity of matter in the attracting body. If the densities of Jupiter and Saturn were the same with that of the Earth, the periodic times of their several Satellites would be shorter than by observation they are found to be. Because the quantity of matter, and consequently the attracting power of each of them, would be as the cubes of their diameters. By comparing the bulks of those Planets, and the periodic times of their Satellites, it is found that, upon the hypothesis of gravity, the density of Jupiter must be greater than that of Saturn, and the density of the Earth greater than that of Jupiter. This seems to establish it as a law in the system, that the nearer the several Planets approach to the Sun, the density of their matter is the greater: a constitution of things which would seem to be the most advantageous of any that could have been established; as water of the same density with that of our Earth, would freeze under the Equator of Saturn, and boil under that of Mercury.

Such is the system of Sir Isaac Newton, a system whose parts are all more strictly connected together, than those of any other philosophical hypothesis. Allow his principle, the universality of gravity, and that it decreases as the squares of the distance increase, and all the appearances, which he joins together by it, necessarily follow. Neither is their connection merely a general and loose connection, as that of most other systems, in which either these appearances, or some such like appearances, might indifferently have been expected. It is everywhere the most precise and particular that can be imagined, and ascertains the time, the place, the quantity, the duration of each individual phenomenon, to be exactly such as, by observation, they have been determined to be. Neither are the principles of union, which it employs, such as the imagination can find any difficulty in going along with. The gravity of matter is, of all its qualities, after its inertness, that which is most familiar to us. We never act upon it without having occasion to observe this property. The law too, by which it is supposed to diminish as it recedes from its centre, is the same which takes place in all other qualities which are propagated in rays from a centre, in light, and in everything else of the same kind. It is such, that we not only find that it does take place in all such qualities, but we are necessarily determined to conceive that, from the nature of the thing, it must take place. The opposition which was made in France, and in some other foreign nations, to the prevalence of this system, did not arise from any difficulty which mankind naturally felt in conceiving gravity as an original and primary mover in the constitution of the universe. The Cartesian system, which had prevailed so generally before it, had accustomed mankind to conceive motion as never beginning, but in consequence of impulse, and had connected the descent of heavy bodies, near the surface of the Earth, and the other Planets, by this more general bond of union; and it was the attachment the world had conceived for this account of things, which indisposed them to that of Sir Isaac Newton. His system, however, now prevails over all opposition, and has advanced to the acquisition of the most universal empire that was ever established in philosophy. His principles, it must be acknowledged, have a degree of firmness and solidity that we should in vain look for in any other system. The most sceptical cannot avoid feeling this. They not only connect together most perfectly all the phenomena of the Heavens, which had been observed before his time, but those also which the persevering industry and more perfect instruments of later Astronomers have made known to us; have been either easily and immediately explained by the application of his principles, or have been explained in consequence of more laborious and accurate calculations from these principles, than had been instituted before. And even we, while we have been endeavouring to represent all philosophical systems as mere inventions of the imagination, to connect together the otherwise disjointed and discordant phenomena of nature, have insensibly been drawn in, to make use of language expressing the connecting principles of this one, as if they were the real chains which Nature makes use of to bind together her several operations. Can we wonder then, that it should have gained the general and complete approbation of mankind, and that it should now be considered, not as an attempt to connect in the imagination the phenomena of the Heavens, but as the greatest discovery that ever was made by man, the discovery of an immense chain of the most important and sublime truths, all closely connected together, by one capital fact, of the reality of which we have daily experience.

Five

Correspondence

Lisle Street, Leicester Fields
12 Apr. 1759

Dear Smith

I give you thanks for the agreeable Present of your theory [i.e., *The Theory of Moral Sentiments*]. Wedderburn and I made Presents of our copies to such of our acquaintance as we thought good judges, and proper to spread the reputation of the Book. I sent one to the Duke of Argyle, to Lord Lyttleton, Horace Walpole, Soames Jennyns, and Burke, an Irish gentleman, who wrote lately a very pretty Treatise on the sublime.[1] Millar[2] desired my permission to send one in your name to Dr Warburton.[3] I have delayed writing to you till I could tell you something of the success of the book, and could prognosticate with some probability whether it should be finally dammed to oblivion, or should be registered in the temple of immortality. Though it has been published only a few weeks, I think there appear already such strong symptoms, that I can almost venture to foretell its fate. It is in short this – But I have been interrupted in my letter by a foolish impertinent visit of one who has lately come from Scotland. He tells me, that the University of Glasgow intend to declare Rouet's office vacant upon his going abroad with Lord Hope.[4] I question not but you will have our Friend, Ferguson,[5] in your eye, in case another project for procuring him a place in the University of Edinburgh should fail. Ferguson has very much polished and improved his Treatise on refinement, and with some amendments it will make an admirable book, and discovers an elegant and a singular genius. The Epigoniad, I hope, will do; but it is somewhat up-hill work. As I doubt not but you consult the reviews sometimes at present, you will see in the critical review a letter upon that poem; and I desire you to employ your

---

[1] [Archibald Campbell, Third Duke of Argyll (1682–1761); Sir George (later Lord) Lyttleton (1709–73); Horace Walpole (1717–97); Soame Jenyns (1704–87); and Edmund Burke (1729–97).]

[2] [John Millar (1735–1801).]

[3] [William Warburton (1698–1779).]

[4] [William Rouet (fl. 1750s–1760s), professor at University of Glasgow and tutor to Lord Hope in 1759.]

[5] [Adam Ferguson (1723–1816).]

conjectures in finding out the author. Let me see a sample of your skill in knowing hands by your guessing at the person. I am afraid of Lord Kaims's law tracts.[6] A man might as well think of making a fine sauce by a mixture of wormwood and aloes as an agreeable composition by joining metaphysics and Scotch law. However, the book, I believe, has merit; though few people will take the pains of diving into it. But to return to your book, and its success in this town, I must tell you – A plague of interruptions! I ordered myself to be denied; and yet here is one that has broke in upon me again. He is a man of letters, and we have had a good deal of literary conversation. You told me, that you was curious of literary anecdotes, and therefore I shall inform you of a few, that have come to my knowledge. I believe I have mentioned to you already Helvetius's book de l'Esprit.[7] It is worth your reading, not for its philosophy, which I do not highly value, but for its agreeable composition. I had a Letter from him a few days ago, wherein he tells me that my name was much oftener in the manuscript, but that the censor of books at Paris obliged him to strike it out. Voltaire has lately published a small work called *Candide, ou L'optimisme*. It is full of sprightliness and impiety, and is indeed a satire upon providence, under pretext of criticizing the Leibnizian System. I shall give you a Detail of it – But what is all this to my book? say you – My Dear Mr Smith, have patience: Compose yourself to tranquillity: Show yourself a philosopher in practice as well as profession: Think on the emptiness, and rashness, and futility of the common judgments of men: How little they are regulated by reason in any subject, much more in philosophical subjects, which so far exceed the comprehension of the vulgar. *Non si quid improba Roma, Elevet, accedas examenque improbum in illa, Perpendas trutina, nec te quaesiveris extra.*[8] A wise man's Kingdom is his own breast: Or, if he ever looks farther, it will only be to the judgment of a select few, who are free from prejudices, and capable of examining his work. Nothing indeed can be a stronger presumption of falsehood than the approbation of the multitude; and Phocion, you know, always suspected himself of some blunder, when he was attended with the applauses of the populace.

Supposing, therefore, that you have duly prepared yourself for the worst by all these reflections; I proceed to tell you the melancholy news, that your book has been very unfortunate: For the public seem disposed to applaud it extremely. It was looked for by the foolish people with some impatience; and the mob of literati are beginning already to be very loud in its praises. Three Bishops called yesterday at Millar's shop in order to buy copies, and to ask questions about the author: The Bishop

[6] [Henry Home, Lord Kames (1696–1782).]

[7] [Claude-Adrien Helvétius (1715–71).]

[8] [Persius, *Satires* I, 5–7: "If confused Rome should make light of something, do not go and correct the deceitful tongue in that balance of theirs, and do not look to anyone outside of yourself."]

of Peterborough[9] said he had passed the evening in a company, where he heard it extolled above all books in the world. You may conclude what opinion true philosophers will entertain of it, when these retainers to superstition praise it so highly. The Duke of Argyle is more decisive than he used to be in its favour: I suppose he either considers it as an exotic, or thinks the author will be serviceable to him in the Glasgow elections. Lord Lyttleton says, that Robertson[10] and Smith and Bower[11] are the glories of English literature. Oswald[12] protests he does not know whether he has reaped more instruction or entertainment from it: But you may easily judge what reliance can be put on his judgment, who has been engaged all his life in public business and who never sees any faults in his friends. Millar exults and brags that two thirds of the edition are already sold, and that he is now sure of success. You see what a son of the earth that is, to value books only by the profit they bring him. In that view, I believe it may prove a very good book.

Charles Townshend,[13] who passes for the cleverest fellow in England, is so taken with the performance, that he said to Oswald he would put the Duke of Buccleugh under the author's care, and would endeavour to make it worth his while to accept of that charge. As soon as I heard this, I called on him twice with a view of talking with him about the matter, and of convincing him of the propriety of sending that young Nobleman to Glasgow: For I could not hope, that he could offer you any terms, which would tempt you to renounce your Professorship: But I had missed him. Mr Townsend passes for being a little uncertain in his resolutions; so perhaps you need not build much on this sally.

In recompense for so many mortifying things, which nothing but truth could have extorted from me, and which I could easily have multiplied to a greater number; I doubt not but you are so good a Christian as to return good for evil and to flatter my vanity, by telling me, that all the Godly in Scotland abuse me for my account of John Knox and the reformation etc. I suppose you are glad to see my paper end, and that I am obliged to conclude with

Your humble Servant
David Hume

---

[9] [Richard Terrick (1710–77).]
[10] [William Robertson (1721–93).]
[11] [Archibald Bower (1686–1766).]
[12] [James Oswald of Dunnikier.]
[13] [Charles Townshend (1725–67).]

London
28 July 1759

Dear Sir

. . . I am told that you are preparing a new Edition [of the *Theory of Moral Sentiments*], and propose to make some additions and alterations, in order to obviate objections. I shall use the freedom to propose one, which, if it appears to be of any weight, you may have in your eye. I wish you had more particularly and fully proved, that all kinds of sympathy are necessarily agreeable. This is the hinge of your system, and yet you only mention the matter cursorily in p. 20. Now it would appear that there is a disagreeable sympathy, as well as an agreeable: And indeed, as the sympathetic passion is a reflex image of the principal, it must partake of its qualities, and be painful where that is so. Indeed, *when we converse with a man with whom we can entirely sympathize,* that is, where there is a warm and intimate friendship, the cordial openness of such a commerce overpowers the pain of a disagreeable sympathy, and renders the whole movement agreeable. But in ordinary cases, this cannot have place. An ill-humoured fellow; a man tired and disgusted with everything, always *ennui;* sickly, complaining, embarrassed; such a one throws an evident damp on company, which I suppose would be accounted for by sympathy; and yet is disagreeable.

It is always thought a difficult problem to account for the pleasure, received from the tears and grief and sympathy of tragedy; which would not be the case, if all sympathy was agreeable. An hospital would be a more entertaining place than a ball. I am afraid that in p. 99 and III this proposition has escaped you, or rather is interwove with your reasonings in that place. You say expressly, *it is painful to go along with grief and we always enter into it with reluctance.* It will probably be requisite for you to modify or explain this sentiment, and reconcile it to your system.

My dear Mr Smith; You must not be so much engrossed with your own book, as never to mention mine. The Whigs, I am told, are anew in a rage against me; though they know not how to vent themselves: For they are constrained to allow all my facts. You have probably seen Hurd's abuse of me.[14] He is of the Warburtonian school; and consequently very insolent and very scurrilous; but I shall never reply a word to him. If my past writings do not sufficiently prove me to be no Jacobite, ten volumes in folio never would. . . .

I am
Dear Smith
Yours sincerely
David Hume.

---

[14] [Richard Hurd (1720–1808).]

Kirkcaldy, Fifeshire
9 Nov. 1776

Dear Sir,

It is with a real, though a very melancholy pleasure, that I sit down to give you some account of the behaviour of our late excellent friend, Mr Hume, during his last illness.

Though, in his own judgment, his disease was mortal and incurable, yet he allowed himself to be prevailed upon, by the entreaty of his friends, to try what might be the effects of a long journey. A few days before he set out, he wrote that account of his own life, which, together with his other papers, he has left to your care. My account, therefore, shall begin where his ends.

He set out for London towards the end of April, and at Morpeth met with Mr.John Home and myself, who had both come down from London on purpose to see him, expecting to have found him at Edinburgh. Mr Home returned with him, and attended him during the whole of his stay in England, with that care and attention which might be expected from a temper so perfectly friendly and affectionate. As I had written to my mother that she might expect me in Scotland, I was under the necessity of continuing my journey. His disease seemed to yield to exercise and change of air, and when he arrived in London, he was apparently in much better health than when he left Edinburgh. He was advised to go to Bath to drink the waters, which appeared for some time to have so good an effect upon him, that even he himself began to entertain, what he was not apt to do, a better opinion of his own health. His symptoms, however, soon returned with their usual violence, and from that moment he gave up all thoughts of recovery, but submitted with the utmost cheerfulness, and the most perfect complacency and resignation. Upon his return to Edinburgh, though he found himself much weaker, yet his cheerfulness never abated, and he continued to divert himself, as usual, with correcting his own works for a new edition, with reading books of amusement, with the conversation of his friends; and, sometimes in the evening, with a party at his favourite game of whist. His cheerfulness was so great, and his conversation and amusements run so much in their usual strain, that, notwithstanding all bad symptoms, many people could not believe he was dying. 'I shall tell your friend, Colonel Edmondstone', said Doctor Dundas to him one day, 'that I left you much better, and in a fair way of recovery'. 'Doctor', said he, 'as I believe you would not choose to tell anything but the truth, you had better tell him, that I am dying as fast as my enemies, if I have any, could wish, and as easily and cheerfully as my best friends could desire'. Colonel Edmondstone soon afterwards came to see him, and take leave of him; and on his way home, he could not forbear writing him a letter bidding him once more an eternal adieu, and applying to him, as to a dying man, the beautiful French verses in which the Abbé Chaulieu, in expectation of his own death, laments his approaching separation from his friend, the Marquis de la Fare. Mr Hume's magnanimity and firmness were such, that his most affectionate friends knew, that they hazarded nothing in talking or writing to him as to a dying man, and that so far from being hurt by this frankness, he was rather pleased and flattered by it. I happened to come into his room while he was reading this letter, which he had just received, and which he immediately showed me. I told him, that though I was sensible how very much he was weakened, and that appearances were in many respects very bad, yet his cheerfulness was still so great, the spirit of life seemed still to be so very strong in him, that I could not help entertaining some faint hopes. He answered, 'Your hopes are groundless. An habitual diarrhoea of more than a year's standing, would be a very bad disease at any age: at my age it is a mortal one. When I lie down in the evening, I feel myself weaker than when I rose in the morning; and when I rise in the morning, weaker than when I lay down in the evening. I am sensible, besides, that some of my vital parts are affected, so that I must soon die'. 'Well', said I, 'if it must be so, you have at least the satisfaction of leaving all your friends, your brother's family in particular, in great prosperity'. He said that he felt that satisfaction so sensibly, that when he was reading a few days before, Lucian's Dialogues of the Dead, among all the excuses which are alleged to Charon for not entering readily into his boat, he could not find one that fitted him; he had no house to finish, he had no daughter to provide for, he had no enemies upon whom he wished to revenge himself. 'I could not well imagine', said he, 'what excuse I could make to Charon in order to obtain a little delay. I have done everything of consequence which I ever meant to do, and I could at no time expect to leave my relations and friends in a better situation than that in which I am now likely to leave them; I, therefore, have all reason to die contented'. He then diverted himself with inventing several jocular excuses, which he supposed he might make to Charon, and with imagining the very surly answers which it might suit the character of Charon to return to them. 'Upon further consideration', said he, 'I thought I might say to him, good Charon, I have been correcting my works for a new edition. Allow me a little time, that I may see how the public receives the alterations'. But Charon would answer, 'When you have seen the effect of these, you will be for making other alterations. There will be no end of such excuses; so, honest friend, please step into the boat'. But I might still urge, 'Have a little patience, good Charon, I have been endeavouring to open the eyes of the public. If I live a few years longer, I may have the satisfaction of seeing the downfall of some of the prevailing systems of superstition'. But Charon would then lose all temper and decency. 'You loitering rogue, that will not happen these many hundred years. Do you fancy I will grant you a lease for so long a term? Get into the boat this instant, you lazy loitering rogue'.

But, though Mr Hume always talked of his approaching dissolution with great cheerfulness, he never affected to make any parade of his magnanimity. He never mentioned the subject but when the conversation naturally led to it, and never dwelt longer upon it than the course of the conversation happened to require: it was a subject indeed which occurred pretty frequently, in consequence of the inquiries which his friends, who came to see him, naturally made concerning the state of his health. The conversation which I mentioned above, and which passed on Thursday the 8th of August, was the last, except one, that I ever had with him. He had now become so very weak, that the company of his most intimate friends fatigued him; for his cheerfulness was still so great, his complaisance and social disposition were still so entire, that when any friend was with him, he could not help talking more, and with greater exertion, than suited the weakness of his body. At his own desire, therefore, I agreed to leave Edinburgh, where I was staying partly upon his account, and returned to my mother's house here, at Kirkcaldy, upon condition that he would send for me whenever he wished to see me; the physician who saw him most frequently, Doctor Black, undertaking, in the meantime, to write me occasionally an account of the state of his health.

On the 22nd of August, the Doctor wrote me the following letter:

> Since my last, Mr Hume has passed his time pretty easily, but is much weaker. He sits up, goes down stairs once a day, and amuses himself with reading, but seldom sees anybody. He finds that even the conversation of his most intimate friends fatigues and oppresses him; and it is happy that he does not need it, for he is quite free from anxiety, impatience, or low spirits, and passes his time very well with the assistance of amusing books.

I received the day after a letter from Mr Hume himself, of which the following is an extract

Edinburgh, Monday 23d August, 1776

> My Dearest Friend,
> I am obliged to make use of my nephew's hand in writing to you, as I do not rise today... I go very fast to decline, and last night had a small fever, which I hoped might put a quicker period to this tedious illness, but unluckily it has, in a great measure, gone off. I cannot submit to your coming over here on my account, as it is possible for me to see you so small a part of the day, but Doctor Black can better inform you concerning the degree of strength which may from time to time remain with me. Adieu, &c.

Three days after I received the following letter from Doctor Black.

Edinburgh, Monday, 26th August, 1776.

> Dear Sir,
> Yesterday about four o'clock afternoon, Mr Hume expired. The near approach of his death became evident in the night between Thursday and Friday, when his disease became excessive, and soon weakened him so much, that he could no longer rise out of his bed. He continued to the last perfectly sensible, and free from much pain or feelings of distress. He never dropped the smallest expression of impatience; but when he had occasion to speak to

the people about him, always did it with affection and tenderness. I thought it improper to write to bring you over, especially as I heard that he had dictated a letter to you desiring you not to come. When he became very weak, it cost him an effort to speak, and he died in such a happy composure of mind, that nothing could exceed it.

Thus died our most excellent, and never to be forgotten friend; concerning whose philosophical opinions men will, no doubt, judge variously, every one approving or condemning them, according as they happen to coincide or disagree with his own; but concerning whose character and conduct there can scarce be a difference of opinion. His temper, indeed, seemed to be more happily balanced, if I may be allowed such an expression, than that perhaps of any other man I have ever known. Even in the lowest state of his fortune, his great and necessary frugality never hindered him from exercising, upon proper occasions, acts both of charity and generosity. It was a frugality founded, not upon avarice, but upon the love of independency. The extreme gentleness of his nature never weakened either the firmness of his mind, or the steadiness of his resolutions. His constant pleasantry was the genuine effusion of good-nature and good-humour, tempered with delicacy and modesty, and without even the slightest tincture of malignity, so frequently the disagreeable source of what is called wit in other men. It never was the meaning of his raillery to mortify; and therefore, far from offending, it seldom failed to please and delight, even those who were the objects of it. To his friends, who were frequently the objects of it, there was not perhaps anyone of all his great and amiable qualities, which contributed more to endear his conversation. And that gaiety of temper, so agreeable in society, but which is so often accompanied with frivolous and superficial qualities, was in him certainly attended with the most severe application, the most extensive learning, the greatest depth of thought, and a capacity in every respect the most comprehensive. Upon the whole, I have always considered him, both in his lifetime and since his death, as approaching as nearly to the idea of a perfectly wise and virtuous man, as perhaps the nature of human frailty will permit.

I ever am, dear Sir
Most affectionately yours,
Adam Smith.